Organisation and Practice of

Modern Indian Education

Organisation and Practice of

Modern Indian Education

J.C. AGGARWAL

SHIPRA

(2019, 17, 10, 07, 05, 2003, First Published in 2002)

Rs. 1400

ISBN: 978-93-88691-00-0

2026
Impression

Organisation and Practice of Modern Indian Education

Published by:
SHIPRA PUBLICATIONS
LG 18-19, Pankaj Central Market
I.P. Ext., Patparganj, Delhi 110092, India
11 47322068; 96500 28065, 98105 22367
info@shiprapublication.com
www.shiprapublication.com

Preface

The problem is that we are organising our educational institutions in the twenty-first century with the educational structure designed, by and large, during the nineteenth century to work well in the twentieth century. Now we need something entirely different.

This publication covers a wide range of issues and themes relating to the organisation and practice of modern Indian education. It highlights the importance of giving a new dimension to problem like the role of the head of an educational institution, the teachers and the community in developing balanced and harmonious relationship in the school so that the pupils develop ideals and values needed in an enlightened citizen of a democratic state.

As a result of the explosion of information technology (IT), the theory and practice of school organisation have undergone sea change and this book duly takes note of it.

'Learning by Doing' 'Learning to Learn' and 'Learning the Art of Living' are the watchwords of the new education. Accordingly an attempt is made here to indicate the new practices, which must be incorporated in the system of school organisation so that it meets the new challenges effectively and efficiently.

Designed as a textbook for students, the book should serve as a handy reference volume for teachers' in-service courses and practising teachers.

The author is greatly thankful to all the authors and publishers whose works he has made use of in preparing this book.

J.C. Aggarwal

Contents

1

Concept of School Organisation

An educational system whose school organisation is unreformed is an unreformed system.

Meaning of School Organisation

School Organisation as an Organised Structure to Fulfil Certain Objectives: School organisation, broadly defined, implies the practical and pragmatic measures which the school takes to ensure that the system of work which it uses will be of the greatest possible assistance in fulfilling its objectives and of the greatest possible value to the students in their all round development.

Organisation may be functionally defined as an organised body or system or structure or arrangement or framework which is used for ensuring unity of effort, efficiency, goodwill, harmonious relations and appropriate use of resources.

School Organisation as an Embodiment of Ideas: School organisation is the embodiment of an ideal and of a spirit. It must enable different limbs of the school organism to function harmoniously in happy coordination, blending themselves into a composite personality like a collage of different colours and shapes which attracts persons of all shades and provides a soothing environment.

School Organisation as a Lens: School organisation may be compared to a lens that brings everything about the school system as well as educational system into focus for faculty (staff), students and the community. If it is a poor lens, the image is fussy and obscure and no one in the school system or the community gets a clear picture of what the educational system or the school system is trying to do. If it is a good lens, the school system becomes a clear-cut and vivid projection of the ideals, ideas and values that have been envisaged to bring into being in the school system.

Objectives of School Organisation

Broadly speaking, the objectives of school organisation may be considered from two points of view which are complementary and supplementary and certainly not competitive.

Objectives of School Organisation from the point of View of the Society

The objectives of school organisation from the point of view of the society are:

1. Consolidating the spiritual strength of the society.
2. Maintaining the historical continuity of the society.
3. Securing the past achievements of the society.
4. Guaranteeing the future progress of the society.

Objectives of School Organisation in Relation to the Development of the Students: A school should be organised to:

(i) To train the faculties of the students.
(ii) To widen their outlook.
(iii) To cultivate their minds.
(iv) To form and strength their character.
(v) To develop and cultivate their aesthetic faculty.
(vi) To build up their bodies and enable them to acquire health and strength.
(vii) To teach them their duties to themselves, the community and the State.
(viii) To enable them to be emotionally well-balanced.
(ix) To prepare them to be spiritually sound.

Objective of School Organisation is not merely to prepare the students for Examination

The objectives and functions of the present day school organisation may be summed up in the words of P.C. Wren as, "Organise the school to benefit the scholar, to train his faculties, to wider his outlook, to cultivate his mind, to form and strengthen his character, to develop his aesthetic faculty, to build up his body, and give him health and strength to teach his duty to himself, the community and the State. Organise the school for this and not to prepare him for the Matriculation Examination."

Main Functions of School Organisation

The main function of school organisation is to make the optimum use of the human elements and material elements of the school system for the optimum fulfilment of the aims of the school system. The human factors include:

(i) Students, (ii) Staff, (iii) Parents, (iv) Community, (v) Board of Education, (vi) Department of Education, (vii) Managing Committee of the School and the Governing Body. (viii) In-service and pre-service training institutes like DIETs etc.

Material elements include: (i) Finances, (ii) School plant, (iii) Instructional supplies and equipment.

The formal structure/organisation of the school system may be illustrated as under:

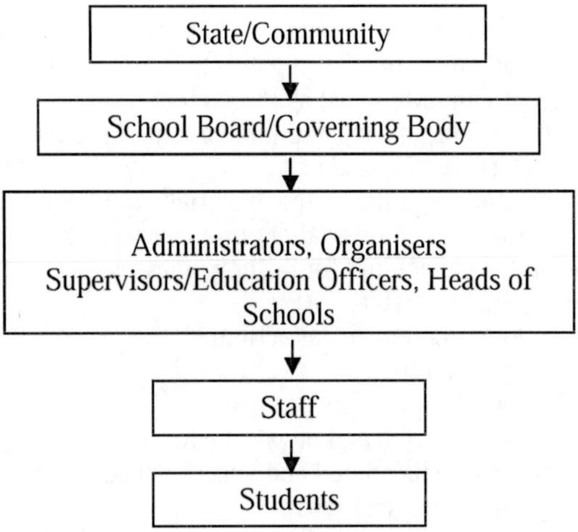

Fig. 1.1: Formal Structure of the School System

Important Aspects and Scope of School Organisation

School organisation includes five elements which may be expressed as 5 M's i.e. Men, Money, Materials, Machines and Methods.

Elements and Scope of School Organisation

Element	*Inputs*	*Process*	*Outputs*
1. Men	Cooperation of students, teachers, parents, community managing committee, Department of Education	1. Planning 2. Organising 3. Staffing 4. Directing 5. Coordinating 6. Reporting 7. Budgeting	i) Aesthetic Development of Students ii) Cultural Development of Students iii) Ethical Development of Students iv) Intellectual Development of Students v) Moral Development of Students vi) Physical Development of Students vii) Recreational Development of Students viii) Social Development of Students ix) Spiritual Development of Students x) Vocational Development of Students
2. Money	Use of school funds		
3. Materials	Use of furniture, stationery, raw materials etc.		
4. Machines	School workshops, Laboratory Apparatus etc.		
5. Methods	Appropriate —Teaching Learning —Management —Evaluation —Supervision		

Scope of school organisation is very vast. As a matter of fact, anything and everything having to do something with the education of the child through the agency of the school comes under the purview of school organisation

Following may be listed as necessary components of school organisation. These are the outcomes of the organisation of 5 M's (Men, Money, Materials, Machines and Methods) as listed above:

1. Providing and organising the human material—teaching staff, non-teaching staff and the students.
2. Providing and organising the material equipment such as school building, furniture, farms, laboratories, library etc.
3. Preparing the curriculum for different classes.
4. Preparing the time-table.
5. Organisation of co-curricular activities.
6. Maintaining discipline.
7. Organisation of student-government.
8. Organisation of health and physical education.
9. Organisation of educational and vocational services.
10. Organisation of mid-day meals.
11. Organisation of various ancillary services like drinking facilities.
12. Organisation of labour and social service weeks.
13. Organisation of home-work time table.
14. Organisation of evaluation machinery.
15. Maintenance of school records.
16. Financing and budgeting.
17. Making purchasing of different kinds.
18. Following departmental rules and regulations.
19. Organising admissions.
20. Organising transport for students.
21. Establishing liaison with several organisations and institutions including parents.

School Organisational Process

Planning	*Organising*	*Motivating*	*Controlling*
Forecasting and fixing goals	Doing division of work	Providing effective leadership	Laying down standards
Collecting and comparing data	Assigning tasks	Communicating effectively	Evaluating performance
Selecting best alterative and decision-making	Delegating authority and responsibility	Providing incentives	Finding out reasons for deviation
Formulating policies, procedures and programmes	Fixing accountability	Humanising organisational process	Taking corrective measures

Fig. 1.2: School organisation is the coordination of various elements

Main Functions of the School Organiser

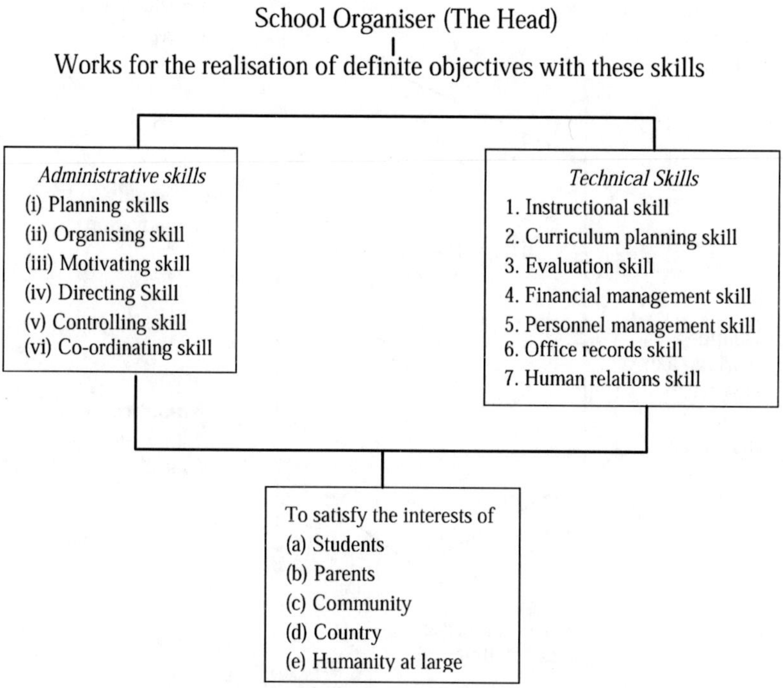

Fig. 1.3: Main Functions of the School Organiser

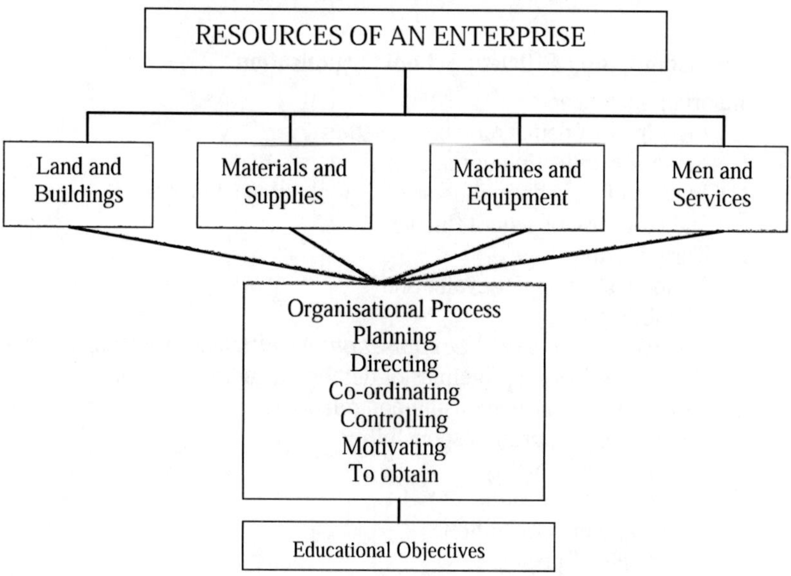

Fig. 1.4: Chief Elements of the Organisational Process

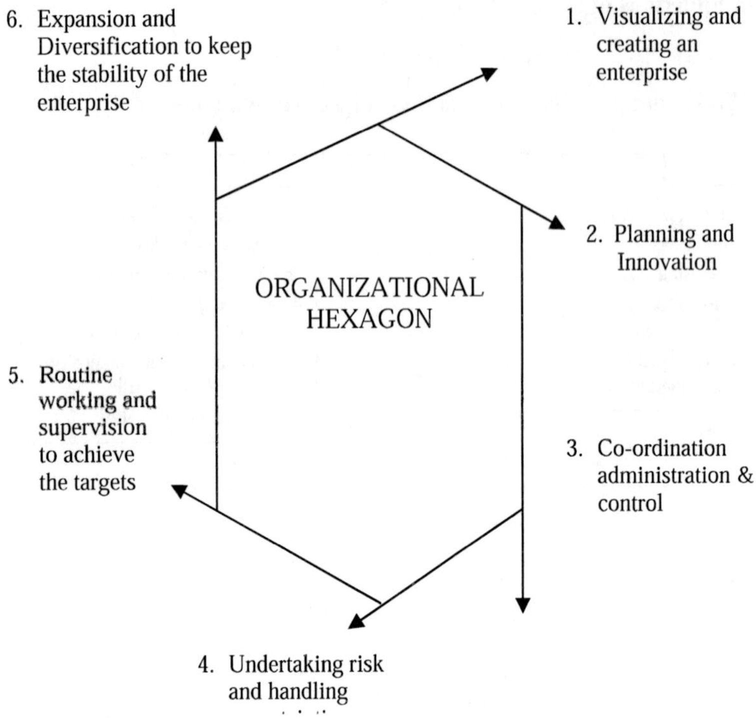

Fig. 1.5: Organisational Hexagon

Factors Comprising Efficient School Organisation

Important factors are:

1. Principles of democratic organisation
2. Scientific collection of the data.
3. Systematic and optimum use of the school machinery.
4. Judicious use of school finance.
5. Target fixing.
6. Periodic checking or evaluation
7. Flexibility.

1. *Principle of Democratic Organisation:* An efficient management must be based on the following principles of democratic administration:

(i) Principle of harmonious human relations.
(ii) Principle of sharing responsibility.
(iii) Principle of equality.
(iv) Principle of freedom.
(v) Principle of cooperation.
(vi) Principle of justice.

(vii) Principle of recognizing individual worth.
(viii) Principle of leadership.
(ix) Principle of coordination

2. *Systematic and Scientific Collection of the Data:* This implies that the school records must be maintained in a proper manner. They must be kept up-to-date, complete in all respects and quite accurate. Any lapse in this direction is likely to upset the whole planning of management. The manager, that is, the head of the school must devote adequate attention to this aspect of school management.

3. *Optimum Use of the School Machinery:* What is school machinery? By school machinery we mean the building, the teachers and the students. The work of the school should be distributed among the members of the staff in such a way that the right teacher teaches the right class. This implies that work should be distributed among the members of the staff according to their qualifications and experience. A good time-table will enable the head to make the best use of the school staff and school building.

Attempt should be made to associate the students with the management of different school activities. A limited form of self-government is very helpful in enlisting their cooperation.

4. *Judicious Use of School Finance:* The school money is a trust in the hands of the school authorities. Most of the troubles in schools may be attributed to the wrong use of the funds, especially the Boys' Fund which gives a handle to the students to create mischief and cause indiscipline. It is, therefore, very necessary that the Boys' Fund must be spent for the welfare of the students.

5. *Target Fixing: Institutional Planning:* Term-wise programme should be chalked out. The entire syllabus to be covered during the academic year should be divided into four terms. Programme of all activities must be carefully planned so as to make the best use of school and community resources.

6. *Periodic Checking:* Terminal and monthly tests should be conducted to judge the progress of the students as well as of teachers.

7. *Flexibility:* It must be stressed that management is a means and not an end. It must not dominate the end. The end is the many-sided development of the personality of the child. The curriculum, the methods of teaching, the evaluation, the time-table and in fact every aspect of school management is devoted to this end. Therefore, it is but proper that the management should be kept flexible.

Flexibility and Not Rigidity in School Organisation: Organisation a Good Servant but a Bad Master

In view of rapid changes, new developments and new situations encountered with while implementing educational programmes, it is essential that we should have an open mind. Planning as visualized may not remain a realistic one with a change in situation. One plan for a particular school system or a class system or teacher may not be suitable for the other. After all school organisation is a means and not an end. The means should not be allowed to dominate school organisation which is for the pupils and its effectiveness and efficiency must be measured to the extent to which it contributes to teaching and learning. No doubt there must be planning but there should be no absolute rigidity in it.

H.G. Stead has rightly said that management should be 'fluid'. In the words of Mort Paul, "Adaptability, stability and flexibility are really facets of the same thing. A school must have these three characteristics if it is to achieve its purposes and at the same time give due regard to all persons immediately or remotely concerned. It must hold fast to the good, change what requires change and be fertile in considering individual differences and in all personalities involved". A fluid system believes in evolution rather than revolution.

Freedom should be given to the teachers to use their own methods of teaching. Similarly, students should not be forced to obey a multiplicity of rules and regulations. Self-discipline cannot be achieved through rod and punishment. It can only be realised through love and sympathy.

Similarly, monthly tests should not be treated all in all. They are a means to the end as enumerated above. All the aspects of school organisation and organisation itself are the servants of the students, the teachers and the Head and as such it must not be given the place of a master. It should be dynamic and not static and should change according to the circumstances.

The end of school organisation is the many-sided development of the personality of the child. The curriculum, the methods of teaching, the evaluation and assessment, the time-table and in fact every aspect of school organisation is devoted to this end. It is, therefore, proper that the management is kept flexible.

Changing Concept of School Organisation: Factors Affecting School Organisation

In view of the new challenges, the roles of the present day school have been radically changed and accordingly the concept of school organisation. Change is the order of the day and the school organisation must reflect a positive note in this regard. The old principles and practices of school organisation are now fading into insignificance in the dazzling light of the new ones.

Organisation of the Traditional School

H.G. Wells has said, "If you want to feel the generation rushing to waste like rapids—you should put your heart and mind into a private school." This remark was meant for some of the private schools of England of the past and is certainly not applicable to the present day school of that country but is absolutely true of the large majority of our schools whether public or private.

A traditional school was considered to be a place where knowledge was manufactured and this used to be bookish, mechanical and stereotyped. Education being uniform; no importance was attached to the individual needs of children. Rote memory and memorisation played the dominant role. Children were regarded just like dumb driven cattle. Examination dominated the entire system of education. Rod was the chief weapon to educate the educand. 'The fear atmosphere' prevailed in the school. The teacher was called a policeman and drill sergeant. Co-curricular activities were unknown. No attempts were made to enlist the co-operation of the parents. Technology of teaching-learning was very simple.

Organisation of the Present-Day Schools

1. *Ideals and Values of Democratic India:* The functions of the present-day schools have undergone a great transformation in India since the advent of Independence. Our is a country wedded to the ideals of democracy. Democracy imposes many responsibilities on the citizens of a country. It is based upon love, cooperation, tolerance, open-mindedness, truthfulness and fellow-feelings. If democracy is to survive, education must develop certain qualities needed for its survival. It must enable an individual to take part effectively and freely in the affairs of the group to which he belongs. Education is essentially a social affair. According to Dr. Radhakrishnan, all education is social. Education is the transmission of technical skill and cultural traditions from one generation to another. Education is literacy plus discipline a kind of an appreciation of the values of society of which we happen to be members. Education is not worth the name, if it does not help an individual to live harmoniously and co-operatively in the society.

2. *Ideals of Socialism and Secularism:* Besides, democracy, we have accepted socialism and secularism as our ideals. Our educational institutions, therefore must serve these ends and produce individuals imbued with the ideals and attitudes of secularism and socialism.

3. *New Concept of Education:* Education in terms of traditional 3 R's has been replaced by the present 7 R's, *i.e.*, Reading, Writing, Arithmetic, Recreation, Right, Responsibility and Relationship.

4. *Guidance and Counselling:* Individual differences of children must be taken into account and diversified courses provided. School curriculum is considered in terms of activities and not subjects. Besides subjects such as English, Mathematics, Hindi etc., it is increasingly being realised that a variety of co-curricular activities must be considered as important as other school subjects. A well organised system of guidance and counselling is needed.

5. *Activity Methods:* New activity methods such as Dalton Plan, the Project Method, the Heuristic Method, the Montessori Method, etc., have brought about far-reaching changes in our methods of instruction.

6. *Impact of New Technology:* New technology has affected the old

system of school organisation. Information technology (IT) has placed new processes and equipments at the disposal of school organiser which must be made use of profitably.

7. *Impact of the New Pattern of Education i.e. 10+2:* Far reaching changes have taken place in the entire philosophy and practices of school organisation. School curriculum and methods of teaching-learning have undergone important changes with the introduction of the new pattern of school education on 1975. All this had implication for principles and practices of school organisation.

8. *Introduction of Vocational Courses and Socially Useful Productive Work:* These two elements have greatly influenced the philosophy and practices of school organisation.

9. *Multifarious Co-curricular Activities:* A present day school is expected to provide for a number of co-curricular activities which need an altogether a new concept of school organisation.

10. *Increase in the School-Going Population:* People are becoming increasingly education conscious. Today we find a large number of students attending the school. They differ in tastes, needs, aptitudes and in various other ways. Family and social backgrounds of the students also vary. This has made the problem of educational management very complex.

11. *Multi-farious Functions of the School:* The school of today is not only concerned with the intellectual development of the child but is also to train him in the 'art of living together' which in itself is a complicated affair.

12. *Role of the School in Fostering Values of Emotional Integration and National Unity:* There is a growing recognition of new demands upon management and the necessity of an imaginative response is transforming the principal's job.

Schools are expected to help in achieving national unity and as such the importance of its impact on educational organisation can hardly be ignored.

Chief Characteristics of a Well Organised School

The pen-picture of a well organised of a school has been outlined by S. Bala Krishna Joshi in the words, "A school is not a mere brick and mortar structure housing a miscellany of pupils and teachers; a school is not a market place where a heterogeneous crowd gathers with diverse objects; a school is not a rigorous reformatory where juvenile suspects are kept under vigilant watch, a school is a spiritual organism with distinctive personality of its own; a school is a vibrant community centre, radiating life and energy all round; a school is a wonderful edifice, resting on the foundation of goodwill—goodwill of the public, goodwill of the parents; goodwill of the pupils. In a word, a well conducted school is a happy home, a sacred shrine, a social centre, a state in miniature and bewitching Brindavan, all beautifully blended into a synthetic structure."

According to the Secondary Education Commission 1952-53, "The secondary school must make itself responsible for equipping its students adequately with civic as well as vocational efficiency—and the qualities of character that go with it—so that they may be able to play their part worthily and competently in the improvement of national life. They should no longer emerge as helpless, shiftless individuals who do not know what to do themselves." The school is one of the most important formal agencies of education. It plays a major role in moulding the ideas, habits and attitudes of the children with a view to producing well balanced personalities culturally sound, emotionally stable, mentally alert, morally upright, physically strong socially efficient, vocationally self-sufficient and internationally liberal. Informal agencies of education such as the church and the home fail to satisfy the increasing educational requirements of a complex society and thus are losing their hold on the people. The school is a social institution set up by the society to serve its ends. It is a place where men of tomorrow are trained and disciplined in certain forms of activities.

It is not without reason that the Education Commission 1964-66 wrote, "The destiny of India is now being shaped in her class rooms. This, we believe, is no more rhetoric. In a world based on science and technology, it is education that determines the level of prosperity, welfare and security of the people. On the quality and number of persons coming out of schools and colleges will depend our success in the great adventure of national reconstruction whose objectives are to raise substantially the standard of living of our people and to create a new social order based on the human values of the dignity of the individual, freedom, equality and justice.

The most important and urgent reform needed in education is to transform it, to endeavour to relate it to the life, needs and aspirations of the people and thereby make it a powerful instrument of social, economic and cultural transformation necessary for the realisation of the national goals. For this purpose, education should be so developed as to increase productivity, achieve social and national integration, strengthen democracy, accelerate the process of modernisation and cultivate social, moral and spiritual values."

The above mentioned objectives can be realised if the school is organised in such a way as it makes provision for the following:

1. Provision of a stimulating environment.
2. Transformation into activity school.
3. Provision for experimentation.
4. Training students in the art of living together.
5. Opportunities for developing self-discipline.
6. Making library as the hub of school activities.
7. Providing work experience and socially useful productive work.
8. Use of progressive methods of evaluation of students' performance.
9. Organising self-government in some select areas of school work.
10. Making school as a centre of community service.

Principles of Effective and Inspirational School Organisation

1. Principle of development of harmonious relationships among all those connected with the school.
2. Principle of forward planning.
3. Principle of realistic target fixing.
4. Principle of periodical evaluation of the planning and implementation of the programmes and activities.
5. Principle of cooperation.
6. Principle of coordination.
7. Principle of democratic philosophy.
8. Principle of equality.
9. Principle of reasonable freedom.
10. Principle of flexibility.
11. Principle of justice.
12. Principle of dynamic leadership.
13. Principle of introspection.
14. Principle of optimum output.
15. Principle of optimism.
16. Principle of recognition of individual differences and worth.
17. Principle of sharing responsibility.
18. Principle of budgeting.
19. Principle of accountability.

Administration, Management and Organisation

Earlier literature on education usually used the word school organisation but in recent literature words 'management' and 'Administration' are increasingly being used in place of school organisation.

In the B.Ed. curriculum of most of the Universities, the word organisation has been replaced by administration and management. In essence, all these three words connote the same meaning.

The *'Webster's New Collegiate Dictionary'* give the following meaning of these terms.

Administer	*Manage*	*Organise*
1. To manage or supervise. 2. To perform the office of the administrator.	1. To handle or direct with a degree of skill. 2. To direct or carry on business or affairs.	1. To cause to develop an organic structure. 2. To arrange or form into a coherent unity or functioning whole. 3. To set up an administrative structure. 4. To arrange elements into a whole of interdependent parts.

Administration: 1. The act or process of administering.
2. Performance of executive duties.

3. The execution of public affairs as distinguished from policy making.

4. (a) A body of persons who administer, (b) a group constituting the political executive in a presidential government, (c) a government agency or board.

5. The term of office of an administrative officer or body.

Management: 1. The act or art of managing: the conducting or supervising of something (as a business).

2. judicious use of means to accomplish an end.

3. capacity for managing: executive skill.

4. the effective body of those who manage.

Organisation: 1. (a) the act or process of organising or of being organised, (b) the condition or manner of being organised.

2. (a) association or society, (b) an administrative and functional structure (as a business or political party: the personnel of such a structure).

The two terms i.e. administration and organisation are not antagonistic but are complementary and supplementary. Organisation appears to be an all inclusive term which exhibits all the working of a school. In other words organisation is a broader concept. It includes administration also.

According to a narrow view, organisation is concerned with the arrangement and re-arrangement of men, material, money, machinery and methods. Administration is concerned with the operative part of organisation i.e. it manages the things so organised.

Some authors are inclined to consider administration as an all inclusive term. Of course, both serve the same purpose.

The following description in a broadly way differentiates between organisation and administration:

— We organise classes in a school and do not administer classes.
— We organise curriculum, methods of teaching-learning and do not administer these.
— We organise students self-government and do not administer it.
— We organise co-curricular activities and not administer.
— We organise subject clubs and do not administer these.
— We organise staff meeting and do not administer these.
— We organise parent-teacher meetings and do not administer them.

By and large, administration is concerned with the appointment of staff, the service conditions etc. Schools are organised according to administrative instructions, rules and regulations.

Autocratic and Democratic School Organisation

Why Democratic School Organisation: We are wedded to a democratic philosophy and a democratic way of life and as such it must prevail in all our institutions and organisations including educational. If this point is lost sight of, the very purpose of school organisation goes into oblivion. As observed by the Secondary Education Commission, "The educational system must make its contribution to the development of habits, attitudes and qualities of character which will enable its citizens to bear worthily the responsibilities of democratic citizenship." The school is an important social agency which provides numerous opportunities to the students to imbibe democratic values and train them in the 'art of living together'.

Democratic School Organisation	*Autocratic School Organisation*
1. 'We feelings' prevail in the school environment.	'I feelings' are predominant. Ego of one individual prevails.
2. An environment of mutual trust exists.	An environment of mutual distrust exists.
3. Cooperative planning is done by the entire staff.	Planning is done by the management.
4. The committees are chosen to do the work.	The head or management chooses committees and dominates them.
5. Organisers discuss problems with teachers and accepts suggestions.	Management tells teachers what to do.
6. The organisers and the Head respect teacher's personality and plans cooperatively with him.	The management/the Head sometimes embarrasses teachers before children.
7. Principal the Head gives co-workers credit for success.	Management/Principal takes credit for all success.
8. Principal encourages faculty to make use of human resources in the community.	Management/Principal gives no recognition to parents and leaders.
9. The budget is prepared cooperatively, with teacher participation.	The budget is prepared by the managerial and administrative staff.
10. Organisers, administrators and principals are educational leaders as well as administrative persons.	Organisers, administrators and principals are concerned only with the details of management and administration.
11. The organisers, administrators and principals make possible an active in-service programme for teachers.	The organisers, administrators and principals take the attitude of 'get it yourself '.
12. Teachers plan with the supervisors in special fields for work to be done.	Special supervisors outline course for teachers to follow in teaching special subjects.
13. The organisation allows teachers to make flexible programmes which best suit the interests and needs of children.	Organisation requires a set type of common programme.
14. Faculty meetings are	Faculty meetings are planned only

Democratic School Organisation	Autocratic School Organisation
cooperatively planned by the entire staff.	by principal.
15. The teachers can adopt an exploratory attitude.	The teachers give directions in a firm manner.
16. Teachers are encouraged to use cumulative records.	Cumulative records are only for the use of principal.
17. Teachers participate in selection of text-books.	Text-books are selected by the management.
18. Audio-visual materials are made available to the teachers.	Audio-visual programme is operated on a rigid time schedule, prepared by the management.
19. The staff and children are allowed to plan social gatherings after school time.	Such occasions are very rare.
20. Students are teacher-guided.	Students are teacher dominated.
21. The students are guided by the teachers in the choice of many activities.	The teacher plans activities without conferring with the pupils.
22. The groups suggest and propose supplementary work.	All the supplementary work is chosen by the organisers.
23. The students assist in planning the academic work, make suggestions and proposals.	The students answer questions asked by the teacher.
24. The pupils share with teachers establishing standards of achievement.	The teachers set up standards of achievement without conferring with the pupils.
25. The students share with the teacher the responsibility of appraising their work.	The students are not conferred with in appraising their growth.
26. Students are encouraged by the teacher to make suggestions concerning their work.	The teacher ignores suggestions of the pupils.
27. Students are encouraged to correct their mistakes.	The teacher directs pupil activities.
28. The daily programme is elastic and can be changed as the group decides.	Daily programme is rigid.
29. The teachers try to understand the child.	The teachers work according to set procedures.
30. The teachers are sympathetic.	The teachers spring awe and fear.
31. Students committees also assume responsibility for selecting equipment and	Teacher or the principal assumes responsibility for selecting and purchasing and supplies equipment.

Democratic School Organisation	Autocratic School Organisation
supplies needed.	
32. The teacher tries to find reasons for misbehaviour.	The teacher arbitrarily punishes pupils for misbehaviour.
33. The teacher takes into consideration the individual differences of the students.	The teacher treats all children alike.
34. Children are naturally affectionate and are encouraged to show affection.	Teacher is cold to child's affection and does not reciprocate.
35. Every child is provided as far as possible with an opportunity to contribute and to lead a group.	Only the aggressive and brighter children contribute and lead.
36. Materials and books are provided for all mental levels in a grade.	One level of supplies is furnished for single grade no matter what the ability range.
37. Students are grouped properly.	Students are grouped on administrative reasons.
38. The students express themselves freely.	There is no such freedom of expression.
39. Curriculum is flexible to meet with the needs of each child.	Curriculum is definite and same goals are set for all the children.
40. Teachers co-operate with other teachers to study problem students.	Teacher does not participate in group study of problem pupils.
41. Teachers encourage parents to visit school for a closer relationship between home and school.	Teachers discourage parents from visiting school because it disrupts the schedule.
42. School atmosphere is reflected by student's remark, "I like school."	School atmosphere is reflected by student's remark "I don't like school."

Concluding Observations: Democratic school organisation looks upon the school personnel as socially equal. It does not believe in taking decisions by itself but with the school family. Responsibility and accountability are shared in managing the school. A code of conduct is prepared and all constituents of the school family are bound to this code. No body is allowed to enjoy any special privilege. An environment of trust becomes the corner stone of school organisation.

2

The School Plant and Equipment

"We shape our buildings in the beginning, and ultimately they shape us" —*Winston Churchill*

Meaning of the School Plant

In the words of Jacobson, Reavis and others, "The school plant is a comprehensive term which includes building, ground, school furniture, other equipment and apparatus. The head of the school must look upon the plant as an integral part of a learning environment". Attractive, well equipped and properly maintained school plant serves as a great motivating factor in the teaching-learning process. It is very important that our school plant and its constituents become the learning laboratories.

Essential Elements of a Good School Plant

A good school plant has the following essential elements:

1. Suitable overall physical environment of the school building—aesthetic and physical.
2. Adequate and suitable site.
3. Structurally suitable building.
4. Proper building services.
5. Sufficient equipment and apparatus.
6. Proper maintenance and repairs.

Suitable Overall Physical Environment

A school is a live-giving and vital environment. Therefore a concerted attempt on the part of all concerned with the school should be put to bring about aesthetic improvement in the drab, dull and ugly environment which most of our educational institutions provide. There must be artistic appeal, beauty and grace in the buildings, furniture, the equipment, the grounds and the general layout of our schools.

A school cannot be put up everywhere and anywhere. The importance of school environment is apparent when we realize that the students spend a good deal of their time in the school premises. A healthy, beautiful and refreshing environment soothes the eyes and pleases the soul. In such an environment the intellectual forces of teachers and students function at their best. It has been very aptly observed by Yeager William, "Nothing in the whole educational programme is more conducive to cooperative attitude among the pupils and a love of school than an attractive and wholesome environment."

K.G. Saiyidain has observed in this regard as, "Ideally a school building should be planned spaciously, functionally and with pleasing architectural features. It should stand out in the village or the city as something of which the local community can be proud. In fact in some educational advanced and wealthy countries, schools are housed in beautiful buildings, which are not only stimulating centres of education for children but also vital centres of community life."

General Principles of Designing School Building

1. *Principle of Adequacy*: The school plant must provide for all the necessary facilities for curricular and co-curricular activities.

2. *Principle of Safety*: The building must be planned in strict conformity with safety and hygienic considerations. Full attention must be given to site, soil, ventilation, light and other allied problems. The school plant must be able to protect the health of the students and teachers.

3. *Principle of Durability*: As far as possible, the building must be 'pucca' rather 'kachcha'.

4. *Principle of Economy*: The school plant should be economical in original cost, upkeep and operation. Economy can be affected by the adoption of a standard classroom unit.

5. *Principle of Accessibility*: The school should be built at a place which is easily accessible to the students and free from road dangers.

6. *Principle of Mobility*: The question of easy movement, particularly in large schools on more than one storey is important.

7. *Principle of Flexibility*: There should be no rigidity in the design and use of the plant. Scope must be left for modification in accordance with the needs.

8. *Principle of Coordination*: There must be full coordination among the various parts and their location at particular place must have a purpose. For instance a workshop will be away from the classroom and staff room very near to principal's room.

9. *Principle of Simplicity*: The design of the building should be simple but artistic.

10. *Principle of Comprehensiveness*: A comprehensive vision is necessary in which function, form/and space are so harmonized that the soil from which the synthesis grows, will be enriched by such a pattern.

11. *Principle of Utility*: It must give the maximum utility to the students as regards accommodation, protection from weather, maximum light and ventilation, free movement and comfortable stay in rooms for longer hours.

Scientific Planning of Schools

In the opinion of the School Buildings Committee, general considerations that should determine the planning of schools of all types are set out below:

1. Due regard should be given to aesthetic standard, e.g., form, design and colour, in school buildings, in order that object lessons in good taste may remain at all times before the eyes of the pupils.
2. The question of easy movement, particularly in large schools on more than one storey, is important. Corridors should be wide enough and staircases should be so placed as to avoid congestion when classes change and above all in the event of fire.
3. Similar considerations should apply to the location of cloak rooms, changing rooms, bicycle sheds, etc., where provided.
4. Latrines, urinals and lavatories should be, from the point of convenience, as accessible as possible from all parts of the schools, subject always to their being so placed as to create neither a nuisance nor an eyesore.
5. The possibility of extension being required at some future date should always be borne in mind.
6. Verandahs can be made a most useful adjunct to almost every school in India.
7. Kindergarten rooms and rooms for young children should always be on the ground floor.
8. Where ample sites are available, single storey buildings have certain advantages. They facilitate elastic grouping of rooms as well as the use of light form of construction.
9. The orientation of all classroom and verandahs and of many practical rooms needs careful consideration. Local climatic conditions will largely determine this and sites should be chosen with this factor in mind.
10. Provided that the arrangement is convenient and design harmonious, the particular shape of the plan is of little importance. The quadrangular plan popular in Western countries has definite disadvantages; the most obvious being that it renders impossible the best orientation of many rooms.
11. Economy can be effected and planning facilitated by the adoption of a standard classroom unit which can be multiplied if necessary where larger rooms are required. It would be an advantage if sound proof adjustable partitions could be provided and where partition walls are provided they should be left free from carrying loads, so that they can be moved if, at some future date, it should be necessary to rearrange the rooms.
12. The plan must provide for a plentiful supply of pure drinking water.

Selection of School Site

In the selection of school site, important considerations which must be taken into account are given below. It must be stressed that the selection of the site which is the first requisite of a good environment needs careful consideration.

1. *Surroundings*: The site should be located in healthy surroundings. It should be near a road so as to be accessible by bus or other means of transport, yet back from the road. It should be located in a quiet and

pleasant environment.

2. *Level*: The level of the area should be little raised so that water-logging does not take place. There should be no danger of floods or breach of any canal.

3. *Direction*: The site selected should permit the construction of the rooms in such a way that no corner remains bereft of sunlight.

4. *Shape*: The shape of the site preferably should be rectangular.

5. *Service Conditions*: Various public services like drainage, water-pipe arrangement and lighting arrangement should be easily accessible.

6. *Scope for Future Expansion*: The site for a school should be so selected as to allow normal expansion towards one direction at least.

Situations to be Avoided in the Selection of Site

1. Noisy and busy roads.
2. Public places like bus stand, railway station, grain market, etc.
3. Places like cremation ground and burial ground.
4. Marshy lands.
5. Uneven and undeveloped lands.
6. Stagnant pools, cattle ponds and other unhealthy surroundings.
7. Places of public entertainment like the cinema houses.

Area Requirements

It is not possible to prescribe any definite limit. The area required for a school site depends upon many factors.

1. *Strength of the School*: As every child is to be provided with 15 square feet of floor space, the area of the site will depend upon the number of students in a particular school.

2. *Type of School*: For residential schools, a big area is required. They will require provision for hostel and staff quarters also. A modern public school which provides a swimming pool etc. needs much large area.

3. *Subjects Taught*: Schools which provide for the teaching of agriculture must have agricultural farm. Naturally, such schools will stand in need of a far greater area than an ordinary school. Likewise vocational subjects would need workshops and various types of equipment. Therefore, their needs would be quite different.

4. *Co-curricular Activities*: Generally speaking greater area is required for the public schools as they organise a large number of co-curricular activities than the ordinary schools. They provide activities like swimming etc.

5. *Other Considerations*: In big cities where land is not easily available, there may be several storeys of schools building. In such cases, the area required would be small. Moreover there is an acute shortage of place for playgrounds. A cluster of schools is provided a common playground. Likewise different yardsticks will apply to schools in hilly areas. In the rural areas, there may not be any problem of getting enough land for school buildings, playgrounds, farms and workshops.

The School Building Committee of the Central Advisory Board of Education suggested the Minimum Area for a Higher Secondary School as under:

No. of Children	*Area of the Building*	*Area for Playgrounds*
160	2/3 Acre	2—3 Acres
320	1 Acre	4—5 Acres
480	1½ Acres	6—7 Acres

Rooms and Their Sizes: Building for 480 Students

Type of Room	*Length (ft.)*	*Breadth (ft.)*
12 Class Rooms	20	20
History Room with Store	40	20
Geography Room with Store	40	20
Craft Room Workshop with Store	40	20
Science Laboratory with Store	40	20
Drawing Room with Store	20	40
Library Room	20	20
Head's Room	20	20
Staff Room	20	20
Office Room	20	20
Dispensary	20	20
General Store	16	12
Computer Room	20	20
Games Room	16	12
Scouting Room	16	12
N.C.C. Room	16	12
Hall	60	40
Science Theatre	20	40

Quarters for the School Staff: The Secondary Education Commission has greatly stressed the necessity of providing suitable quarters to the teachers as near the school as possible. The Commission writes, "We feel that the presence of the headmaster and at least some of the staff in or near a school, particularly if there are hostels attached or where the schools are residential, will be of the greatest benefit to the school going population."

Minimum Size of a Classroom: Minimum size of a classroom depends upon the number of students to be accommodated. On the basis of the 10 sq. ft. each for 40 pupils in a Primary School and 12 sq. ft. each for 35 in a Middle, High and Higher Secondary school the minimum area of a school room will vary between 400-420 sq. feet.

Dimension of a Room: The standard classroom unit of approximately 400 sq. ft. should be 20"-20". The length and breadth may be varied by 2" on either side.

Lighting: Short-sightedness is very common among children of school-going age. This imposes additional responsibilities upon the school authorities for providing proper means of lighting. Important considerations are: (a) Light should be well diffused. (b) It should not fall directly on the eyes of the students. (c) Light should come from the left. (d) Where left light is not possible, right light may be allowed. (e) Direct front light is not allowable in any case. (f) The colour of the walls should be such as it does not tax the eyes of the pupils.

Windows: The windows serve two purposes: (a) admission of light, (b) admission of air. The window area should not be less than one-fifth of the floor area. Every part of the school should be well lighted. The window sills should be placed at not more than four feet and not less than three feet and a half above the floor of rooms in which the pupils are seated at desks.

Ventilation: There are two methods of ventilation, natural and artificial. Natural ventilation depends upon natural forces while artificial ventilation is brought by the use of fans etc.

Following points should attended to:

(i) Ventilation is of use only when there is cross ventilation. Doors and windows provided only on one side of the room will not serve the desired purpose.

(ii) The window should be fixed at three to four feet above the floor level. They should be sufficiently wide and high to allow adequate air to come into the room.

(iii) The windows should be wire-gauzed so that it is possible to keep them opened in the event of dust also. The wire-gauzed provides protection against excessive cold, heat, dust, rain and insects.

(iv) There should be supplementary arrangements for ventilation such as the ventilators which serve as outlets for foul air and the floor ventilators which allow plenty for fresh air from outside.

(v) When there is the possibility of smoke and gas inside the room, an outlet should be provided in the form of a chimney.

Flooring: The floors should be such as can bear the wear and tear and can be cleaned easily. Cemented floor is the best floor. It is durable and can be swept and washed conveniently Brick floors should be the last alternative. In hilly areas, asphalt tiles or linoleum blocks and wooden sleepers can be used.

Types of Building Design of a School

Important types of design are:

I Type: This is the simplest form of school building. It consists of a number of classrooms in a single row. This can be a temporary arrangement and allows scope for further expansion.

L Type: This is an improvement of I type. In this pattern I type will have an expansion on one side.

T Type: This consists of I type with extension on one side both ways.

U Type: This has two I's joined on one side.

E Type: In this design I type will have three extensions on the same side of the main block.

H Type: This consists of two I's joined in the centre with the block of rooms.

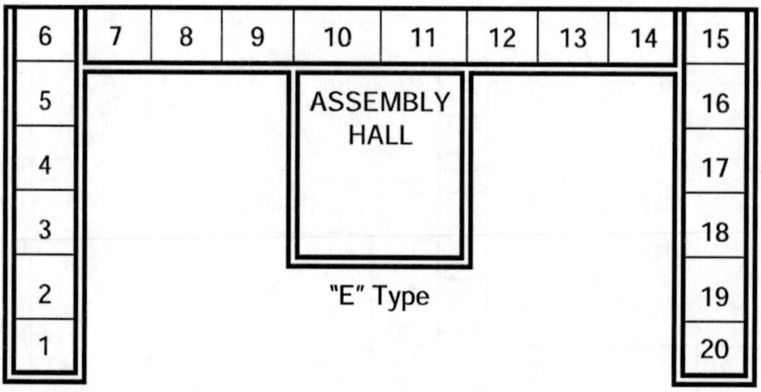

Fig. 2.1: E Type School Building

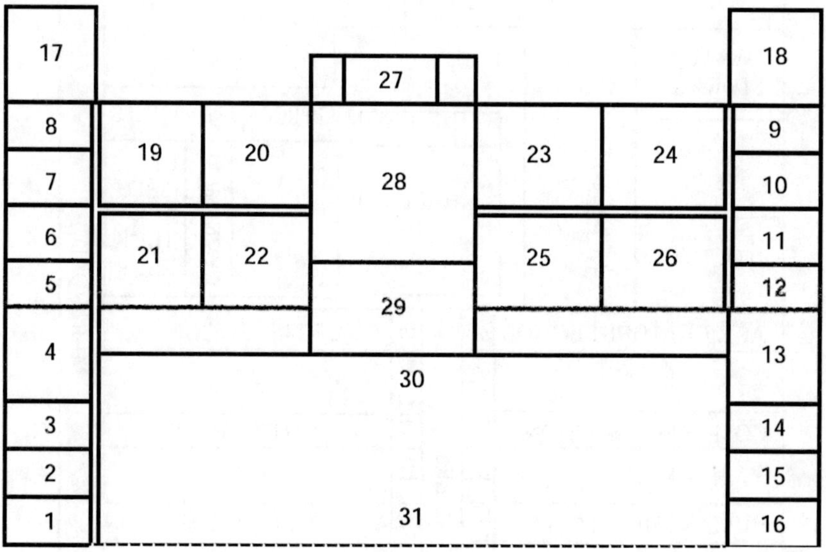

Fig. 2.2: H Type School Building

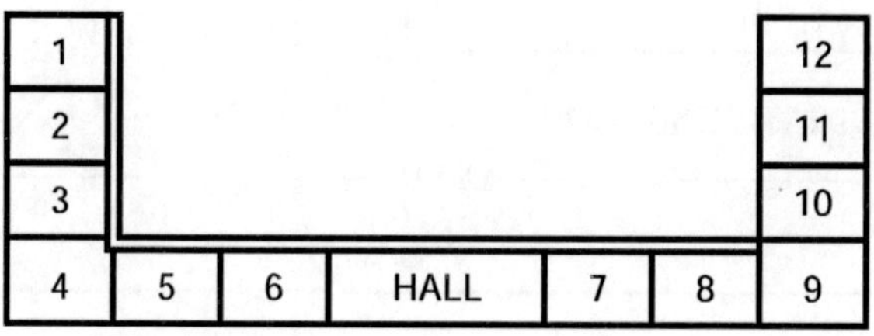

Fig. 2.3 U Type School Building

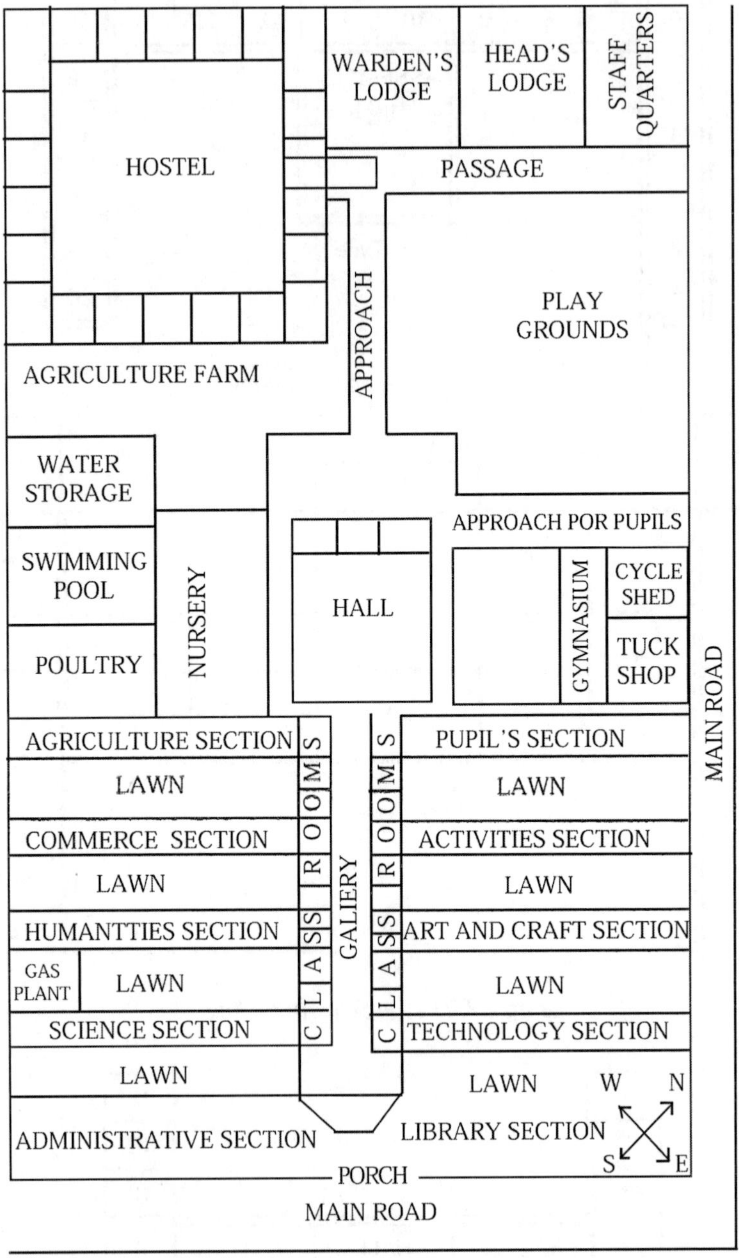

Fig. 2.4: Master Plan for a Progressive School

Classroom Equipment

The classroom equipment is usually divided into three categories i.e. essential, less essential and desirable.

Essential equipment: It includes:

- (i) Desks and chairs for the pupils or matting if they are required to sit on the floor.
- (ii) Block-board, preferable a wall black-board.
- (iii) A chair and a table for the teacher.
- (iv) A map stand or a chart stand.
- (v) Dust bin.

Less essential equipment: This includes:

- (a) A bulletin board.
- (b) Foot pad, door mat, wash basin etc.
- (c) Decorative items such as flower pots, table cloth etc.

Desirable

- (i) Curtains
- (ii) Matting under the desks.
- (iii) A dais or a raised platform for the teacher.
- (iv) An almirah or cup-board carved into the walls for chalk duster, Illustrative aids etc.
- (v) An attendance board.
- (vi) A notice board
- (vii) Wooden railings round the walls of the room with hooks and nails for display of charts, pictures and portraits.

Problems of School Buildings and the Recommendations of the Education Commission (1964-66)

The Education Commission that was appointed to consider all aspects of education at all levels made important recommendations on school buildings.

State of School Buildings and three Aspects: About the existing state of school buildings, the Education Commission observed, "The provision of school buildings is extremely unsatisfactory at present. At the primary stage, only about 30 per cent of the schools are stated to have been housed in satisfactory buildings. The corresponding proportion at the secondary stage is stated to be about 50. This shows the great backlog of unconstructed school buildings which has to be cleared during the next few years. In addition, buildings will have to be provided for the additional enrolments which will come in with increasing speed. The problem, therefore, has three aspects: (1) provision of the necessary funds; (2) reducing the building costs to the minimum level possible; and (3) devising a suitable machinery which can implement the programme expeditiously and economically."

Major Recommendations of the Commission on School Buildings

I. *Funds for School Buildings*: The Education Commission recommends that the allocations for construction of school buildings in the Central and State budgets should be increased. This is one area where the local community can make a significant contribution. Schemes of grant-in-aid should, therefore, be devised under which assistance from the State will be available to local communities, on a basis of equalisation, for the construction of school buildings. Wherever possible, loan programmes for the construction of buildings should be encouraged. Grants-in-aid and loans should also be available to private schools, on a fairly liberal basis, for building constructions.

II. *Less Costly Buildings*: The Education Commission feels that the prejudice against the use of 'temporary' buildings or thatched huts for school purposes is totally unjustified. Designed and constructed with a raised floor and high doors and windows with plenty of ventilation, these structures serve more than adequately as school building. This should not, however, be misunderstood to imply that *kachha* buildings are always better. This is not so; and some *kaccha* buildings prove costlier in the long run because of heavier costs of maintenance. What we wish to emphasize is the need to accept well-planned *kaccha* structure as part of our system and highlight simplicity and utility rather than ostentation in the construction of buildings.

III. *Buildings in Rural Areas*: *Local Initiative:* The problem of school buildings has been discussed by the Commission separately for urban and rural areas.

In the former case, land values are high; and very often enough land is not available at all. Sophisticated structures are, therefore, necessary, even in order to keep in tune with the immediate environment. In the rural area on the other hand, land is cheap and readily available; and sophisticated structures often look grotesque in a village atmosphere.

The Education Commission recommends that everything should be done to encourage local initiative and local contribution (in cash, kind of labour) for the erection of schools. A special device that can be of great use is that Government should supply only the framework, which can be pre-fabricated, and the local people should be expected to raise the plinth and fill up the walls.

IV. *Buildings in Urban Areas*: For urban areas, the Commission suggests that the following steps should be taken for achieving economy in the construction of education buildings:

(a) *Judicious selection of specifications and local materials.* The existing practice of playing safe by adopting conventional specifications is not conductive to economical construction. The economy can be achieved through the selection of locally available materials, use of cheaper materials and omission altogether of certain finishes and acceptance of a lower standard of construction.

(b) *Techniques of construction*: With careful planning and designing, even the so-called 'temporary' structures can be made to serve a better purpose than many of the rented buildings in which schools are often housed. Such structures should be built, wherever climatic and other conditions permit. If *pucca* buildings are absolutely necessary, an increasing reliance is needed on the improved techniques of construction such as the use of framed structures, cavity, walls, pre-fabricated components, R.C.C. frames for doors and windows and components evolved by the Central Building Research Institute and other research organisations.

V. *Expeditious Construction*: In order to expedite the construction of school buildings, the following steps are recommended by the Education Commission.

(a) *Rural areas*: In rural areas, there are no local contractors available. Contractors from urban areas generally charge higher rates when they are required to work in villages. The departmental machinery is also not adequate to reach most of the outlying villages. For the construction of village school buildings, therefore, the Commission recommends that the agency of the local communities or village panchayats should be utilised to the fullest extent possible.

(b) *Urban areas*: In urban areas, it has been recommended that the local agencies like Municipalities and Corporations should be utilised fully for construction of school buildings. They have the necessary technical staff and can also contribute towards the cost of such buildings. If the responsibility for providing buildings for local schools is placed on municipalities and if a suitable system of grant-in-aid is devised, the progress in this sector would be accelerated.

VI. *Supervision and Standardisation of School Buildings*: The Commission recommends the adoption of the following additional measures:

(a) *Formation of educational building development groups*: Each State should have Educational Building Development Group within the Public Works Department but working in close association with the Educational Department and consisting of an architect and educationist, all working on a full-time basis (with power to co-opt representatives of special technical skills) whose main function would be to improve the planning and construction of Government school buildings and whose advice should be available for private school also. There should also be a Building Development Group working at the Centre, for effectively coordinating the working of state levels Groups. These groups should be assigned the following functions:

(i) To study building requirements in the light of new teaching techniques,

(ii) To develop in cooperation with manufacturers new building techniques and specifications,

(iii) To evolve functional and economic type plans for various types of educational buildings,

(iv) To arrive at a correct assessment of costs of materials and labour required.

(v) To conduct field trials,

(vi) To evaluate the plans, specifications and building techniques already in use, and

(vii) To study methods of maximising the use of indigenous materials.

The Group at the Centre could profitably bring out a journal highlighting the latest techniques of construction, researches at home and abroad on conventional buildings.

The State Government should ensure that the recommendations of these Development Groups are followed.

When the Groups in different States are well established the possibility of making them function within a rigid framework of "maximum cost per place and minimum standards" as is being successfully done in the United Kingdom, should be explored.

(b) *Separate school unit of P.W.D.* To avoid delays in the construction of government buildings a separate unit of P.W.D. should be set up for execution of educational building programme.

VII. *Formation of Educational Building Consortia*: After the Educational Building Development Groups have standardised the plans and the techniques of construction, the possibility should be examined of establishing Educational Building Consortia (on the lines of similar associations, popularly known as CLASP, in the U.K.) to exploit fully the advantages of industrialized building.

VIII. *Standardization*: Lay-outs, dimensions, specification and methods of construction of any particular region should be as mentioned above so that mass production of the different components on a factory scale can be undertaken resulting in economy as well as speed of construction. Considerable work in the field of standardization has been done by organisations like the Indian Standards Institution which could serve as a basis for further studies.

IX. *Building for Private School*: These economy measures worked out by the Educational Building Development Group in each State for reducing the cost of educational buildings should be made known to the managements of private educational institutions in the State, and the grant-in-aid given to a private management for a building subject to upper cost limits worked out.

School Building and Health of the School

Following points should be taken note of:

(i) Healthy surrounding of the school.
(ii) Airy and well-ventilated rooms.
(iii) Suitable colour of the walls.
(iv) Cleanliness of the school building.
(v) Good seating arrangements.
(vi) Suitable chairs and desks.
(vii) Right type of black-boards and use of right type of chalk.
(viii) Fresh drinking water.
(ix) Sanitation of latrines and urinals.
(x) Spacious playgrounds.

Aesthetic Aspect and School Building

Our present system is dominated by a material outlook and affords very little scope for the growth of aesthetic sense in our students. Aesthetic education has a great value in life. Man does not live by bread alone. He has to satisfy his other senses also. Aesthetic education enables us to appreciate the wonderful face of nature. Delightful scenes whether in nature, painting, photography or poetry have cheering influence on the body, as well as the mind. Aesthetic value sometimes provide relief to the students from the dull and dreary life of the school. Aesthetic imagination if properly developed can become one of the greatest assets of man. Appreciation of 'truth', 'beauty' and 'goodness' is the watch-word of aesthetic education.

Following factors can be very conveniently employed for the introduction of aesthetic elements in our schools.

1. Healthy school surroundings.
2. Buildings well designed and tastefully decorated.
3. Occasional excursions to places of natural scenery, e.g., valleys, lakes, river sides, open fields etc.
4. Introduction of activities such as gardening, photography etc.
5. Well-furnished reading rooms.
6. Teaching of poetry and other subjects like nature study, arts and drawing.
7. Musical competitions.
8. Organisation of various programmes like dramatics.
9. Arranging competition in art and craft work.
10. Giving due appreciation to the activities of children.
11. Planning and execution of various projects like the pageant on the life of Buddha.
12. Emphasis on personal cleanliness.
13. Orderly arrangement of desks.

Desks

Desks have a great bearing on the health and especially of the postures of the students. As a child spends a good deal of his time at desk, it is but obvious that right postures can be maintained only when good seats are provided. A child who is comfortable is likely to pay more attention and concentrate on his work than one who is not. The seat and the desk should be made to fit the child—not the child to the seat and the desk. J. Mace Andress states, "If a child is properly seated he should be able to rest his feet comfortably on the floor without pressing upon the nerves and blood vessels under the knee; the seat should be so shaped as to encourage the sitter to it with the pelvis well back in the chair, the distance of the chair from the desk, its height and slants should be such that bending forward will not be encouraged."

Dressler states, "If the back of school bench or chair be just a little lower than the shoulder blades of the pupils when sitting properly, the best results, other things being equal, may be obtained."

P.C. Wren has described the importance of good furniture for the students in these words, "Furniture plays an extremely important part in the physical, moral and mental welfare of scholars. If the desks be of the wrong kind, or if benches be used instead of desks, curvature of the spine, contract of chest, roundness of the shoulders and a confirmed stoop may result as a physical injury; bad discipline, irritation, discontent and discomfort may result as moral injury and inability to sustain attention and concentration owing to lack of bodily ease may result as mental injury."

Following points should be borne in mind while providing furniture to the students:

(i) There should be, as far as possible, single desk with a slight slope towards the seat.
(ii) The seat should be supported by a back.
(iii) The maximum length of the desks should be twelve feet.
(iv) Inkpots should be fitted in the desks.
(v) The desks should not be arranged more than six rows deep.
(vi) 18" of space should be provided to each pupil.
(vii) There should be sufficient space between the rows of desks as well as between desks and walls so as to have free movements.

Black-board

The black-board plays a significant role in making the teaching efficient and effective. It is a necessary equipment of a class-room and a handy apparatus at the hands of a teacher.

Types of Black-boards

Following are the various types of blackboards:

(i) Fixed black-board.

(ii) Easel or removable.
(iii) Roller black-board.
(vi) The sliding black-board.

Use of Black-board

Black-board should be placed at a place from where the writing on the black-board could be seen very easily. It should never be placed between windows. Its back should not be towards the light as in this position its surface would be in the dark and it will tax the eyes of the students in trying to read what is written on the black-board. It should be either black or green in colour and should not be glossy, otherwise it will adversely affect the eyesight of the pupils. Its height from the floor should vary from 26 to 39 inches according to the height of the students. It should be four feet wide. Easel black-board is better as its both sides can be used and it can be raised or lowered. It is also easily removable. Damp duster should be used to clean it so as to avoid the inhalation of chalk dust which leads to consumption.

Seven factors to be kept in view in the use of black-board are:

(i) Location
(ii) Distance
(iii) Colour
(iv) Surface
(v) Dimension
(vi) Chalk and duster
(vii) Washing and varnishing

Sanitation Facilities: Toilets and Lavatories

It is universally agreed that the provision of proper and adequate sanitary facilities is essential. But it is only here that there is a wide gap between the standard recommended by different authorities and the actual conditions. An ideal toilet room should consist of flush latrines, urinals, wash basin etc. However, this is not possible. The lavatory block should be located at a place easily accessible from all the sings of the school buildings.

In several urban areas and rural areas, there is no water supply arrangement. The dry latrines will be the only alternative. These latrines require cleaning every two to three hours. Phenyl and other disinfectants must be used regularly.

Following are the desirable provisions:

i) Latrines of W.C. : One for every 100 students or part thereof.
ii) Urinals : 1 One for every 25 students or part thereof.
iii) Water tap with troughs : 1 for every 50 students or part thereof. For girls separate arrangements should be made.

SCHOOL HOSTEL

Significance and Need for a School Hostel

It is universally accepted that a good hostel can serve as an enlarged ideal family for developing a spirit of corporate living, self reliance and self-discipline in the students. An ordinary school sets limits to the possibilities of developing the 'art of living' amicably and graciously.

A well-supervised hostel is very conducive to the training of ideals and values of citizens.

A well-organised hostel can serve as a great cementing factor in uniting students coming from different regions with their distinct languages, customs and manners etc. Values of appreciation of varying cultures is developed. Ideals of emotional integration and national unity are strengthened.

Hostel becomes a necessity in the event of frequent transfer of parents of students.

Sometimes parents send children to protect them from unhappy and unhealthy home environment.

Role of the Hostel Superintendent

The proper management and organisation of a hostel depends to a great extent on the personality and character of the hostel superintendent. He is the person who can provide an appropriate environment for the desired development and training of the students.

Sympathetic and enlightened supervision of the various activities of the hostel life by the superintendent with the help of students' committees will go a long way in making the lives of the hostellers, riches, fuller, nobles and conducive to the ideas of citizenship.

If the superintendent is careless, negligent and devoid of psychological knowledge, the boarders are likely to go astray. Broadly speaking the hostel superintendent must be a parent substitute. All the essentials of home life must be made available to the students so that they may not think that they are living at a place which is quite separate from them. To develop this kind of attitude, introduction of self-government in hostels is very helpful.

Too much of liberty regarding their stay outside the hostel is very harmful. No student should be allowed to spend the night away from the hostel except with the prior permission of the hostel superintendent.

A proper check on the visit of the friends of the hostlers should be kept. Undesirable elements should be disallowed to visit the hostel.

To minimise the chances of extravagant expenditure, the hostel superintendent should act as a banker. He should teach them the virtues of thrift and economy.

Proper time-table for studies and games, provision for co-curricular activities, formation of students committees for the management of different activities, etc. are very essential for organising hostel life.

Following are some of the important duties of the hostel superintendent:

1. To look after the morals of the students.
2. To look after the studies of the students.
3. To look after the diet of the students.
4. To look after the health of the students.
5. To look after the cleanliness of the hostel.
6. To look after the recreational activities.
7. To look after the spending habits of the students.
8. To look after the corporate life of the students.

The hostel superintendent is expected to possess the following qualities:

i) He should be a man of vision.
ii) He should be democratic in his outlook.
iii) His treatment with the students should be parental.
iv) He should be academically and professionally well qualified to guide students in their intellectual pursuits.
v) He should command respect and obedience through his qualities of head and heart.
vi) He should understand the adolescence psychology.

Self-Government in the Hostel

Principle of sharing responsibility with the students should be the key-note of the functioning of hostel.

Following committees may be constituted to carry on various activities of hostel life.

(a) *Mass Committee*: The function of this committee will be to prepare a suitable menu, to make necessary purchases in connection with the meals and to supervise the preparation of meals. It will be its concern to see that wholesome diet is supplied to the boarders.

(b) *Sanitation Committee*. Its function will be to look after the general cleanliness of the hostel, urinals, lavatories etc.

(c) *Literary Committee*: It will be entrusted with the task of supervising the study habits of the students. Perhaps this is the most difficult task.

(d) *Cultural Committee*: It will be entrusted with the work of organising daily prayers and arranging talks on moral and spiritual matters. Social and religious functions may also be planned by this committee.

(e) *Dramatic Committee*. This will organise dramatics to make the hostel life richer from the recreational point of view.

(f) *Games Committee*: This Committee will be entrusted with organising games regularly.

(g) *Discipline Committee*: This Committee will frame general rules and code of conduct to be observed in the hostel.

These committees are intended to provide opportunities to students to develop the ideas of cooperation, mutual help, fellow feeling and love for rules and regulations. The students will feel that they are residing in their own homes and it is their responsibility to enhance the reputation of this home, i.e., hostel. By obeying the laws framed by different committees, they will develop an attitude of respect to laws whether framed by the superintendent or school authorities. Dignity of labour will also be developed in them. They learn how to adopt the policy of 'give and take'.

A Word of Caution

Lack of appropriate supervision by the hostel superintendent may lead to the following undesirable elements:

1. Indulgence in gossips.
2. Undesirable habits.
3. Mutual bickerings and jealousies.
4. Extravagant expenditure.

To avoid ugly situations and indisciplinary tendencies, it is very essential to prepare proper time-table for studies, provision for co-curricular activities and formation of students committees to look after various activities.

3

School Time-Table

Well arranged time is the surest mark of a well arranged mind.

—Pitman

Meaning of School Time-Table

The school time-table is a chart which indicates all the activities undertaken by each member of the staff and the student in each class or on farm or workshop at a particular time of the day when the school is functioning. It is the school mirror which reflects the school programme. It is called the 'Second Clock' of the school on the face of which is shown the daily schedule of the school. In the words of H.G. Stead, "It is the time-table that supplies the frame-work within which the work of the school proceeds. It is the instrument through which the purpose of the school is to function."

Time table is an outline of the day's work in a school which indicates:

1. Time of the beginning and ending of the school day.
2. Time of beginning and ending of each class period and the activity of the class.
3. Subjects and activities being undertaken by students in each class, in each period and by an each teacher.
4. Days on which every subject is taught.
5. Name of the teacher teaching a particular subject in a particular period and in a particular room.
6. Room or place where each activity is going on.
7. Recess Break or interval time.

Significance of the School Time-Table: Spark Plug of the School

Dr. Jaswant Singh regards the time-table of the school as the "spark plug of the school which sets into motion its various activities and programme." Some educators regard it as the 'mirror' that reflects the entire daily schedule of the school.

Time-table is an indispensable document of the school. The main points of the significance and value of time table are discussed below.

1. *Brings System in the School:* Without the time-table, there will be chaos and confusion all around in the school. In the absence of the time

table, the school life will come to a stand still and become a free for all affairs.

2. *Eliminates Wastage of Time and Energy:* Undoubtedly all planned programmes eliminate wastage of time and energy and it is equally true in the case of a school time-table. The entire school work is, by and large, equitably distributed among the members of the staff.

It directs the teacher's and students energy and attention to one thing at a time by placing proper persons at their proper places at the proper time and in the proper manner.

3. *Ensures Due Attention to Every Subject or Activity:* In framing the time-table, due attention is given to every subject. Periods are allotted to different subjects according to their importance and their fatiguing nature.

4. *Develops Moral Values.* It helps to develop qualities like punctuality and regularity both in the teachers and the taught by placing before them a set programme of activities.

5. *Ensures Regular and Even Progress:* Regular and even progress is ensured because time-table prevents laxity and shortages.

6. *Provides a Psychological Environment:* It has got a psychological value leading to the removal of fatigue which may occur due to prolonged hours of teaching and learning. It brings new motivation and stimulation to teachers and students.

7. *Ensures Equitable Distribution of Time to Different Subjects and Activities:* Time-table helps in avoiding the allotment of took much or too less work to one teacher.

8. *Develops Good Habits:* It helps in developing regular habits of work in students as well as teachers.

9. *Facilitates advance Planning by the Teachers and Students:* Time-table helps in chalking out plans in a systematic manner.

10. *Ensures Efficiency:* There will be no looseness, duplication of effort and repetition of items and activities. Everybody in the school system knows what to do at a particular time.

11. *Helps in Maintaining Discipline:* Since the students are kept gainfully busy in desirable activities, they have little excuse to loiter about. When they are busy, they do not think and act in wrong directions.

12. *Facilitates Supervision:* The head finds it convenient to supervise the work of the teachers and students and offer appropriate guidance to them. He can have individual consultation with the teachers when they are not busy with their classes.

13. *Necessitates Advance Planning:* This urges upon the school management to plan in advance and prepare for various activities and courses.

14. *Leads to Even and Regular Process:* It avoids imbalances and leads to even and regular process in all areas of school curriculum.

Form of a School Time-Table

The form of a time-table depends upon the nature of activities carried on in a school. The more the number and variety of activities, the more types of time-tables. In an ordinary school four forms of time-table i.e. consolidated time-table of the school, class time-table, teachers' vacant period time-table and teachers' time-table will serve the purpose. Time-table for co-curricular activities is coming into vogue in view of their importance in the field of education. Similarly in schools where games are properly organised, the need for games' time-table can hardly be stressed. The progressive schools maintain special room time-table. Time-table for homework is also maintained by some schools.

Ideally speaking there should be seven types of time-table.

1. Master time-table indicating the entire programme of the school.
2. Class time-table.
3. Teachers' time-table.
4. Vacant period time-table.
5. Games time-table.
6. Co-curricular activities time-table.
7. Home work time-table.

One copy of the class time-table should be kept in the class-room concerned. A copy of the teachers' time-tables should be put in the staff-room. One copy of each of the time-table should be kept in the Head's office so that he may know at a glance what work a particular class or teacher is doing at a given time.

General Considerations Underlying School Time-Table Construction

The construction of time-table makes large demands on the ingenuity and skill of the Head. Framing of a time-table is a time absorbing task. Some of the chief factors which determine the construction of a time-table are:

1. Departmental regulations.
2. Type of School.
3. Amount of time available.
4. Relative importance of a subject.
5. Incidence of fatigue.
6. Principle of justice.
7. Principle of variety.
8. Principle of free period for teachers.
9. Principle of play and recreation.
10. Principle of optimum utilisation.
11. Principle of local variation.
12. Principle of initiation.
13. Principle of elasticity.

1. *Departmental Regulations:* Generally, the State Department of

Education issues directions regarding the number of working hours of a school, examination and evaluation schedule and holidays to be observed etc. It is obligatory for the schools to obey these regulations.

2. *Type of School:* The type of school *i.e.* a boy's school or girl's school, urban or rural, infant school or school for girls, public or ordinary, will determine the nature of activities of the school and accordingly time-table will be framed. The double shift will call for shortening the duration of the school hours. Similarly, co-educational school will necessitate numerous changes so as to meet the specific needs of both the boys and the girls. In the higher grades of schools the duration of the periods will be longer than in the lower grades of schools.

3. *Amount of Time Available:* The amount of time to be given to each subject or activity is determined by the total amount of time available at school. Generally speaking, the higher the grade of the school, the longer the school day. There are certain departmental regulations concerning school timings which have got to be obeyed. According to the Punjab Education Code, the hours for opening and closing Government schools shall be fixed by the Inspector and other recognised schools by the Local Bodies or Managers concerned after consideration of the season, locality and class of pupils and subjects to the restriction that the total weekly period of instruction (excluding the time allotted to drill and recess) does not exceed the following limits:

Class I	16 Hours
Class II and III	19 Hours
Class IV	24 Hours
Secondary classes	30 Hours

Recommendations of the Education Commission 1964-66: The Commission made the following recommendations:

(A) The working hours per day should vary from four hours at the pre-primary stage to about six hours at the higher secondary stage.

(B) The total period does not include the time for co-curricular activities.

(C) The period includes the time for library period or the guided studies.

(D) At the lower primary stage the hours of instruction should be about 900 and at the higher primary and secondary stages they should be not less than 1,000 and preferably raised to 1,100 or even 1,200 if conditions are favourable.

4. *Relative Importance and Difficulty of Subjects:* There are certain social and economic considerations that determine the importance of a subject in the school curriculum and accordingly time is allotted to each subject in the school time-table. Subjects like English and Mathematics which are considered to be important and difficult are allotted more time.

5. *Incidence of Fatigue:* The element of fatigue influences the construction of the school time-table in a number of ways. Subjects

requiring more brain-work are placed on the time-table when the brains of the students are quite fresh and when they are capable of doing hard and difficult work. Each part of the morning is considered better than the corresponding part of the afternoon. In other words, the middle or the morning is better than the middle of the afternoon although the middle of the afternoon is better than the end of the morning and the end of the morning is better than the end of the afternoon. It is a common feeling to think that mental freshness is the greatest in the morning. It gradually increases until it reaches its maximum about the middle of the morning. That is the case after recess. Mental freshness is greater not just after recess but in the second period after recess. The best periods for fatiguing subjects are, therefore, the second, and third periods in the morning and second period after recess. The order of subjects causing fatigue is as follows: Mathematics, English, Indian Languages, Science, Nature Study, Science practical, Drawing, Crafts, Music, etc. The second and the third periods in the morning and the second in the afternoon are considered to be the best periods for the fatiguing subjects. English and Mathematics should, therefore, be placed as far as possible in these periods. The worst period is the last period in the afternoon and it may be given to manual work, science practical, physical exercises, etc.

The 'fatigue principle' is true of the days of the week also. Tuesday and Wednesday are considered to be the best days in which maximum work could be done. The end of the week is like the end of the day and fatigue is the greatest.

The younger are quickly fatigued, and therefore, the duration of the period in the lower classes should not exceed thirty minutes and in the higher classes it should not exceed forth minutes. In the summer season, the duration of the period should be reduced.

Likewise teachers are not given four periods continuously to teach.

6. *Principle of Justice:* Work among the members of the staff should be equitably distributed. Unequal distribution of work causes frustration among them and hampers progress. Similarly, time should be allotted for different activities according to their importance in the school curriculum.

7. *Principle of Variety:* It should always be remembered that to keep the children sitting the whole day long at the same place is in no way a wise procedure. As often as possible and convenient, the classes should change place. It has been stated "Change of room, of seat, of posture is an antidote against weariness." Change of occupation is one of the best forms of rest. This applies to both students and teachers. The children should not be kept at the same subject or type of subjects or at subjects which have high fatigue element. Variety can be introduced in the following manner:

(a) No subject except in case of science practicals should be kept for two consecutive periods as it is likely to cause monotony in the class.

(b) Variation in the subjects should be aimed at in order to avoid boredom, e.g., Ancient History should not be followed by Medieval History.
(c) The same class should not, as far as possible, sit in the same room for the whole day.
(d) The same teacher should not have consecutive periods in the same class, as far as possible, except in the primary classes.
(e) If a subject is taught only two or three times a week, the periods should follow at intervals.
(f) The drill period, science practicals and craft work, all provide for a change of the nature just referred to above.

8. *Free Periods for Teachers:* Free periods for the teachers should be provided so as to increase their efficiency and also for correction work. The free periods of the teachers should be scattered all over the week as far as possible. The language teachers should be given more free periods as they have to do a lot of correction work. In the period immediately preceding the science and other practical periods, the teachers concerned should be kept free to enable them to make the necessary preparation for the work to be undertaken in the coming period. On an average teachers should be allowed two vacant periods per day.

9. *Principles of Play and Recreation:* Attention is to be given to provide for rest and recreation. The children should not be deprived of play. It affords them a good opportunity for enjoying fresh air outside and mixing freely with each other besides giving them time to have something for replenishing their energy. The recess period provides for rest and recreation and its duration should not be less than half an hour.

Provision for Radio and Television Broadcasts should also exist wherever possible.

Provision for various co-curricular activities should also be made in the time-table.

10. *Principle of Optimum Utilisation of School Building and Equipment:* The number of students in a school, the number of teachers for various subjects the number of room, laboratory (arrangement and furniture etc.), also affect the framing of the school time-table. The time-table of a single teacher school will be quite different from that of other schools having many teachers. Sometimes, due to paucity of rooms, two classes are held in the same room. Time-table should in such cases be arranged in a manner that when one class is busy at writing work, the other should be doing reading work and the like.

11. *Principle of Local Variations:* The hours of work and the duration of recess may be marginally adjusted to suit local conditions, i.e., distance of the school especially in rural areas, train timings, rainy days etc.

12. *Principle of Initiation:* Interesting programmes in the beginning of the day provide motivation to work enthusiastically.

13. *Principle of Elasticity:* The time-table should not be kept rigid but flexible and fluid. In view of the various difficulties that are likely to crop up, a fluid time-table is always desirable. Some times specific needs of many children have got to be met and it becomes inevitable to make some variations. The transfer of teachers also necessitates to bring about variation in the time-table. It is not necessary that the time-table should show the time allowed for the sub-branches of a subject. If we allot 12-periods to English per week, it should be left to the teacher to decide how many periods he shall give to grammar, translation and composition and how many to text.

We should always remember that the time-table is a tool and not the master and as such it should never be allowed to dictate procedures and methods.

Tyranny of the School Time-Table and Modern Protests: Flexibility of Time-Table

Many modern psychologist and educationists think of the curriculum in terms of activities instead of subjects. They advocate the abolition of the time-table and want to liberate the child from its limitations.

According to modern psychology, each individual is unique in certain respects. Each child has his own nature, his own preferences and his own rate and speed of working. When he is left to himself, he continues what he starts. He leaves it only when he loses interest or feels fatigued. If he is interested in his work, he is alert and active. This interest gives him psychological satisfaction. But when work is regulated, by a rigid time-table, a child might have to stop at the time when he has begun to take interest in a subject due to the ringing of the bell or the other way that is to feel fatigued with the subject before the period is over. Since the period is meant for a particular subject, he has to continue even though he is disgusted. It is for this reason that some educational reformers would like to abolish time-table altogether. According to them if a child is left to himself, he would give more time to those subjects in which he is interested and give up those in which he is not interested to come back at a more favourable time.

Several modern educationists do not prescribe any collective time-table as they think that education must cater to the individual need of the students. The very fact that no two individuals are alike necessitates that to meet the specific needs of many children, different methods will have to be devised and accordingly a new conception of time-table will serve the required purpose.

Usually the modern protest is due to the following defects in the rigid time-table:

1. The co-curricular programme hardly finds any mention in the time-table:
2. By dividing the school day into uniform chunks of 35 to 45 minutes,

allocating certain hours per week to the study of individual subjects, the time-table places pupils and teachers in a kind of lock-up.

3. A rigid time-table militates against the integration of various experiences.
4. A rigid time-table is a great hindrance in the total growth of the pupil's learning experiences.
5. In the conventional time-table there is hardly any co-ordination of the efforts of teachers.
6. The conventional time-table does not provide time for teacher-pupil conferences.

The present emphasis is on methods like the Dalton Plan, the Project Method and the like which are a great departure from the time-honoured time-table. 'Contract' is the important feature of the Dalton Plan. Class as a unit of a organisation remains but as a unit of instruction vanishes. Child promises to do the given work in a specific period which is usually a fortnight and works according to his intellectual attainments. No collective time-tables are formed in such methods of education. During this time, the child is free to work in whatever subjects he wishes, when he wishes and as long as he wishes. The only condition is that he must complete all the work in his various subjects before another contract can be undertaken. In this way, each child can progress in the school at his own rate.

Many programmes have been evolved in progressive schools which provide flexibility and the common features are:

First, the instructional material is organised into larger meaningful units built round the needs and interests of the students.

Secondly, there is provision for some long periods for practical activities.

Thirdly, there are certain "unassigned" periods in which the students may engage themselves in some worthwhile hobby.

Finally, there is no rigidity and the teachers are at liberty to alter the daily programme according to the special circumstances connected with the needs and interests of the students. Of course this has to be pre-planned and in consultation with other teachers so that they may accordingly modify their programmes.

Summing up

The task of a time-table framer is very delicate and challenging. It involves the interlocking or weaving of different subjects, teachers and classes into the school fabric.

The time-table maker should be a man of vision and must be open-minded. He should take into consideration the human factor. He should not try to 'boss' over other teachers. A good time-table maker makes the optimum use of men and materials.

4

Co-curricular Activities or Extra-curricular Activities

They (Co-curricular activities) are as an integral part of the activities of a school as its curricular work and their proper organisation needs just as much care and for Secondary Education Commission thought.

Importance of Co-curricular Activities

All-roundness is the theme of the modern education which recognises that when the child comes to the school, he comes in *mentally, physically, socially, spiritually* and *vocationally* and as such he must be educated and nourished in all of them. According to the modern concept of education, the three traditional R's should be replaced by 7R's i.e. Reading, Writing and Arithmetic (denoting school subjects in the old concept of education), Rights, Responsibilities Recreation and Relationships (new 4 R's in the context of democratic values). This can be achieved only by providing a well organised and supervised programme of co-curricular activities along with curricular programme.

The remarks of the Secondary Education Commission (1952-53) in respect of the co-curricular activities are worth noting: "The school is not merely a place of formal learning whose main concern is to communicate a certain prescribed quantum of knowledge but rather as a living and organic community which is primarily interested in training its pupils in what we have called the 'gracious art of living'. Knowledge and learning are undoubtedly of value but they must be acquired as a by-product of interested activity because it is only then that they can become a vital part of the student's mind and personality and influence his behaviour. But the 'Art of living' is much more comprehensive concept than the acquisition of knowledge, however intelligently planned. It includes training in the habit and graces of social life and the capacity for cooperative group work. It calls for patience, good temper, sincerity, fellow-feeling and discipline. These objectives can only be cultivated in the context of the social life and the many co-curricular activities must find a recognised place in any schools."

The Indian Education Commission (1964-66) stressed the importance of co-curricular activities in these words, "We conceive of the school curriculum as the totality of the learning experience that the school provides for the pupils through all the manifold activities, in the school or outside, that are carried on under its supervision. From the point of view, the distinction between curricular and extra-curricular work ceases to exist, and a school camp and games are curricular or rather co-curricular activities."

Changes in the philosophical and psychological ideas have now given a new direction to the school curriculum.

Philosophical ideas have brought about a change in the concept of education. The crying need of the hour is the 'education for democracy' and hence education must aim at producing those individuals who can intelligently and amicably participate in the various activities of life. Traditional curriculum has failed to meet the demands of the changing concept of education. The co-curricular programme is a convenient tool by which an inadequate curriculum may be modified.

A consideration of psychological factors urges upon us of the necessity of giving more and more attention to understand the individual differences of the children and of providing proper outlets for the flow of the energies of the children. These activities are very helpful in this regard.

'Learning by Doing', 'Learning by Living' and 'Learning without Tears' are the main characteristics of new education.

Types of Co-curricular Activities

Broadly speaking co-curricular activities may be categorised under thirteen heads, although there are no water-tight compartments as the activities overlap.

Academic Development Activities

- Preparation of Charts, Models etc.
- Subject Club, e.g. Economics Clubs, Geographical Clubs
- Projects
- Symposiums
- Surveys
- Quiz

Aesthetic Development Activities

- Sculpture
- Dramatics
- Drawing
- Exhibitions
- Fancy Dress
- Music
- Painting
- School Decoration

Citizenship Training Activities

- Visit to Assembly and Parliament
- Cooperative Store
- Students Council
- Youth Parliament
- Social Service

Cultural Development Activities

- Dancing
- Drawing & Painting
- Celebration of Festivals
- Visits to Cultural Places

Emotional and Integration Development Activities

- Camps
- Celebration of National and International Days
- Educational Tours
- Speeches

Leisure Time Activities

- Album making
- Coin Collecting
- Photography
- Stamp Collecting

Literacy Utilization Activities

- Brain trusts
- Declamation contests
- Debates
- Recitation
- Library work
- Public speaking

Moral Development Activities

- Celebration of birth days of great men
- Lectures
- Morning assembly
- Social service

Productive Activities

- Card board work
- Clay work
- Embroidery
- Craft work
- Leather work
- Kitchen gardening
- Soap making
- Toy making

Physical Development Activities

- Athletics
- Cycling
- Mass drill
- NCC
- Swimming
- Yogic
- Indoor & Outdoor

Social Value Development Activities

- Girl guiding
- Scouting
- Labour weak
- First Aid
- Red Cross
- Community service

Scientific Temper Development Activities

- Science clubs
- Science quizs
- Science fairs
- Visits to places of scientific importance
- Science models

Multipurpose Activites and Projects

- Beautification & cleanliness of school campus
- Social service
- Social surveys
- Tree plantation
- Adult education
- Community service and awareness

Co-curricular Activities as an Integral Part of Education

In the past, co-curricular activities were mainly organised after school hours and, therefore, were called extra-curricular. But now they are treated as integral a part of the activities of the school as its curricular work and their proper organisation needs just as much care and fore-thought." The Secondary Education Commission remarks, "Given a clean, pleasant and well-maintained school building, we would like the school to see if it can provide a richly varied, pattern of activities to cater to the development of their children's entire personality. It has to formulate a scheme of hobbies, occupations and projects that will appeal to, and draw out the powers of children of varying temperaments and aptitudes".

Origin of Co-curricular activities: These activities are as old as education itself though their sphere was not so vast as it is today. *Monitor system* was one of the important institution of the ancient Indian system of education. The Gurukulas of old were residential institutions providing opportunities of social contacts on a large scale.

In Athens and Sparta, student participation in organising activities like athletics and music was very common.

Values of Co-curricular Activities

The educational values of co-curricular activities are many as well as varied. Some of the important values derived from these are detailed here.

1. *Academic Development and Growth:* The teaching of civics, composition, history, geography, etc., can be greatly supplemented. Election to the students council would give them a picture of Central and State elections. Excursions to historical, geographical and industrial places enrich the experience of the students. Writing for the school magazine supplements the teaching of languages. Similarly there are many practical activities which afford opportunities to supplement classroom work.

2. *Development of Aesthetic Values:* It is common knowledge that aesthetic sensibility cannot be taught but it is caught and developed through real programmes. Participation in dances, dramatics, fancy dresses, flower

shows etc. by the students provide them opportunities to appreciate and develop aesthetic values.

3. *Civic Training:* The school should be a training ground for democracy. It should be organised and administered on democratic lines. The introduction of self-government provides experience of the life of a democratic society. In this, pupils determine the policies and the programmes. They plan and present assembly programmes. The individual pupil learns how to conduct a meeting in an approved parliamentary style. It gives him an opportunity to exercise his vote. While working together, the students learn that rights involve responsibilities. They get valuable lessons in cooperation which can be learnt by practice. In order to retain his position as a member in a Students Council, Athletic team, etc., a student has to learn to cooperate.

4. *Community Relations:* Social service activities bring closer the school and the society. Students also earn appreciation of the society for the good work done by them.

5. *Cultural Values:* Activities like visits, celebrations of community festivals, dance, drama etc. enable the students to appreciate cultural heritage and develop cultural values.

6. *Dignity of Labour:* In activities like camps and social service, students develop the value of dignity of labour.

7. *Disciplinary Values:* Discipline becomes self-discipline. The students remain busy and different kinds of activities develop their talents in different directions. They make laws for the various societies and come to realize the need for showing respect to other school laws.

8. *Followership Qualities:* By participating in student government, students learn that followership and leadership go hand in hand. Both are complementary and supplementary.

9. *Guidance and Counselling:* Students get opportunities to know their assets and liabilities. The teachers and especially the school counsellor come to know them better and accordingly suggest programmes for their development.

10. *Instruction becomes Pleasurable.* Pleasure and interest combined with instruction and guidance sugarcane the pill of learning and experience.

11. *Leadership qualities:* Many programmes have to be organised. Many situations have to be faced in the running of various societies. All these inculcate in the students the virtues of initiative, clear thinking, originality, resourcefulness, good judging power, tolerance, patience, enthusiasm, self-confidence and reliance which are very essential in a leader.

12. *Learning and Earning:* Many activities provide opportunities to the students to earn also.

13. *Loyalty:* The more the students run the school affairs, the more they feel that the school belongs to them and they belong to the school. The labour week, *i.e.,* cleanliness of the school by the students themselves

develops the ideas: 'This is my school because I have made it with the sweat of my brow.' Tournaments and activities like school function also foster this sentiment.

14. *Moral Training:* Students get opportunities of social contact. They also get opportunities of doing social service. This teaches them the lesson of morality. They acquire the virtues of honesty, sympathy and good euquettes.

15. *Physical Development:* Games, N.C.C., Physical Drill, etc., contribute to the physical development of the individual.

16. *Self-Expression:* Someone has a talent for writing, another for speaking, a third for music and so on. These activities bring out these qualities and develop them. This self-discovery and self-knowledge will tell them in what direction they should turn their ability and talent to advantage and help them to make wise vocational choice.

17. *Recreational Interests:* Education for leisure is as important as education for work. If recreational interests are developed during school life, they prove to be very beneficial in the leisure hours of adult life and make life fuller and richer.

Mohi-ud-din has described the recreational value of these activities as "Provision in the school of a programme of free and creative activities, by way of crafts and hobbies, give direction to youthful enthusiasm and training for healthy occupation..... The last, but certainly not the least important function of extra-curricular activities is thus to convert the leisure in after-school life from a curse into blessing, from a burden into an opportunity for a fuller, richer and nobler life."

A good deal of educative work can be accomplished through recreation. In the opinion of G.D. Sondhi, "So wide is the field of recreation that there is no school, no teacher, no student that cannot find something of interest in it. If there are no playgrounds, yet there are school courtyards and school-rooms where some form of recreation can be introduced—be it group dancing, play-acting, clay modelling, paper cutting, painting, group-singing, carpentering, spinning, weaving and the like. Opportunities for joy-giving will be provided and boredom eliminated and invention, initiative and emotional control developed."

"Then there are outdoor activities like camping and hiking, gardening and even cycling and mountaineering which build up some of the basic requirements for success in life—the spirit of service, observation, grit, determination and courage." Further he observes, "Pleasure and interest combined with some instruction and guiding, sugar-coat the pill of learning and of discipline."

The fundamental point that these activities are means and not ends, should not be lost sight of.

Knowledge and learning are acquired as a by-product of interesting activity.

18. *Psychological Values:* Co-curricular activities provide the children a psychological compensation from the usual dull, routine like and monotonous classroom environment in the following manner:

(a) The co-curricular activities provide much needed channels or outlets for sublimation.

(b) These activities play a significant role in training the emotions of students.

(c) They cater to the various aptitudes and interests of the students.

(d) They are a potent means of developing and ensuring mental health.

19. *Social Training:* Co-curricular activities are very useful in giving training in 'Art of Living'. According to the Secondary Education Commission, the 'Art of Living' is a much more comprehensive concept than the acquisition of knowledge, however, intelligently planned. It includes training in the habits and graces of social life and the capacity for co-operative group work; it calls for patience, good temper, sincerity, fellow feeling and discipline. These can only be cultivated in the context of the social life and the many curricular and co-curricular activities that must find a recognised place in every good school. By participation in co-curricular activities pupils learn valuable lessons in practical co-operation and the habits of team work; they realise the relation of the society to the individual and of the individual to the society.

Mohi-ud-din states that these activities have a social appeal, "By reason of the social appeal of extra-curricular activities, their co-operative method, their spontaneity and their intrinsic interest, they are a significant social medium for the civic training of the young".

To be a good member one must sacrifice one's immediate interests if need be, for the welfare of the group. It is well known that boys and girls in the process of maturity, move from sheer individualism to social awareness.

20. *Sublimation of Instincts:* Gregarious instinct in the adolescent is very predominant. This tendency expresses the desire of the growing boys to behave socially. If no opportunities are provided to them, they will form their own groups. This grouping may be harmful to them and the society also and may take the shape of gangs etc. Their energies will be misdirected and they will indulge in anti-social acts. Without proper guidance, they are likely to develop wrong scales of social values and they may direct their energy and enthusiasm towards one end that will be harmful and even disastrous to them and to society at large. Various co-curricular activities, *e.g.,* self-government, social service leagues, scouting, etc., will be very conducive to sublimate this instinct by providing them a field for doing something socially worthwhile through group activities. Similarly, their other instincts of self-assertion, sex and self-abasement will be sublimated.

21. *Team Spirit:* In the beginning every player wishes to carry the ball himself and does not realize that he must depend upon others to realize the goal. But with the passage of time an individual discovers that one must

play in a team if one is to win anything worthwhile. Thus a team spirit develops in him. Spirit of 'give-and-take' takes the place of selfishness.

22. *Vocational Development:* Through participation in several co-curricular activities like craft work, dramatics, dance, music, gardening, photography etc. students develop vocational interests which greatly help in career planning.

Inadequacy of Popular Support to Co-curricular Activities

In general it is noticed that the importance of co-curricular activities has not been appreciated to the desired extent by teachers, students, parents and in fact several other sections also.

Causes of Lack of Due Interest among the Students in the Co-curricular Programme

1. Interference with studies.
2. Inconvenient hours of activities.
3. No credit in the examinations.
4. Inadequate provisions regarding these activities.
5. Lack of suitable play-grounds in the crowded cities.
6. More emphasis on intellectual development of the child and very little emphasis on his other developments, e.g., physical, moral, aesthetic, social etc.
7. Poor economic conditions of the students compelling them to work in their homes after school hours and thus leaving a very little time at their disposal for participating in the activities which are organised after school hours.
8. Indifference of parents rather discouragement sometimes.

Causes of the Lack of Interest among Teachers

1. No extra pay or credit is usually given to them for organising such activities.
2. Teacher's teaching hours are not reduced.
3. A majority of the teachers does not possess the proper training for organising such activities.
4. Some of the teachers do not see any good coming out of these activities as they do not fully realise that they should aim at the all round development of the personality of the student.
5. Due to the rigid outlook of the teachers and the Heads the idea of the self-government is not allowed to creep into the minds of the students of the school. They feel that the students are not sufficiently mature and may misuse power vested in them.
6. The vain idea of superiority among the teachers parents them from allowing the students to share responsibility with them.

Limitations of a Co-curricular Programme

1. *Disregard of Institutional Conditions:* Many schools undertake activities simply because other schools have started these. They do not take into consideration their assets and limitations.
2. *Lack of Accommodation:* Some schools do not have adequate playgrounds; no space for indoor games; no space for mass drill.
3. *Lack of Funds:* Several schools lack finances for purchasing equipment for sports, craft work, hobbies, workshop material, etc.
4. *Lack of Variety:* Some schools organise a few activities only with the result that students with diverse interests do not get opportunity to participate.
5. *Lack of Adequate Staff:* The number of teachers who can provide effective guidance to student in this field is limited.
6. *Conservative Attitude of Authorities:* Many heads and teachers do not find any good coming out of a co-curricular programme and they are rather indifferent to it.
7. *Over-emphasis on Academic Work:* Generally speaking no regular time is allotted to the organisation of these activities and undue stress is laid on academic achievements.
8. *Overemphasis on Co-curricular Activities:* Some schools follow the extreme course. They over-stress this programme.
9. *Heavy Load on Teachers:* These activities put a heavy load on the teachers and they feel over-burdened.
10. *No Credit in the Annual Examination:* Usually very little consideration is shown to students' performance in these activities while promoting them.

Essentials of a Programme of Co-curricular Activities

1. *Guidance of Teachers:* The co-curricular programme should be strictly under the guidance of teachers.
2. *Variety of Activities:* A wide variety of activities should be planned in order to meet the different needs of a large number of students.
3. *Activities During School Hours:* As far as possible activities should be organised in school time.
4. *Teacher as an Adviser:* The teacher should not play the role of a dominator rather that of an adviser.
5. *Facilities to Teachers:* Some credit either in the form of less teaching periods or in the form of extra-payment to teachers should be given.
6. *Participation of a Large Number of Teachers:* As far as possible each member may remain incharge of a particular activity of his interest.
7. *Equal Opportunity to Students:* All the students should have equal opportunity to be a member of school club.
8. *Gradual Growth of the Programme:* Activities should be started in a

small way and developed gradually.

9. *Careful Consideration:* Every careful consideration should be given when a new society is to be started. Normally, when once an activity is organised and scheduled, it should not be allowed to die.
10. *Maintaining Records:* Record of the various activities must be kept by every society.
11. *Reasonable Expenditure:* Activity should be less expensive as far as possible.
12. *Provision for Funds:* Sufficient funds to meet the expenditure involved on various activities should be raised by the society concerned.
13. *Balanced Stress:* Funds should not be spent on a few stars (a few players or debaters etc.)
14. *Regular Work:* Regular time should be devoted to these activities.
15. *Evaluation:* Provision should be made for periodic appraisal of the services and value of these activities.
16. *Activity Time-Table:* An activity time-table and a calendar for activities may be prepared.
17. *No Show Work:* These activities may not be started merely for 'show work'.
18. *Publicity:* Publicity should be given to the activities of these societies and the community should be well-informed.
19. *Means not Ends:* Co-curricular programme must be organised and considered as a means to the educative process.

Providing Advise—Activity Director or Co-ordinator

To make the activity programme effective, the head would do well to appoint a teacher as an activity director or co-ordinator. His teaching load must be so that he may give sufficient time to the planning and execution of various activities in the school. His duties would be:

(i) To plan the schedule of the year's activities to; set dates of special activities, such as concerts parents days, school dances etc.
(ii) To secure a list of clubs that the teachers desire to offer.
(iii) To take care of special discipline cases during club periods.
(iv) To co-ordinate with transport service to take students to various places.
(v) To issue bulletins of club activities.
(vi) To select only those activities which are by and large related to the school curriculum and community needs.
(vii) To make the programme as inexpensive as possible.
(viii) To ensure that each student of the school participates in one activity at least according to his interest.

Concluding Observations

Harry C. Mckown has very aptly observed, "A school with only extra-curricular activities (co-curricular activities) would be as absurd as a school without them". In other word an ideal balance has been struck between the curricular and co-curricular programme.

DESCRIPTION OF VARIOUS CO-CURRICULAR ACTIVITIES

I. Clubs in the School or School Clubs

Clubs may be constituted for undertaking different co-curricular activities in the schools. Every club must have its constitution. Its specific aim must be clear. It must meet the needs of the students. Johnson and Faunce give the following objectives of the school clubs:

1. They provide opportunities to the students for learning experiences based on their interests. Students are attracted to a club because of their enthusiasm for the programme it offers.
2. They supplement the curricular work. Visits to places of historical or scientific importance, etc. can be organised by these clubs.
3. They provide opportunities for the development of pupil abilities.
4. Clubs are very helpful in making the constructive use of leisure time.
5. Clubs may help in the exploration of occupational interest of the students.
6. Clubs provide opportunities for the practice of group planning and decision.

Leadership of the Sponsors or the Teachers-in-Charge of the Club

Leaders or sponsors must possess the following qualities:

1. They should be able to enlist the co-operation of the students.
2. They must be able to offer constructive suggestions for activities of the club.
3. They must be able to guide without dictation.
4. They must have the ability to plan systematically.
5. They must be willing to give time and thought in making the work of the club a success.
6. They must be democratic in spirit.
7. They must possess a sense of humour.
8. They must have the necessary talent and skill so that their performance is higher and better than their pupils and they look upon to them as a model.
9. They should help the clubs and societies to make a wise choice of office bearers indicating what qualifications are necessary in an office bearer but should do nothing to force their choice in favour of any individual student.

10. They should make as careful a preparation for participation in co-curricular activities as they do for their teaching work.

Clubs may be organised for a variety of activities and school subjects.

II. Dramatics or Dramatisation

Meaning: Dramatisation has been described as "a synthetic art, involving the purposive co-ordination and control of the delicate organs of speech and muscles of the body combined with a sense of rhythm, with a view to free and intelligent expression of emotions and ideas."

Values of Dramatisation

(i) Dramatic art affords innumerable opportunities for the correlation of a large number of subjects.
(ii) In the preparation of their roles, the students indirectly and unconsciously improve their speech habits and language.
(iii) A systematic study of historical events has to be made when pageants of the life of great persons are prepared, *i.e.,* pageant on the life of Buddha, Chandragupta, Vikramaditya, Gandhiji etc.
(iv) Children prepare consumes suiting different ages and thus come to know about the dresses of the people during different periods of history.
(v) Dramatics also add to the geographical knowledge of the students.
(vi) Carpentry and other mechanical arts facilitate the work of construction of the stage. Dance and music add to the beauty of a drama.
(vii) Drama has its great social value. It is a co-operative enterprise and develops qualities of co-operation and social understanding.
(viii) It helps in fostering *'esprit de crops'* among the students. In various school functions dramas form the chief items of the programme. For the honour of the school, every student works to the best of his capacity.
(ix) Dramatics afford the students many opportunities for training in team work.
(x) There are many activities in a drama and as such student of diverse aptitudes get chances to choose items for which they are best suited and satisfy their urges, *e.g.,* self-expression through the various activities of a drama.
(xi) Dramatisation provides a healthy and rich entertainment.
(xii) From literacy points of view, it provides practical opportunities for improving speech, expression, intonation etc.
(xiii) It may prepare for a vocation.
(xiv) It provides attraction to the guardians of the students and other dignitaries to visit the school and promote it.
(xv) The staging of dramatic performance provides valuable experience to students in organising programmes.

Essentials for the Success of Dramatics

A number of rehearsals bring grace and success to the play when it is staged. Pupils should prepare as much stage material as they can.

Children should be encouraged to write their own plays. The usual participants in this activity should be given opportunities to play different roles. The same pupils as far as possible should, however, not be allowed to play the role of villain.

Selection of Play

1. Only competent teachers should undertake this programme.
2. Plays chosen should depict the evils of the social customs and promote social reforms.
3. A play should have a literary value.
4. The students should be able to understand and appreciate the play.
5. It should have also entertainment values.
6. It should be free from objectionable subject matter.
7. There should be no vulgarity in the play.

III. Educational Excursions and Tours

Meaning of Educational Excursions: Educational excursions imply small journeys which are undertaken to agricultural, cultural, geographical, historical and industrial places which are not very far off from the educational institution. However educational tours may be, for far off places.

Significance of an Educational Excursions and Tour: W.M. Gregory evaluates school excursion in these words, "Education has been too far removed from the basic experiences of modern life. Many students are quite deficient in opportunities for some perception exploration and raw experiences. They need fewer words and more activities with things situations, conditions and relations. For useful learning, pupils require experiences with the raw materials of life. A garden, a shop, a live animal collection, a trip to a farm, a mill, a store, a park, a museum—all must have a place in the modern school." Following are some of the main advantages of excursions:

(i) *They supplement class work:* Visits to museums, forts, temples, caves, mountains, valleys, canals and fields help in supplementing the teaching of social studies by providing first-hand information. Industrial establishments and laboratories etc. are very useful places to the students of science. Excursions to these places bring reality, clarity and vividness to the 'dead matter' of various subjects, and provide for valuable correlation of subjects.

(ii) *They introduce variety in the school programme:* These excursions infuse a new life and vigour in the children and give them some relief from the dull and monotonous life of the classroom.

(iii) *They develop qualities of leadership:* Excursions help in developing qualities of initiative and leadership in the students by affording them opportunities to make necessary arrangements. These also encourage a spirit of co-operation among the students.

(iv) *They acquaint the pupils with the environment:* Excursions enable the students to know intimately their environment by putting them in direct touch with the things, persons, organisations and institutions.

(v) *They develop self-activity among the students:* Excursions make pupils active agents rather than passive recipients. Students get opportunities to plan various programmes connected with excursions. Besides they get opportunities to develop keenness and accuracy of observation. All their senses are at work and they experience the joy of discovery.

(vi) *They develop the aesthetic sense of the students:* Excursions to natural settings and places of beauty create love for nature and develop aesthetic sense.

(vii) *They foster ideals of emotional and national integration:* The students come into contact.

Proper Planning of Excursions: To derive the maximum benefit from excursions, it is essential that these should be properly planned. The teachers and the students may work out the plan of the excursion jointly. An excursion must be wisely conceived, properly planned and well conducted. It must be a result of careful thinking. The organisers would do well to obtain sufficient information before hand regarding the importance of places to be visited so that they may be able to give suitable replies to the various queries of the students.

The fact that the excursions are arranged for educational-cum-recreational purposes should not be lost sight of and therefore, if possible, student singers, titbit tellers and photographers should find a place in the party so that learning and laughing should go hand in hand.

The appointment of group leaders facilitates work to a considerable extent. The group leaders should preferably be those students who have some knowledge of the locality or who know the technique of explaining things in a clear way.

The importance of maintaining discipline in an excursion can hardly be ignored and a sympathetic and resources teacher shall not find it difficult to do so.

IV. Labour Week

Regarding this type of work, K.G. Saiyidain writes, "I feel strongly that not only in this country, but in the whole world, we have to make an earnest and concentrated effort to give a new orientation to the social ideology of our children and youth particularly in the direction of inculcating a sense of the dignity of labour and cultivating the capacity to work together for constructive and socially worthy causes. I cannot think of any better method of doing so than by bringing all school children together into a fellowship of work and service where the meanest work will be undertaken in a spirit of adventure and comradeship because it is useful and provides healthy outlet for their energies and talents."

Following types of work may be done during a labour week:

(a) Cleaning and white-washing the school building.
(b) Decorating the rooms.
(c) Removing stones, iron nails, waste paper, etc. from the school compound, playground, lanes and streets.
(d) Filing pits in the streets and lanes, and cleaning roads.
(e) Organising first-aid centres for the public.
(f) Teaching adults.
(g) Improving drainage of selected localities and drying marshy land created by open drains.
(h) Turning school compounds.
(i) Propaganda amongst the public regarding the importance of personal cleanliness and social sanitation in order to ward off common diseases.

To make this programme a success, the teachers themselves should take an active part in activities stated above. This will give incentive and encouragement to the students.

V. Morning Assembly/School Assembly

Meaning: Flora T. Cook describes the morning assembly as "The morning assembly is a common meeting ground to which each brings his offerings, the fruit of his observation and studies or music, literature, and art that delight him, a place where all co-operate for the pleasure and well-being of the whole."

Prof. Fretwell calls the assembly as "Town meeting of the school."

In the words of W.R. Smith, "School assembly can serve as a focussing centre of all form of extra-cullilar life."

Nature of Activities of the Assembly: Common activities of an assembly are:

(i) School prayer.
(ii) Singing of national anthem.
(iii) Singing of devotional song.
(iv) Roll call.
(v) Checking of cleanliness.
(vi) Checking of school uniform.

(vii) Short speech or some moral aspect by the head or the teacher or the student or the guest speaker.
(viii) Announcements.
(ix) Commendations.
(x) Mass drill.
(xi) Daily news.

Objectives, Purposes and Values of the School Assembly

(i) *To provide a solemn occasion:* The singing of morning prayer and devotional songs provides a very solemn and elevating occasion and makes a good beginning for school work.
(ii) *To develop devotion to God and Spirituality:* If can be used to create in the students an urge of prayer and meditation which also helps in emotional stability.
(iii) *To develop spirit of patriotism:* Singing of some patriotic song or narration of some patriotic event inculcates the sentiment of patriotism and love for the country.
(iv) *To celebrate festivals and days:* Some of the important national days and religious festivals can be celebrated.
(v) *To unify the school:* An assembly is very helpful in developing a community spirit among the students. They get occasions to see, feel and know the school as an organised group. An average student remaining in his class does not appreciate his relationship to the school as a whole.
(vi) *To serve as clearing house:* The school assembly serves as a clearing house for all school activities both curricular and co-curricular.
(vii) *To familiarise the students with the common rules and ideals of the school:* Every child must become a full-fledged citizen of the school. In a school assembly, the students should be told about the traditions, rules and ideals of the school.
(viii) *To develop correct audience habits:* To be socially efficient, every child must know how to behave in a gathering. Social etiquette demands that children must listen to the speakers with courtesy and patience. When and how to applaud is another quality that must be developed. The school assembly trains the students in this art.
(ix) *To give due recognition to worth-while achievements publicly:* Prizes to the students for outstanding accomplishments of any nature, curricular or co-curricular should be given before the entire school. This action will motivate other students to perform outstanding accomplishments.
(x) *To give opportunities to students to face the audience:* It gives training to a large number of students in effective appearance and expression before a critical audience. Students advanced in

different spheres present their programmes and give stimulus to others to emulate their example.

(xi) *To widen interest:* Assembly experience deepens and widen student interests.

(xii) *To develop good habits:* Habits of punctuality and regularity are developed.

(xiii) *To motivate students:* Announcement and public recognition to outstanding performance of some students in academic and co-curricular programmes motivate other students to work hard.

(xiv) *To make general announcements:* Changes in the school schedule, preparation of any special programme can be announced in the morning assembly.

Edmonson and others expect the assembly to discharge the following functions:

1. To develop school unity.
2. To encourage school spirit.
3. To motivate curricular functions.
4. To stimulate extra curricular activities.
5. To motivate expression and overcome self-consciousness.
6. To develop proper habits and attitudes in audience.
7. To share information.
8. To influence public opinion.
9. To develop aesthetic sense.

Essentials for Ideal Assembly Programmes

1. All programmes should be carefully planned and executed.
2. Sufficient care should be exercised to ensure that the students observe disciplinary etiquettes.
3. The assembly should not be made a forum for saying unpleasant things.
4. One of the worst things a head would do in an assembly is to find fault openly with some staff member or to criticize the entire student population of the school. This unpleasant element should be avoided.

VI. National Cadet Corps (NCC)

The National Cadet Corps Directorate, Ministry of Defence, has enunciated the following objectives of the National Cadet Corps:

Firstly, to develop character, comradeship, the ideal of service and capacity for leadership in young men and women;

Secondly, to provide service training to young men and women so as to stimulate interest in the defence of the country; and

Thirdly, to build up a reserve of potential officers to enable the Armed Forces to expand rapidly in a national emergency.

Membership: The membership of the N.C.C. is entirely voluntary and there is no liability for military service. It undertakes the training of the young between the age of 13 and 20. Free training is imparted to the cadets. Free uniforms are issued to them and all expenses on account of messing and amenities for them during their camps are met by the State Government.

Divisions: The National Cadet Corps consists of three divisions.

Junior Division: In the Secondary and Senior Secondary Schools and the Public Schools, Junior Divisions have been raised. It comprises three units—Army, Navy and Air Force.

Senior Division: This is also composed of three wings—the Army, the Naval and the Air Force Wings. The maximum tenure of service for a cadet in the Senior Division is four years. This unit is raised in the colleges.

Girls Division: Though the present strength is not an encouraging one, yet it is hoped that more units will be raised before long as it is becoming increasingly popular.

VII. School Magazine

Significance and Values of School Magazine: A school magazine is the embodiment of the corporate life of an institution and affords suitable opportunities to the students for giving expression to their thoughts and ambitions.

In the words of Jacobson, "The school magazine offers great opportunities for those who participate in it. It is not uncommon to find that pupils and their parents consider the editorship of the school paper the most valuable experience which has come to a pupil, particularly when directed by a wise sponsor who makes it a very purposive educative experience. All pupils who serve on the magazine secure some experience in creative writing, usually the form of their writing improves because a powerful incentive for correct form exists when the material is to be printed or mimeographed for public examination."

It serves as a link between the school and the parents as it reaches them through the students.

A school magazine supplements class work to some extent. The students learn to write their thoughts in an effective, clear and concise manner. Study habits are developed as the students consult some books or journals to write for their school magazine and make the best use of their leisure time.

Spears and Lawshe list the following functions of the school paper as an aid to the school:

1. To educate the community as to the work of the school.
2. To publish school news.
3. To create and express school opinion.
4. To capitalise the achievements of the school.
5. To act as a means of unifying the school.

6. To express the idealism and reflect the spirit of school.
7. To encourage and stimulate worthwhile activities.
8. To aid in developing right standards of conduct.
9. To promote understanding of other schools.
10. To provide an outlet for student suggestions for the betterment of the school.
11. To develop better inter-school relationships.
12. To increase school spirit.
13. To promote co-operations between parents and school.

Factors Essential for the Success of the School Magazine: Contributions from the students should be corrected before their publication. The school magazine should include a variety of articles. Not only short stories, essays, poems, titbits but current news, school news about curricular and co-curricular activities, photos, designs and cartoons, etc. should also find place in the school magazine. Student editors should be carefully appointed. Prize for the best contributions may be given to the students to give them an incentive to write. The teachers should not make the school magazine as their organ.

The teacher incharge of the magazine should be a man of vision, of literary taste and well-versed with the current events.

In schools where the number of students is small and the financial position does not permit the publication of a full-fledged magazine, it will be advantageous to take resort to wall magazine.

Black-board or wall-magazine greatly help in the preparation of the printed magazine. News on boards may be written every day in the morning. Daily news should be illustrated with the help of a map. Important places where important events take place should be shown on the map. Other boards dealing with facts and figure regarding our natural resources, development projects, inspiring thoughts from religion, history or ethics may be prepared weekly or fortnightly as the case may be. The students should be made responsible for preparing these boards.

VIII. Scouting and Girl Guiding

Values of Scouting: Prof. Bertrand Russell has very beautifully commended the value of scouting: "The naturalist may praise it for its success in putting the boy close to Nature's heart, the moralist for its splendid code of ethics, the hygienist for its method of physical training, the parent for its ability to keep his boy out of mischief: but from the stand-point of the educator, it has marvellous potency for converting the restless, irresponsible, self-centred boy into the straight-forward, dependable, helpful young citizen. To the boy who will give himself to it, there is plenty of work that looks like play, standard of excellence which he can appreciate, rules of conduct which he must obey, position of responsibility which he must occupy as soon as he qualifies himself, in a word: a programme that appeals to a boy's nature."

Another writer Dr. L.D. Coffman writes: "Scouting gives us no lecture on vocational guidance, and yet it teaches the meaning, the importance of the dignity of work; it operates no bank and yet it teachers the meaning of thrift; it contains no jails and yet it teaches the meaning of self-control; it does no preaching and yet it teaches devotion to a cause and loyalty to a purpose; it is founded upon no religious creed or sectarian doctrine and yet it emphasizes above all things the importance of religion. It is universal in appeal, natural in its methods, progressive in its outlines, strengthened and cemented by the bonds of fellowship and the idealism of the movement.

Following are some of the important contributions of scouting:

1. *Social Service Training:* Scouts render a very useful service in the fairs and gatherings. Anti-malaria work, flood relief work, adult literacy work and cleaning campaigns are the other fields of their activities.

2. *Good Fellowship:* A good deal of the sufferings of the world is due to the absence of fellowship feeling. If humanity is to survive, a spirit of good fellowship must be developed in the students who in a few years are expected to play an important role in the world. Scouting knows no barriers of caste, creed and colour. Camp life and other co-operative activities are the means to develop this quality of brotherhood.

3. *Dignity of Labour:* It is an open secret that an average student shirks work. He does not take pride in doings thing for himself. This movement is the best one to provide practical opportunities to the students to throw themselves with vigour and derive pleasure from work.

4. *Sublimation of Instincts:* Patrol contest and games take the place of gang fights. Sex instinct is sublimated through contact with Nature. Self-assertion finds its outlets in producing patrol and troop leaders. Similarly, other instincts finds suitable channels.

5. *Love of Nature:* Various outdoor games, camp life and excursions bring the students in close touch with nature and develop their aesthetic sense and engender in the minds of the students love for Nature.

6. *The Spirit of Adventure:* Students are by nature restless and curious to know new things. They like to explore and face difficulties. The outdoor life provides worth-while opportunities to satisfy their lust for enterprise and discovery: "The outdoor life is the life blood of scouting." Writes F.G. Pearce.

7. *Practical Efficiency:* There are many activities like health training, first-aid, home nursing, rescue and emergency aid, swimming, riding, etc., which greatly increase the practical efficiency of the scouts.

History of Scouting: Sir Robert Baden Powell (1857-1941) founded the Boy Scout Movement in 1908. However in India, the movement was introduced in 1911 at Bangalore. Many rival organisations such as the 'Seva Dals', 'Bharat Youth Sangha,' Seva Samiti, Boys Scout Association and finally, the Hindustan Scout Association, came into existence.

Baden Powell had served the army in India, Afghanistan and then in South Asia.

In India it was considered for long that the movement was alien in its character.

The movement has received a great setback with the starting of N.C.C. and other organisations.

The movement is non-political, non-official but voluntary.

How to Start a Scout Troop

(i) It should be started by a teacher who himself possesses the spirit of service and is really interested in scouting. 'Come on', and never 'Go on', should be his watchword.

(ii) There should not be more than thirty-two boys in a troop. This number can easily be managed by one scout master.

(iii) Generally speaking, a troop should not be instructed as a whole. The scouts are to be trained through patrol leaders and directly by the scout master.

(iv) Right type of boys should be selected for scouting.

(v) Preliminary training should start with outdoor life. A picnic may be arranged and scouting may be talked about. Thus gradually the students should be made conversant with scout law, scout uniform and scout promise.

(vi) Twice a week, an hour and a half before or after school will suffice for the training in scout tests (Tender Foot and Second Class Tests). Time should be adjusted in co-operation with other teachers.

(vii) Inter-patrol competitions should be held as these are very helpful in maintaining keenness and promoting efficiency.

(viii) Scouts should be motivated to take a pride in their uniform from the very start.

(ix) A scout troop must have ropes, flags, bandages, compass, first-aid material, books and camping and picnicing equipment.

(x) A suitable room in the school should be provided and known as scout room.

(xi) Practical opportunities should be provided to the scouts to do social service.

(xii) Camp fires should be organised.

(xiii) Records of the work of the troop should be kept.

(xiv) Too many rallies should be avoided.

(xv) Scout troop should not be started merely for the purpose of show or at the time of inspection.

(xvi) The scout-master himself should follow the scout laws.

IX. Social Service and Community Development Activities

School as an Social Institution: School is set up by the Community/Society to serve its needs. One of the important ways to serve the community is to render social service by the students. There are several areas in which the students can render very useful service to the community.

The Education Commission (1964-66) laid a great emphasis on labour and social camps of the students. It suggested the following programme.

During the period of the camp, students should be expected to put in 8 hours of work per day and the general routine would be as follows:

2 hours—personal time in morning.
2 hours—rest and relaxation in the afternoon.
6 hours—manual work.
2 hours—intellectual work not connected with school studies.
2 hours—personal time in the evening.
8 hours—sleep.

Values and Advantages of Camps and Community Development Programmes

(i) They inculcate in students the spirit of community service.
(ii) They develop in the students the spirit of self-sacrifice.
(iii) They give children a scope for the exercise of initiative.
(iv) They build up an attitude of co-operation and fellow-feeling.
(v) They help to built an environment of co-operation in the home and the outside world.
(vi) They train students in leadership.
(vii) They give children training in citizenship and in the art of self-government.
(viii) They develop wider outlook.
(ix) These activities help in the many-sided development of the pupil—physical, mental, moral, religious and social.
(x) These activities foster dignity of labour.
(xi) These directly and indirectly impart moral education.

In short, these activities develop virtues of give and take, co-operation, participation in social life, sharing responsibilities, co-operative endeavour, mutual adjustment, internal self-discipline friendly disposition, ideals of service, proper attitudes, etc.

Financial Aspects: A part of the funds for the programme could be obtained from the local Rural Works Programme. All the overhead charges—which will come to a very small amount—should be met by Government. The student should be required only to bear: (1) transport charges to the camp site and back, and (2) food charges during the stay at the camp. Even these could be subsidized to some extent on the basis of the work that the students put in. A student who holds freeship or half freeship should be given similar concessions in the camp. Adjustments could also be made by requesting the students to bring some articles of foodstuffs etc. from home. On the whole, an attempt should be made to keep the cost of this camp down to the minimum for each period. Moreover, camps for boys and girls will have to be organised separately; and there need not be much difference between the types or programmes undertaken for them.

(*See also Labour Weeks*)

5

Self-Government in Schools

A school, city state, a student council or any other form of student government requires a constant and intelligent supervision in which neither dictation nor aloofness is conspicuous. —*W.R. Smith*

Significance and Need for Self-Government or Student-Participation in School Affairs

The Secondary Education Commission (1952-53) has pointed out the importance of student self-government or student-participation in the affairs of the school as, "Nothing in more calculated to develop a proper sense of self-discipline, and proper behaviour than their enforcement not by any outside authority with any symbol of punishment but by the students themselves. They should choose their own representatives to see to it that proper codes of conduct are observed, both for the sake of the individuals and for the good name of the school. It is from this point of view that we commend what is known as the house system in schools, with prefects or monitors or student councils, whose responsibility will be to draw up a code of conduct and to enforce its observance in the school". Student participation in the government of the school is an effective method of citizenship training and is a means of keeping the energies of the pupils canalised for useful purposes in the development of a wholesome personality through a definite, constructive, well-planned programme. The Report of the Secondary Education Workshop held a Hyderabad in April-May 1955 states that the student government gives, "opportunities to pupils to learn the skill in electing leaders and of conducting their deliberations on democratic lines, thereby giving ample scope for self-expression, evaluation and judgment."

University Education Commission states, "Good Student Government integrates the college community, imparts a wholesome social atmosphere, fosters common ideals and pride in an institution but most important, provides training for good citizenship and social responsibility. It gives scope for the right type of student political activity, which helps to develop the capacity to play the role of citizens in a republican form of government and a democratic society. It replaces the undesirable tendencies toward undermining respect for constituted authority and leaving youth a prey to propaganda of conflicting ideologies."

E.B. Castle explains the importance of self-government as, "Edicts from above do not conduce to the best human relationships, no one man or small group of adults working in a hierarchical formation can produce the pleasantness of tone that usually results from common purposes commonly achieved. Where a hierarchy of status exists and orders are received from above, these in the lower ranks of the hierarchy are almost certain to impose good behaviour instead of attempting to evoke good feelings." The educators and others experienced in social relations feel that the greatest unity of spirit and self-discipline results when members of the group have a voice in making decisions which affect them.

Democracy and Self-government: School life must reflect democratic values. An ideal school in a democracy must present a segment of real life. Its activities must be geared to the needs of social life around and it must present an idealised epitome of the social life. In bureaucratic and autocratic set-up there is a great distance between the teachers and the administrators on the one hand and the teacher and the children on the other hand. Teachers look to their superiors for every kind of detail while they themselves are just like jailors for the children. The head being the absolute monarch, the teachers his ministers and the monitors his executive officers. The pupils had no responsibility for the school management. They simply obey the monitors, the teachers and the head. Such an organisation in a democratic set-up which aims at preparing the young children as efficient members of a democratic society, does not work. Just as we cannot learn speaking or writing a language without practice, in the same way our children cannot learn how to govern themselves and to get training in the democratic way of life unless they are provided opportunities for practical training in the democratic way of life. Therefore we must make the children themselves responsible for most of the activities concerning school management. When the students plan, execute and assess various activities and projects, they learn and practice democratic ideals and practices and their sense of social and civil responsibilities.

Meaning of Self-government: Student's government has been defined in Goo's Dictionary of Education as "the maintenance of order and regulation of matters of conduct in school by elected representatives chosen from the students body by the students themselves."

Types of Self-government

P.W. Terry describes the following five types of self-government:

1. *The Informal Type:* It is a temporary organisation. It is formed as occasions arise. Some senior students or other outstanding pupils are invited to co-operate with the members of the staff in helping them on certain occasions such as to receive and accommodate guests on the school function day, etc.

2. *The Specific Service Type:* Certain duties such as to mark attendance, to supervise study rooms, to maintain cleanliness, etc., are assigned to some students who are either selected by the members of the staff or elected by the students themselves.

3. *The Simple Council Type:* In this form of self-government there is a certain unit of student organisation called the students' council to deal with the different activities of the students.

4. *The Complex Type:* Under this form, there are two or more central bodies of the students. One is a small body doing executive business and the other a bigger one exercising legislative powers. The former may be compared to that of a Cabinet and the latter to a Legislative Assembly or House of Representative.

5. *The School City Type:* The administration of the school is carried on the lines of city administration. It is an elaborate form of student government. The whole of the student population of the school is divided into wards which elect municipal councillors.

Student Participation and Not Student Self-Government

According to H.C. Mckown, student self-government is not possible on account of the following reasons:

1. Students lack the judgment that may accompany executive, legislative and judicial power.

2. The Head of the school is officially charged with the responsibility for the school, its equipment and its students' welfare. The students are not so charged and cannot be.

Student Council

Complete government by the pupils is not possible even in well established progressive schools in our country. There are nevertheless practical undertakings in the schools to train pupils for future citizenship. The organisation of co-curricular activities offers a field in which student government could function very effectively. The Simple Council Type of self-government is easy to practise.

Objectives of Student Council or School Sabha or Parishad

1. To promote worthwhile student activities.
2. To develop harmonious relations among students and the staff.
3. To assist in the management of school affairs concerning students discipline and welfare.
4. To develop values of good citizenship in students.
5. To promote the overall welfare of the school.
6. To provide a forum to the students for the expression of their problems.
7. To develop initiative and responsibility among students.

8. To provide a laboratory for learning democratic values through practical activities.
9. To provide an opportunity to the student for developing qualities of democratic leadership.

Constitution of Student Council

To start with, a school may have school Sabha. Each class or section elects one representative to the Sabha. Some talented students may be nominated by the head of the school in consultation with the staff adviser. The Sabha may have six Boards under it and the members may be elected from among the elected representatives. One staff member may act as an adviser to each Board. The following activities may be undertaken by these Boards:

(a) Games and sports.
(b) Health and sanitation.
(c) Activities like debates, dramas, magazines, hobbies, etc.
(d) Discipline.
(e) Social welfare activities like Adult Literacy campaigns, Flood Squads, Labour Weeks, etc.
(f) School Cooperative Store.

No rigid rules can be laid down for the range of activities to be undertaken by the Sabha. Every type of activity which has some educational significance may come under its purview.

Important Activities of the Council

H.C. McKown has given a list of 147 activities which can be undertaken by the Sabha or the Council. Some of these activities are given here:

1. To welcome new students.
2. To supervise and help in the maintenance of good sanitary conditions in the school.
3. To decorate the class-rooms and the school premises.
4. To visit sick students.
5. To meet and welcome the visiting teams.
6. To provide assurance to the weak and handicapped students.
7. To plan campaigns—Courtesy, safety, punctuality etc.
8. To organise contests and competition.
9. To publish school magazine.
10. To organise and manage a lost-and-found department.
11. To promote better lunch-room and cafeteria manners.
12. To promote good manners at athletic contests.
13. To appoint library and reading-room monitors.
14. To promote good behaviour at assembly, public events, before, in and after school.
15. To arrange lectures.
16. To organise exhibitions.

17. To organise the school store.
18. To organise the school-bank.
19. To introduce students to new trends in education.
20. To promote and arrange inter-school visits.
21. To arrange inter-school sports tournaments.
22. To promote inter-home room programme exchanges.
23. To hold academic contests.
24. To organise excursions and trips.
25. To provide for publicity of commendable school work.
26. To promote good dress and neat appearance.
27. To look after school bulletins.
28. To collect material for school museum.
29. To supervise ventilation.
30. To discourage smoking.
31. To discourage seeing bad pictures.
32. To look after the school garden.
33. To promote good habits.
34. To arrange medical aid for the needy.
35. To assist health and police authorities.
36. To organise health social service on various occasions.
37. To assist in community-fund drives.
38. To organise school functions.
39. To organise literacy campaigns.
40. To budget its finances.
41. To conduct campaigns to improve school spirit.
42. To plan and promote a "better manners campaign".
43. To visit other schools to gain new ideas.
44. To run school government for a day.
45. To design student awards and emblems.
46. To run campaigns for new cheers, songs for school.
47. To act as coaches.
48. To act as tutors of weak students in studies.

Principles of Organising Students Council

H.C. Mckown has suggested the following principles of organising students council effectively:

(i) *Principle of need:* The school must feel a continuous need for the council.

(ii) *Principle of gradual introduction:* Participation by the students should be introduced gradually.

(iii) *Principle of Objectives:* A study of objectives should precede any attempt at definite organisation.

(iv) *Principle of whole representation:* The council should represent the school as a whole.

(v) *Principle of recognition:* The average student should feel that he is represented.

(vi) *Principle of balanced representation:* Both student body and faculty should be fairly represented.

(vii) *Principle of Moderation:* The council should not be too large.

(viii) *Principle of real powers:* The council should have definite powers and duties.

(ix) *Principle of Sincerity:* The council should not be considered a dumping ground.

(x) *Principle of Veto Powers:* The head of the school should retain veto power.

(xi) *Principle of evaluation:* The work of the council should be continuously evaluated.

(xii) *Principle of responsibility:* Each member of the council should assume some specific responsibility.

(xiii) *Principle of accountability:* Each committee should be held strictly accountable for its particular responsibility.

(xiv) *Principle of training:* Officers and committee chairman should receive specialized training.

(xv) *Principle of co-operation:* The co-operative aspects of participation should continuously be emphasized.

(xvi) *Principle of regularity:* Council meetings should be held regularly and during school time as for as possible.

(xvii) *Principle of publicity:* The council should give continuous publicity to its ideals, activities and problems.

With a view to training the school students in the art of self-government, some enthusiasts recommend the Parliamentary system of government in schools and they want to see it run on the basis of parties in the Parliament. Theoretically speaking this may look very sound but its introduction is fraught with grave dangers. Such a system is likely to introduce politics into the school and this imitation is neither necessary nor helpful. Without adopting such a system, the students can very conveniently be trained in the art of self-government as enumerated earlier.

A scheme of youth parliament for the promotion of democratic values and procedures has been introduced in some states by the Parliament of India.

Problems in Organising Student Self-Government/Student Participation

(i) *Apathy of the Staff:* The members of the staff and the head are hesitant to part with power. They think that their prestige is in danger when students share powers with them.

(ii) *Immaturity of the students:* The students are immature and lack power of independent and critical thinking.

(iii) *Reluctant bright students:* Good students sometimes are reluctant to hold office as they think that this will have an adverse effect on their studies.

(iv) *Wrong election of representatives:* Many a time it is seen that the students fail to elect their representatives who can handle various offices satisfactorily. This leads to constant troubles between the students and the educational authorities and the standard of education deteriorates.

(v) *Interference of politicians:* The politicians try to use student's council as a tool to further their ends and this discourages the educational authorities to allow the formation of student's unions in educational institutions.

(vi) *Student groups:* The elections of the student's council create bad blood among the students themselves. Not infrequently they come to blows.

(vii) *Absence of facilities:* The student's council can function effectively under ideal conditions. At a time when most of our schools are ill-equipped and understaffed it will not be advisable to introduce such councils.

Factors Essentials for Successful Working

1. *Faith in the Programme:* For the successful working of this programme it is very essential that the teachers must confide more in their students. The sense of responsibility can only grow and flower in an atmosphere of trust and freedom. The responsibility should be really handed-over to the students and there be no pretext about it, "It is useless to institute self-government in name only *i.e.* to call self-government system where the Head-teacher impresses his or her views upon the prefects and they accept them and impress them on the pupils. Nor is it of any value to have a system of self-government with a master or mistress always just round the corner to exercise authority," writes H.G. Stead.

G.R. Dustin is of the opinion, "A successful scheme requires a demonstrative organisation of the teaching staff of the school. The principal must first realize the meaning of democratised education. Teachers must also democratise their teaching and class-room management. Autocracy will never cooperate to make a democratic form of government a success."

2. *Gradual Introduction of the Programme:* Heavy responsibilities on the shoulders of children should be placed gradually. We should not demand too much from children who are immature in their judgment. It is wrong to think that a teacher's work is reduced by the introduction of self-government or a student's participation programme. Students need constant help and guidance from the teachers. The students must be told that the efficiency of an organisation depends upon the personnel of committee for the selection of which sober judgment is required.

3. *Talks on Student Self-government:* The teachers would do well if they

acquaint the students with the general principles which govern the selection of suitable representatives. This will help the students in selecting their representatives. They should also acquaint the student with the merits of student involvement in the management of their affairs.

4. *Constant and Intelligent Supervision:* In connection with the supervision work of these activities, W.R. Smith writes, "A school, city state, student council or any other form of student management, requires a constant and intelligent supervision in which neither dictation nor aloofness is conspicuous."

Of course strict supervision should be made of the financial aspect of the Sabha.

5. *Regular Meetings:* The meetings of the various Boards should be held regularly. Each Board, committee or sub-group should be given specific responsibility and held accountable for it.

6. *Very Few Restrictions on Students:* Every good system of self-government should provide opportunities for as many pupils as possible to participate in its programmes. No restrictions on council membership should be imposed as far as possible.

7. *Due Publicity:* The activities of the Sabha should be continuously published.

8. *Non-Involvement of Students in Politics:* Care should be taken to see that the Sabha does not become a tool in the hands of the politicians to grind their own axe.

9. *Constant Evaluation:* The work of the council should be continuously evaluated.

Main Characteristics of Student Council or Student Self-Government or Student Participation Programme

1. It has clearly defined powers and responsibilities.
2. It is democratically organised.
3. It gets due support from the head and the staff.
4. It enlists the willing co-operation of the students.
5. It is suitably guided and supervised by a staff member.
6. It maintains detailed account of its proceedings.
7. It exercises strict control on financial matters.

Advantages of Student Self Government

1. The students develop love and *esprit de corps.*
2. They realise the necessity of having rules and regulations for the efficient and successful working of an institution.
3. They learn to respect authority.
4. They learn to tolerate difference of opinion and develop tolerance.
5. They learn the principle of 'give' and 'take'.
6. They learn to rise above casteism and communalism.

7. They get opportunities to make decisive choices.
8. They learn to lead others and develop qualities of leadership.
9. They learn to handle public money.
10. They learn to prepare themselves for future life as enlightened citizens of a democratic country.
11. They get an idea of the actual working of the panchayat, Assembly and Parliament.
12. They learn to discipline themselves.
13. They realise their rights and responsibilities as citizens.
14. They learn the mechanics and devices of government and develop true spirit of citizenship.

House System and Self-Government

The organisation of house system in a school is a simplified form of student self-government. According to this system, all the classes are divided into houses for carrying out some affairs of the school. Students belonging to different classes are placed in each house. There is no fixed number of houses to be constituted in a school. However, there should be at least four such houses. Each house is given a name after the name of some eminent personality, mountain or river etc. House captains/prefects etc. for each house are chosen or elected by the students composing the house. Houses functions under the guidance and supervision of a teacher called the house master who is assisted by other teachers. Each house is put on duty for a month or so. Students from each house look after the cleanliness of the school, school beautification and school discipline etc. Games and supports are also organised on house basis. The responsibility of the prestige of the house falls upon its members and they ensure that they will not do anything which may bring discredit to it. The house system greatly helps in developing a sense of discipline among students. Earlier house system was the most important feature of residential public schools. Now this is being adopted by day schools of all types.

6

Rewards and Punishments

The child is immature and helpless and he must not be given a long rope with which he may hang himself. —*W.C. Bagley*

There are misfit schools, misfit tests and studies, misfit dogmas and traditions of pedants and pedantry. There are misfit homes, misfit occupations and diversions. In fact, there are all kinds and conditions of misfit clothing for children, but in the nature of things, there can be no misfit children. —*Frederick Burt*

Divergent View

Case for Rewards: Divergent views are expressed by educators on the issue of rewards and punishments. While the naturalists dub all rewards as bribery, the protagonists of rewards argue that since the society as a whole is governed by a system of rewards and punishments, they have an important place in the school system.

Psychologically the system of rewards and punishment is justified when we take into account the Law of Effect (or the Law of Pleasure and Pain) as enunciated by Thorndike.

Rewards provide incentives for more efforts and healthy emulation among individuals and groups.

The students feel encouraged when their work is appreciated in the presence of others. This helps in infusing all the more confidence in them.

Rewards give happiness to the parents when their wards receive prizes. They encourage them to put in all the more labour.

Reward is considered a higher motive to desirable conduct than punishment.

Rewards motivate the pupil's work and conduct on desired lines.

Reward is a positive instrument to develop discipline and punishment a negative one in this direction.

The spirit of competition is awakened in the students and they get incentive to work hard.

Opposition to Rewards: Usually following arguments are put forward against the system of awards.

1. Reward is a sort of bribe given to the child.
2. Rewards provide temptation to work not for the sake of duty but for the sake of prize.
3. Rewards lead to unhealthy competition and jealousy among the students.
4. Winning of awards become the end-and-be-all of school system students use fair or final means to get awards.
5. Sometimes accusations of favourtism are levelled on those who choose the awardees.
6. There remains some scope for subjectivity in the system of awards.

Purposes of Giving Awards

Rewards may be given for:

(a) Good conduct.
(b) Progress in studies.
(c) Proficiency in games and sports.
(d) Achievements in co-curricular activities.
(e) Service rendered for a good cause.
(f) Regular and punctual attendance.
(g) Overall good performance in the school.

Types of Rewards

Rewards are mainly of two types:

1. *Material wards:* These comprise articles, badges, books, cash, cups, medals, scholarships etc.
2. *Non-material wards:* There are incentives like appreciation, commendation, encouragement, position of importance and honour and ranks etc.

General Principles of Awarding Prizes

1. System of awarding prizes should be as objective as possible. The rewards should be free from the element of favouratism and partiality.
2. The students should be made to realize that rewards are given to them as tokens of good appreciation and they are meaningful only to this extent. What is more important is the formation of good habits and hard work and this pays them most in life.
3. Rewards for efforts rather than attainments should be given.
4. Group rewards should be preferred to individual rewards.
5. Rewards should be of small intrinsic value. They should not appeal to material consideration.
6. They should be given immediately to the younger students.
7. They should be a few in number.

8. Rewards should also be given for usually considered as minor virtues of school conduct such a punctuality, regularity in attendance and personal cleanliness.

Punishments

Opponents of Punishments: Freedom to the Child: Educators like Fredrick Burt, Rousseau, Froebel, Montessori, Spencer and Russell critise the institution of punishments and rewards. They have waged a bitter war against repression and unnatural methods of disciplining the child. Their watchword is *'Freedom to the Child'* because they think that by nature a child is innocent and noble and adult restrictions and discipline simply spoil the intellect of the child and stand in the way of his progress and happiness. They believe in the 'discipline of natural consequences' and are convinced that natural punishments are the best and leave no room for punishments in the life of the school. Rousseau says, "Children should never receive punishment as such—it should always come as the natural consequence of their fault."

Sir T. Percy Nunn writes, "The conviction that punishment and the fear of punishment are the natural foundation of school government, is gradually being recognised as merely a barbarous superstition."

A.S. Neill in his book *The Free Child* writes, "My contention is that unfree education ignores almost entirely the emotions of life, and because these emotions are dynamic, their lack of opportunity for expression must and does result in cheapness, ugliness and hatefulness. Only the head is educated, but if the emotions are free, intellect will look after itself."

Herbert Spencer would like the child to suffer the unavoidable consequence of his conduct.

Plato writes, "A free man ought not to be a slave in the acquisition of knowledge of any kind. Bodily exercise, when compulsory, does no harm to the body, but knowledge which is acquired under compulsion, obtains no hold on the mind. Then, do not use compulsion, but let early education be a sort of amusement, you will be better able to find out the natural bent."

Froebel thinks, that control over the child was to be exercised through a knowledge of his interest and by expression of love and sympathy.

S. Bala Krishna Joshi feels, "The unwritten moral code of the institution must be more binding on the members than the rules of conduct in vogue."

Koos and others state, "To impose control on the pupil wholly from without is to deny him his most essential and effective learning experiences and to nullify the educative influence of the school."

No misfit Children but misfit system: Fredrick Burt has observed, "There are misfit schools, misfit tests and studies, misfit dogmas and traditions of pedants and pedantry. There are misfit homes, misfit occupations and diversions. In fact, there are all kinds and conditions of misfit clothing for children, but in the nature of things, there can be no misfit children." Writes

Frederick Burk. Educationists representing such a school of thought protest against all sorts of well established systems of rewards and punishments.

Bertrand Russell remarks, "The man whose tongue is constricted by laws or taboos against free speech, whose pen in constricted by the censorship, whose laws are constricted by an ethic which considers jealousy a better thing than by affection, whose childhood has been imprisoned in a code of manners, and whose youth has been drilled in cruel orthodoxy, will feel against the world that hampers him with the same rage that is felt by the infant whose arms and legs are held motionless. In this rage he will turn to destruction becoming a revolutionary militarist, or a prosecuting moralist according to temperament and opportunity."

Similarly the votaries of "Free discipline", would dub all rewards as bribery.

Arguments against punishment to children may be summarised as under:

1. Punishment is against the very nature of the child who is innocent.
2. Punishment is an animal tendency. It has no connection with human values.
3. Children are very tender by nature. They become timid from the fear of punishment.
4. The children become stubborn through punishment.
5. Sometimes from fear of punishment students leave educational institutions.
6. Punishment cannot inculcate love for discipline.

Punishments are Indispensable

Educators like Bagley, Bray, Thring and Wren are of the view that punishments have an importance place in the school system.

Bagley puts it, "The child is immature and helpless and he must not be given a long rope with which he may hang himself."

Bray justifies punishments with these words, "Punishment is the lesser evil applied to avoid the greater one that lives in the future." It is always seen that evil of not checked in time brings havoc ultimately. "Nip the evil the bud" is an old saying.

P.C. Wren, though admits that punishment is an evil thing to be avoided, yet says that it is a necessary evil like the surgeon's knife.

According to H. Thring, school punishment is not vengeance. Its object is training, first of all the training to the wrong-doer; next the training to other boys by his example. Both he and other are to be deterred from committing the offence again.

Theories of Punishment: Justification of Punishment

Following are some of the theories and purposes of punishment:

(i) *Retributive Theory:* This is based upon the idea that the offender must suffer as such pain as his victim. If a student has slapped another he should be given a slap by the teacher. The tendency behind this form of punishment is purely a revengeful one. It believes in the saying, "An eye for any eye and a tooth for a tooth." The tendency has been described as low and selfish.

(ii) *Vindication of Law Theory:* According to the view, the purpose of punishment is to punish the offender because he has violated the law. This view is opposed on the grained that school is not a court.

(iii) *Exemplary Theory:* The court purpose of punishment according to theory is to deter others from repeating the same kind of offence. A child may be fined for coming late to school so that he may not come late again for fear of the same punishment and example may be set for others.

(iv) *Preventive Theory:* The aim of punishment according to the theory is to prevent the wrong-doer from repeating the offence and thus to protect others from harm.

(v) *Natural Consequences Theory:* This consists in letting the Child from the penalties as natural consequences of his fault. The penalties of nature are inevitable. But nature's penalties are too uncertain, too delayed and often too severe.

(vi) *Reformatory Theory:* The positive and correct view of punishment in a school is that the child should be reformed by means of punishment if at all its need arises.

Causes of Punishment

(i) Absence without leave.
(ii) Absence from the examination.
(iii) Bullying.
(iv) Calling names.
(v) Damaging the school property.
(vi) Disobeying the school laws.
(vii) Inattentiveness.
(viii) Late coming.
(ix) Misbehaviour with other students, teachers and others who come into contact.
(x) Negligence in the matter of home-task.
(xi) Running from the school.
(xii) Stealing.
(xiii) Using unfair means in the examination.

Forms of Punishment

Following are the various forms of punishment depending upon the nature of offence.

1. *Moral Punishments:* Sometimes moral punishments such as apologies, public or private, are accepted from the students.

2. *Reproof:* Tongue is said to be the most patent weapon in the armoury of a teacher. 'A world to the wise' is an old proverb. Sometimes a mild reproof to sensitive and intelligent student may achieve the desired results and a vulgar abuse to an obstinate student may prove to be futile. But rebukes are to be used as sparingly as possible. Mohiyuddin says, "Sareasm, ridicule and abuse are cowardly weapons to employ and psychologically they are very unwholesome and ineffective means of correction."

3. *Deprivation of a Privilege:* The wrong-doer may be prohibited from playing any game in the school for some time, may be deprived of his position if he is holding any and may also be denied certain concessions like fee, etc., if enjoyed by him.

4. *Fines:* Absence fines, late fee fine or some other kind of fines depending on the nature of the offence may be imposed on the wrong-doers. It is true that this kind of punishment imposes a burden on the parents but occasions may necessitate the levy of fines.

5. *Loss of Marks:* Sometimes marks are deducted when students use unfair means.

6. *Making Good the Loss:* The student who destroys some property may be asked to make good of the loss.

7. *Detention after School Hours:* When students fail to do their home-task, they may be detained to sit after school hours and be made to do the work under the supervision of a teacher deputed for the job. The avoid hardship to teachers, teachers' time-table specifically providing for such type of job will be very helpful. But the danger, sometimes, is that pupils may not form unpleasant associations in connection with the work given to them. They may not develop a taste for that work which has been given as punishment.

8. *Isolation:* In this respect the views of Russell are worth noticing when he writes, "When a child persistently interferes with other children or spoils their pleasures the obvious penalty is banishment." A child who repeatedly makes a noise in the class may be asked to sit in one corner of the room—away from the class.

9. *Position of Disgrace:* For certain acts of indiscipline, students are made to stand on the bench or stand outside the class.

10. *Exposure to Social Disapproval or 'Saturation':* When a student draws pictures or caricatures etc. in the class instead of being inattentive to the teacher, he is asked to repeat the same act before the class. Thus he gets a public censure.

11. *Repetition of Tasks:* The child who is inattentive in the class may be asked to repeat the lesson. *i.e.*, may be asked to repeat lines of poetry, or the spellings of a difficult word, etc.

12. *Corporal Punishment:* Slapping, canning, hands up, kneeling down, boxing the ear etc., are some of the usually employed forms of this punishment.

13. *Suspension and Expulsion:* Sometimes there are certain incorrigible students who undermine discipline and adversely affect the morale of the students. Their presence in the institution is considered to be undesirable and as such the authorities are left with no alternative but to suspend or expel them. These are the two extreme forms of punishment. Great care should be taken to ensure that these are resorted to very cautiously and rarely.

Forbidden Practices (Indisciplinary Acts) according to Delhi Education Act and Rules

(1) No student shall indulge in any of the following practices, namely—
   (a) spitting in or near the school building except where the spitting is made in any spittoon provided by the school.
   (b) disfiguring or otherwise damaging any school property;
   (c) smoking;
   (d) any form of gambling;
   (e) use of drugs or intoxicants except on prescription by a registered medical practitioner;
   (f) rowdyism and rude behaviour;
   (g) use of violence in any form;
   (h) casteism, communalism or practice of untouchability.

(2) The Administrator may, on the advise of the Advisory Board, amend or add to the forms of practices forbidden under sub-rule (1).

(3) If any student, who has not attained the age of fourteen years, indulges in any of the practices referred to in sub-rule (1), the Director may shift him to such special school as he may think fit.

Forms of disciplinary measures: (1) The following shall be the disciplinary measures which may be adopted by a school in dealing with:—
   (a) all students—
      (i) detention during the break, for neglect of class work, but no detention shall be made after the school hours,
      (ii) corporal punishment,
   (b) students who have attained the age of fourteen years—
      (i) fine,
      (ii) expulsion,
      (iii) rustication,

(2) For the avoidance of doubts, it is hereby declared that the disciplinary measures specified in clause (b) of sub-rule (1) shall not be imposed on any student who has not attained the age of fourteen years.

(3) Fine may be imposed on a student who has attained the age of fourteen years in the following cases, namely:
   (i) late attendance;

(ii) absence from class without proper application from the parent or guardian;
(iii) truancy;
(iv) wilful damage to school property;
(v) delay in payment of school fees and dues;

(4) (a) Corporal punishment may be given by the head of the school in case of persisting impertinence or rude behaviour towards the teachers, physical violence, intemperance and serious form of misbehaviour with other students.
(b) Corporal punishment shall not be inflicted on the students who are in ill health.
(c) Where corporal punishment is imposed, it shall not be severe or excessive and shall be so administered as not to cause bodily injury.
(d) Where cane is used for inflicting any corporal punishment, such punishment shall take the form of strokes not exceeding ten, on the palm of the hand.
(e) Every punishment inflicted on a student shall be recorded in the Conduct Register of such student.

(5) Expulsion shall debar a student from being re-admitted to the school from where he is expelled but shall not preclude his admission with the previous sanction of the Director to any other school.

(6) Where a student is rusticated, he shall not be admitted to any school till the expiry of the period of rustication.

(7) No student shall be expelled or rusticated from a school except after giving the parent or guardian of the students a reasonable opportunity of showing cause against the proposed action.

Notes:
(i) Expulsion or rustication shall be resorted to only in cases of grave offences where the retention of the student in the school is likely to endanger its moral tone of discipline.
(ii) Except in the case of any expulsion or rustication from an unaided minority school, the punishments of expulsion and rustication shall not be imposed without the prior approval of the Director.

Precautions in Awarding Punishment

1. Punishment should be resorted to very rarely.
2. Punishment should be given only when it is assured that the desired aim would be fulfilled.
3. The accused student should be provided opportunity to explain his point of view before inflicting punishment.
4. Punishment should be proportionate to the degree of the offence.
5. Punishment should be according to the nature of the child. Punishment for the same type of offence may differ from child to

child.

6. Punishment should be given immediately when a wrong act has been done.
7. Punishment should not be given in anger.
8. Sarcastic remarks should not be needed.
9. Punishment may be given in the form of making good of the loss done.
10. Expulsion or rustication should be restored to very rarely.
11. As far as possible corporal punishment should not be given.
12. Punishment should not be given in the spirit of vengeance.
13. Punishment should be reformatory.
14. A 'punishment register' should be maintained and the names of the students punished should be recorded in that register. The nature of the offence and the form of punishment should be recorded.

Corporal Punishment

A sharp controversy has raged on the issue of corporal punishment. In the traditional educational system, it occupied a very prominent place and was considered to be an indispensable instrument or weapon in the armoury of the teacher, to reform the child. 'Spare the rod and spoil the child' was the favourite slogan. It was believed that he who had not been chastened was not educated.

Most of the modern educators consider corporal punishment to be outmoded and call it a barbaric act. They condemn it outright. According to Alless, "Severity and lack of sense can permanently destroy a man's ability of life, people emerge from such an upbringing as moral cripples."

Russell doubts very much whether punishment need ever be severe. Physical punishment believed to be never right. "In mild forms it does little harm, though no good; in severe forms, I am convinced that it generates cruelty and brutality," he writes.

Similarly B. Hamley states, "Whatever may be our opinion of the need for corporal punishment, it will do us no harm to admit that its necessity is a sign of weakness in the school."

Hobbes is of the view, "The fool cannot be mended by flogging and he who flogs is the greatest fool."

H.G. Stead has dubbed this type of punishment as a lazy means of control.

E.B. Castle condemns corporal punishment as "I find little weight in the arguments of those who support the practice of corporal punishment. For minor offences it is too harsh; for serious moral delinquency, it is irrelevant and may be positively evil, as a stimulus to learning it has been proved to be in the long run a deterrent, rather than an encouragement. When inflicted in public it may excite the wrong emotion—morbid excitement, repulsion, anger, fear, and pity or admiration for wrong-doers. It is an interrupting and disturbing rather than a binding influence in a community and plays no useful part either in promoting lasting good social relationships or sound learning."

Chief Objections to Corporal Punishment

Following are some of the chief objections to corporal punishment:

1. It is not in consonance with the creed of non-violence.
2. It coarsens the child and the person who inflicts punishment.
3. It is a negation of co-operation.
4. It has an appeal to the brutal instincts only.
5. There is no proper standard of applying it.
6. It is negative in effect.
7. It sometimes gives rise to permanent injuries.
8. It is degrading to both, *i.e.,* the one who inflicts and the other who receives it.
9. It is not corrective.
10. It is based on the psychology of fear.
11. It is confession of failure on the part of the teacher.
12. It evokes resentment rather than repentance.

Conditions and Principles to be Observed While Inflicting Corporal Punishment

1. It should be given only by the head of an institution.
2. Neither party should be in anger.
3. The instrument of punishment should be very light.
4. The child, the head and the staff should be very clear about the cause of punishment.
5. Its scope is limited to moral offences.
6. In no case it should be applied to scholars other than those between six and twelve years of age.
7. There should not be long interval between the time of offence and punishment.
8. It should not be applied to the delicate parts of the body.
9. It should not be administered to highly emotional and delicate children.
10. It must be suited to individual temperament and physical and emotional development of the offender.

Departmental Regulations Regarding the Infliction of Punishments

The Education Codes of various Education Departments empower only the Head to inflict corporal punishment of misconduct in Upper Middle and High Departments of recognised schools for boys. The corporal punishment must take form of strokes, not exceeding ten, with the cane on the palm of the hand. Every such punishment is to be recorded and a report sent to the parent or guardian of the boy punished. Corporal punishment has no place in Primary or Lower Middle Departments of schools.

The penalty of expulsion or rustication of a student for serious misconduct may be imposed by the Inspector or Inspectress, as the case may be, in the case of Government and Local Body schools, and in the case of privately managed schools by the Managing Body of the schools. Disciplinary action against students of privately-managed schools can be taken by the Inspector or Inspectress if the case of misconduct comes to their notice at the time of their visit to the school. There is no appeal against the order of punishing authority but a copy of the orders passed by the Inspector or Inspectress and Managing Committee shall be forwarded to the Director and Inspector or Inspectress respectively for information. The orders must state the nature of the offence committed by the student concerned.

The Indian judiciary made history in the school system in 2000 A.D. when it gave its landmark judgment against corporal punishment.

School Discipline: Traditional and Modern Concept

There has been a sea change in the concept of school discipline. It has passed through the following stages:

Stage 1. Flogging theory.
Stage 2. Impression rather than repression theory.
Stage 3. Laissez Faire Theory.
Stage 4. Self discipline and social discipline theory.

To quote the Secondary Education Commission, "Discipline is the fruit, the valuable by product of cooperative work willingly and efficiently undertaken."

Discipline according to modern concept is a co-operative mental attitude in which each member of the class freely gives his best because he feels himself a member of corporate body whose aims are recognised as worthy. The aim of such discipline is to produce self-controlled students who will work without supervision.

Discipline from without is always temporisation.

Constructive discipline, like religion cannot be taught but only can be caught and practised. It is the outcome of activities and experiences that inculcate in the students virtues of self-control based on reason and not on force. It is the outcome of persuasion and not compulsion.

Discipline in the school should not be a matter of arbitrary rules and regulations enforced through the authority of the teachers, helped by the lures of rewards or the fear of punishment. The students should be given considerable freedom to organise functions to conduct many of the school activities through their own committees and even to deal with certain types of small disciplinary cases. Disciplines, thus should be maintained through the influence of the social group and gradually led to the development of self-discipline.

Old Concept and New Concept of Dissipation

	Old Concept of Discipline	*New or Modern Concept of Discipline*
1. *Aim*	Making the child obey.	Enabling the child to appreciate the necessity of obeying.
2. *School Environment*	1. Fearful. 2. Repulsive.	1. Full of cheerfulness. 2. Receptive and attractive.
3. *Role of the teacher*	(i) Teacher as a fearful person. (ii) Teacher as an autocrat.	Teacher as a friend, guide and philosopher.
4. *Methods of control*	(i) 'Do note move' (ii) Do not talk (iii) Scolding (iv) Punishment	(i) Freedom to work. (ii) No physical punishment. (iii) Social control
5. *Curriculum*	Rigid	Flexible
6. *Co-curricular Activities*	(i) Activities mostly confined to the classroom (ii) Very few.	(i) Variety of activities. (ii) Several indoor and outdoor activities.
7. *Students' Participation*	No scope or very little or negligible scope.	Involvement of students in sharing responsibility self-government.
8. *Place of the child*	(i) Passive listener (ii) Like a bird in a egg	(i) Active being. (ii) Full of life in free environment

Methods of Achieving Self-Discipline and Social Discipline

Following measures are considered to be of great significance in achieving the goal of self-discipline and social discipline.

1. Overall co-operative and vibrant environment of the school.
2. Philosophy of human relations as the guiding force under the humanistic leadership of the head of the school.
3. Enlightened and sympathetic attitude of the teachers.
4. Students' involvement in running some affairs of the school i.e. self-government.
5. Provision of rich and varied co-curricular activities.
6. Flocible school curriculum.
7. Dynamic and progressive methods of teaching.

8. Co-operation among the members of the staff.
9. Suitable material conditions of work.
10. Provision for social service activities.

Summing Up

The Secondary Education Commission very rightly has observed, "Discipline, they say, should be a responsibility of parents, teachers, the general public and the authorities concerned."

The problem of discipline is not an isolated one. Many-sided attempts will, therefore, have to be made. If we are to revive a spirit of idealism among students a favourable social environment based on higher values of life will have to be created. Leaders of all shades must set high ideals before the students. Nevertheless, there is much a school can do for raising the tone of discipline among the students and the school staff must play a constructive role to achieve this end.

7

Principal-Teacher-Pupil-Parent Relationship

In the Context of Administrative Styles of Leadership

The Authoritarian Administrator and the Democratic Administrator

"The boss drives his men; *the leader coaches them.*

The boss depends on authority; *the leader on good-will.*

The boss inspires fear; *the leader inspires enthusiasm.*

The boss assigns the task; *the leader sets pace.*

The boss says, "Get here on time"; *the leader gets there ahead of time.*

The boss fixes the blame for the breakdown; *the leader fixes the breakdown.*

The boss makes works a drudgery: *the leader makes it a game.*"

Concept of Human-oriented Organisation/Administration and Leadership

School organisation is not an end in itself. It must serve the objectives of education.

Since education is a tool for social transformation, it must explicitly inculcate and generate a sense of identification, a sense one's of fellow-being. This can only happen if we completely change or bring, about a radical change in the pattern of educational organisation, administration and style of leadership. J.M. Hughes observes in *Human Relations in Educational Organisation* that "every educational personnel is characterised by a system closely interlocking roles." The school programme involves the participation of the head of the school, the teachers, the students, the parents, the community leaders, government officials and the managing committee and its success depends upon the competency of the educational administrator to make all efforts to maintain good human relationships. The head of the institution as the educational administrator of the school must make all efforts to create good-will, understanding and will to cooperate between himself and each category of the participants and among the participants themselves. It must be remembered that in an educational organisation like the school, it is the quality of personnel relations which exists among its members that has a direct relation to the achievement of the school. Sustained co-operation is a fundamental requirement of efficient working of a school.

Ernest O. Melby has described in *Administering Community Education* the importance of human relations as "If a school system has a good general administration of education, with good human relationships, regardless of race, colour or creed or race, difficulties are not likely to occur. Similarly, if the human relations in a particular school administration are less than satisfactory, the incident of conflict will be higher."

Prof. S.N. Mukerji thinks that "Education administration is concerned with the management of things as well as with human relationships, *i.e.* the better working together of people. In fact, it is more concerned with human beings and less with inanimate things. It is, therefore, primarily a social enterprise."

K.G. Saiyidain states, "The educational administrator must learn that his concern is not only—or even mainly—with files, procedures and techniques or even the tackling of human relations. He should endeavour to become a living bridge between ideas and tested scientific knowledge, on the one hand, and practical problems and situation, on the other. Practice without enlightened theory is apt to become dull and lifeless and theory without practice runs the risk of losing social significance. We must all combine in the attempt to radiate our school practice with the play of creative ideas that would meet the new situations as they arise."

According to Dr. Sampurnanand—educational administration should be such that it makes the teacher believe in his work, brings out the best of which he is capable, stimulates him to bigger and better efforts, comes to his rescue when his courage begins to falter.

Leadership and Human Relations

Meaning of leadership: According to La Piere and Farmsworth, "Leadership is a behaviour that affects the behaviour of other people more than their behaviour affects that of the leader."

In the words of Pigor, "Leadership is a concept applied to the personality—environment relation to describe the situation when a personality is so placed in environment that his well-being, and insight direct and control others in the pursuit of common cause!'

Ralph M. and Stogdill views leadership, "as a process of influencing the activities of an organised group in the task of goal setting and goal achieving." *Good's Dictionary of Education* reads, "Leadership is the ability and readiness to inspire, guide, direct or manage others.'

Leslie D. Zeleny's definition is the most appropriate one. It states, "A group member whom others follow because he has demonstrated mastery of social relations in the group, and as a consequence, becomes its 'centre of living.'

Administrative Styles of Leadership

Nomothetic leadership	Auto-cratic leadership
Ideographic leadership	Anarchic leadership
Transactional leadership	Laissez Faire leadership
Democratic leadership	Symbolic leadership

Nomothetic Leadership: The status of the leader is based on his legal position. Such a type of leader believes in rules and procedures. He ensures that his subordinates must conform to a pattern of behaviour which he expects from them.

Ideographic Leadership: The leader does not exercise his authority for conformity.

Transactional Leadership: This is a compromise between the two extremes of leadership. Such a leader appreciates the necessity for achieving institutional goals, but at the same time hopes that individual personalities will not be violated as they strive towards these goals.

Democratic Leadership: This type of leadership is characterised by the emphasis on group decision or group action. The leader seeks co-operation and does not try to dominate. The personality of the members of the group is respected.

Autocratic Leadership: Autocratic leadership is characterised by the authoritarian attitude of the leader. The leader assigns tasks without consulting the members of the group. He seeks conformity.

(See the beginning of the chapter for comparison. Also see Chapter One)

Anarchic or Laissez Faire Leadership: The leader allows complete freedom to the members for arriving at decisions.

Symbolic Leadership: According to Knezevich, in this type of leadership, "the leader is perceived as a kind of 'might' or a 'whit horse' and described as being larger in physical size, stronger, more intelligent, more matured, more cultured and more impressive than you or I or any other of his followers. The longing of followers for security and dependence is satisfied through the development of such a symbol."

Desirable Qualities of an Effective Leader

1. Assertiveness
2. Attractive appearance
3. Cooperative nature
4. Determination
5. Emotional stability
6. Fearlessness
7. Group dynamism
8. Intelligence
9. Moral standard

10. Organising ability
11. Patience
12. Professional knowledge
13. Sympathetic outlook

Difficulties In Developing Harmonious Human Relations

1. Different social, economic, religious and educational background of the persons involved in educational administration.
2. Immature pupils with their typical and peculiar problems.
3. High expectations of the community from the school.
4. Desire of the leaders of the community to play dominant role in educational matters.
5. Limitations of the administration to provide good conditions of service to the teachers.
6. Separatist tendencies among the persons involved in educational administration.
7. Clash of personalities when the members differ widely in their frame of reference towards various matters in education.
8. Inability of the educative process to give immediate turnouts.
9. Various backgrounds composing the educational enterprise.
10. Interpersonal conflicts due to unforeseen circumstances.
11. Interpersonal conflicts due to prejudice and group prejudices.
12. Interpersonal conflicts due to frustration.

Role of the Head of the School: His Supreme Position

As the Head, so is the School

In the words of the Central Advisory Board of Education, "No scheme of educational reconstruction will produce the desired result unless it is administered with vision and efficiency." The school is aptly called the lengthened shadow of the Head because the environment of the school reflects the personality of the Head.

Will French and others stress the role of a principal as "If a teacher fails, the principal fails, if the teacher succeeds, the principal succeeds. To sum up what the principal's job is, we may call him a referee—the captain of the ship—the boss of the firm—a juvenile judge before whose tribunal come not only the culprits but the adults who frequently contribute to the pupils' shortcoming. He is a promoter who must project the future of his institution and convert the public to this plan. He is a social physician to every parent who has a wayward son who needs attention. He is a friend in need to pupils and to all the homes in which misfortune comes. His power, his activities, even the good he does, cannot be measured by a measured yardstick."

General Grant is said to have remarked that there are no poor regiments but poor colonels. Sultan Mohi-ud-in rightly states that no school can succeed if the teachers in it work only as individuals and not as a group. But just as every group needs a leader, so also a school must have a leader who would stimulate and direct its work. Such a leader is the Headmaster. And so is the case with the school. He is the hub of the education process. The success of the school system depends on his ability and skill as a sound and effective educational leader. The success or the failure of the school depends upon its Headmaster.

Great Headmasters make school great, "The reputation of the school and position that it holds in the society depends in a large measure on the influence that he exercises over his colleagues, the pupils and their parents and the general public," observed the Secondary Education Commission.

W.M. Ryburn compares the position of the Headmaster in a school to the Captain of a ship.

P.C. Wren sums up the importance of the job of the Headmaster, "What is main spring is to the watch, the fly when to the machine or the engine to the steamship, the Headmaster is to the school."

It is stated, "He is organiser, leader, governor, business director, co-ordinator, superintendent, example, teacher, guide, philosopher and friend."

He is responsible for the smooth running of the school. He is responsible for carrying out the policies and programmes of the Department of Education. He is the co-ordinator of educational work. He sets the tone of the school. He acts as a 'liaison' between the Education Department and the management or the general local community. His influence necessarily depends upon the qualities of head and heart he possesses.

Hundreds and thousands of eyes watch him, judge him, measure him and are eager to follow his noble example.

He has to be sweet and soft as well as stiff and stem.

Goldsmith said "Oil, vinegar, sugar and saltness in him do agree!"

Unless he has a seeing eye, an understanding heart and an all adjusting mental poise, he is bound to falter and tumble.

Duties, Functions and Responsibilities of the Head of the School

In the past, the duties of the Head were confined mostly to routine work at school and beyond that he had practically no responsibilities. The new ideal of secondary education entails heavy responsibilities. Now he is required not only to deal with correspondence, office work, scholar's registers and cash books but also to discharge his duties to the society. He has to co-ordinate the efforts of teachers, students and the community at large.

The functions of Headmaster are very complex. He has to supervise each and every activity in the school. He has to play a very delicate and critical role. He has always to work with four varied interest and groups: pupils, people, teachers and the authorities. He has often to come across and strike a balance in the practical fields among quarrelling and fighting students, complaining parents and exacting departments. He is expected at various times and various interests to play different roles. He must, by nature of his position, be—

1. A *teacher* of teachers.
2. A *supervisor* not only of teachers but of service personnel.
3. A *disciplinarian,* just but effective.
4. A *psychologist,* at least to the extent of being able to detect maladjustment, especially of teachers, which definitely hinder effective instruction and achievement of desired goals.
5. *A financier* in organising the school budget.
6. A *lawyer* at least to the extent of knowing his obligations, rights and legal liabilities as well as those of all school personnel.
7. A *sociologist* to the extend of at least being able to understand the relation of school with social forces.
8. A *technical expert* is educational measurement and evaluation.
9. An *expert in group dynamics* to the extent of working effectively with staff, pupil, parents, public and the authorities.

The Head and Human Relations

I. *General Principles of Developing Human Relations*

The success of the head of the school depends on the extent to which he brings out the best of the staff, students and their parents and the community and develops wholesome relationships. Following are the important practices which the head should adopt to develop human relations with all the groups he comes into contact.

1. The principal should be ever ready to consider new ideas on education coming from others and should be willing to try out those which seem to be useful.
2. He should consistently hold a "progressive" view in educational matters.
3. He should try to apply such new methods as are suitable to Indian conditions.
4. He should encourage teachers to experiment with new procedures and techniques of education.
5. He should keep in touch with the latest developments in the field of education.
6. He should be democratic in his relations with teachers.
7. He should prove by his actions that he always means what he says.
8. He should not favour any of the teachers unduly.
9. He should show by his actions that he has confidence in his teachers.
10. He should give proper recognition to the good work done by the teachers.
11. He should not keep himself aloof from the other members of the staff.

12. The principal should show in his dealings a real respect for the opinion of others.
13. He should not attempt to dominate his teachers by the force of his position.
14. He should have a due regard for the feelings of others.
15. He should never play one teacher against another in order to maintain his official superiority.
16. He should try to mutually reconcile differences, if they arise among teachers, between teachers and parents, and between teachers and the employer.
17. He should be ready to share with his co-workers the responsibility for any deficiency or weakness in the school programme.
18. He should share his work with and delegate responsibilities to suitable staff members and committees.
19. He should provide all possible assistance to new teachers.
20. He should encourage and provide opportunities for in-service education of teachers.

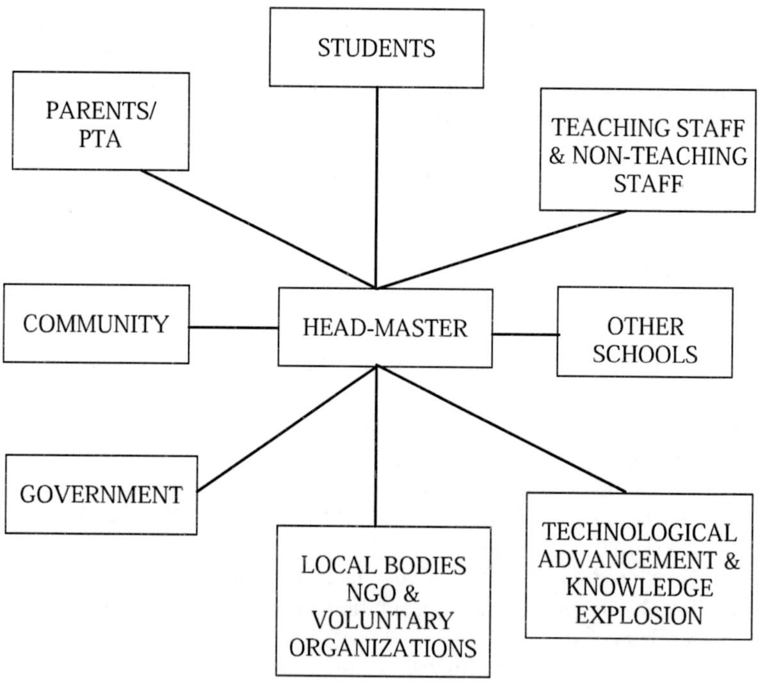

Fig. 7.1 : Multiple Responsibilities and Relationships of a School Head

Major Characteristics or Qualities of the Head of the School for Developing Balanced Human Relations

1. *Considers the Administrative Machinery as an Instrument of Social Service:* "An educational administrator is more than an official punctilious about administrative routine, he is a leader guiding and directing a sacred undertaking. The official apparatus that is at his disposal, the education department that is under his control, is more than a bureaucratic machine. It is an instrument of social service." —*Chitra Naik*

2. *Co-operative Attitude:* "The leader of the school can be successful only when he secures willing co-operation from his co-workers; when he makes those co-workers feel that the problems of the school are theirs and not his own." —*Mohi-ud-din*

"Dignity does not consist in aloofness and in maintaining an air of superiority; It rather consists in being helpful and doing the right thing." —*Mohi-ud-din*

3. *Democratic Attitude:* "A democratic administrator should look upon the personnel as socially equal to himself; he should not take decisions by himself; but with his colleagues, he should make them feel responsible and share in administration, he should have code of set rules of administration which he and his colleagues should follow rigidly, making no discrimination in their application, and lastly, he should have no special privilege." —*R.R. Kamria*

4. *Educational Statesman:* In the words of E.P. Cubberly, "He must learn to lead by reason, by his larger knowledge and courageous enthusiasm rather than to drive reason of his superior power.... He must reach up out of the routine of school supervision and execute duties into the higher level of educational statesmanship."

5. *Expert in Human Psychology:* An ideal head always remembers that all people cannot be equally intelligent and hard working. A trouble shooter needs to be handled firmly in the very beginning praise and appreciation sometimes help even if a person does not deserve it. Sometimes sympathetic hearing is all that is needed to blow off the steam of emotions. Sometimes valuable suggestions help in easing the tension.

6. *Faith in Human Nature:* "It is essential, therefore, that he be a man of faith, faith in his vocation, faith in his pupils, faith in human nature and faith in himself." —*W.M. Ryburn*

"He must unlimited faith in himself and his creator." —*Jaswant Singh*

7. *Recognition to Good Work Done:* Ryburn writes, "Nothing will more encourage a man or woman, a boy or girl, to greater effort than an encouraging recognition of good work done, of sincere effort made, or good qualities shown. If those in charge of institutions and those carrying on the administrative work of departments wish to enable those working with them to do their best, they should always realize the value of ungrudging recognition of all that merits recognition."

8. *Judicious Decision Making:* (i) Decides cases promptly. (ii) Gives judgment only after weighing and considering relevant evidence. (iii) Perceives true nature of cases. (iv) Decides cases on the basis of principles rather than expediency. (v) Makes decisions without bias and prejudice.

9. *Headmaster not by Appointment but by Superior Ability.* "It must not be known by his staff and scholars that he is their headmaster by appointment but felt that he is their master by superior ability, energy and character." —*P.C. Wren*

"He is the organiser, leader, governor, business director, co-ordinator, superintendent teacher, guide, philosopher and friend."

10. *Health:* "A person with indifferent health and poor stamina will not be able to discharge his own or discharge the multifarious and heavy responsibilities of his office." —*Jaswant Singh*

11. *Life one of Immolation:* In the words of S. Balakrishna Joshi, "The progress of the school community is his thought by day and dream by night, and his aching passion is to wear himself out in the service of the shrine in which he feels spiritually wedded. It is his conviction that while the life of a teacher is one of consecration that of the Headmaster should be one of immolation."

12. *Leader by Courage and Reason and not by Power:* "He must learn to lead by reason, by his larger knowledge and courgeous enthusiasm rather than to drive by reason of his superior power.... He must reach up out of the routine of school supervision and execute duties into the higher level of educational statement." —*E.P. Cubberly*

"The successful administrator gets people to work with him, not primarily because he has power over them and can order them about, because he is the kind of leader for whom they want to do their best." —*Pagors and Myers*

13. *Man of Integrity:* He fights all temptations to pad his purse with money to which he is not entitled. The quote S. Balakrishna Joshi, "He does not try to exploit school influence for private gains because he realizes that if he does it, he signs his moral death-warrant. The result is that no amount of pressure can wean him from the path of duty and justice. Authority, cannot coerce him, nor can temptation reduce him into any course of conduct, nor conductive to the highest interests of the school."

14. *Optimistic Outlook:* He has unlimited faith in himself. He does not accept defeat. He always think of success all the time. Ryburn stresses, "It is essential, therefore, that he be not only a man of high character but also that he be a man of faith; faith in his vocation, faith in his pupils, faith in human nature, and faith in his staff."

15. *Patience:* "Patience is a virtue that will pay very generous dividends to assists, not to control the educative process." —*Reaves*

"Go slow the first day, the first week, the first month, and even the first year, make changes slowly and always with the co-operation of the faculty."

—*William T. Melchor*

16. *Philosophy of Education:* "A good Headmaster needs to have a sound philosophy of education." —*Jaswant Singh*

17. *Planning Capacity:* "If a principal is not careful, he will find himself spending much of the time in answering telephone, running errands for teachers, signing excuses, making repairs to the buildings, handling money, raising campaigns, and performing other minor duties and then budget his time accordingly." —*Margaret Grag*

18. *Professional Devotion:* "He should drive the same satisfaction from working for institution as the artist or the sculptor derives when working late hours over his handiwork, fully attentive to the smallest details, never tiring." —*Jaswant Singh*

19. *Progressive Outlook:* "It is reasonable to expected that a headmaster should be progressive in his outlook." —*Mohi-ud-din*

20. *Due Appreciation to Others:* "Nothing will more encourage a man or woman, a boy or a girl, to greater effort, than an encouraging recognition of good work done, of sincere effort made, or good qualities shown. If those in charge of institutions and those carrying on the administrative work of departments wish to enable those working with them to do their best, they should always realize the value of ungrudging recognition of all that merits such recognition. —*Ryburn*

21. *Rises Equal to any Occasion:* "He rises equal to any occasion, and by his resourcefulness and readingness to render service, solves knotty problems. To him it is not beneath his dignity to strike the going in time if the peon is engaged otherwise, or to lead a band of devoted volunteers to flush the latrines if scavenger is absent. Again he is prepared to 'referee' a match if the umpire has not turned up or step into a class and teach any subject if a teacher is called suddenly. Thus his willingness and ability to do any piece of work pertaining to the school, wrest for him the confidence and regard of all concerned."

22. *Scientific Attitude:* An ideal head is particularly careful in making judgment about persons for whom he cherishes a positive like or dislike. He observes correctly without letting personal feelings, prejudices, and wishes to influence him, draws valid conclusions from give facts and makes sound generalizations as the facts warrant. He does not see things through coloured spectacles. He is able to detach his personal likes and dislikes from the performance of others. He is conscious of the fact that monopoly of truth is not held by any one.

23. *Sense of Humour:* Dr. Jaswant Singh writes about this quality, "It will enable him to get over an impassee with the help of a smile, a light hearted chuckle, or a jocular remark which will ease the tense atmosphere. The sense of humour will help break resistance, overcome opposition by

injecting a spirit of comraderie into the situation. Many a difficult situation can be resolved by a witty remark."

24. *Sensitive to the Needs of the Community:* "In whatever community the principal finds himself, he should study the characteristic social conditions and needs of his pupils and endeavour in appropriate ways to secure increased co-operation between the school and the community in meeting these needs." —*W. Johnson Frank*

25. *Sensitive to the Needs of the Students:* A good Headmaster should be profoundly sensitive to the physical, mental, moral, intellectual and spiritual needs of his pupils and should know how to minister to them." —*V.S. Jha*

26. *Sensitive to the Needs of Teachers:* "The Principal should not interrupt classes, unless invited to do so." —*Jacobson and Others*

"If the Principal stays to the end of the class period he should observe good manners by expressing in a sentence or two his pleasure on visiting the class." —*Jacobson and Others*

27. *Sensitive to the Needs of the Parents:* "He should always treat parents with scrupulous courtesy. —*W.M. Ryburn*

28. *Sensitive to the Need of the many Sided Development of the Child:* According to Dr. V.S. Jha, "He should be profoundly sensitive to the physical, mental, moral, intellectual and spiritual needs to the pupils and should know how to minister to them."

29. *Source of Inspiration:* The members of staff should look to him for guidance, help and inspiration. "Under any authoritarian regime, where basis of relationship is fear of one sort or another, it is often possible to get certain routine done efficiently. But under such conditions it is impossible to bring into rapport the best elements in the personality of the teacher—thus education loses its formative influence."

"He gives up the time-old tradition of checking his teachers, frightening his teachers, weakening his teachers and examining them; but manipulates things so as to train his teachers, inspire his teachers, encourage his teachers and trust them." —*D.I. Lall*

30. *Thinking Capacity:* "Experience in an indispensable qualification for a headmaster. This is certainly true. But experience alone without the capacity to think out and plan out new progressive programmes is inadequate." —*Mohi-ud-din*

31. *Vision and Imagination:*

(a) Makes decisions which later events show to be sound and reliable.
(b) Searches new practices and techniques.
(c) Seizes opportunities to develop new patterns of action.

32. *Not an Awful man.* "In a school worth its name the Head will neither sit in his room like a large spider waiting for a chance to pounce on his prey nor he like an awe inspiring God on the Olympian Heights who visits the earth once in a way to thunder disapproval or to subjegate the people by his presence." —*A. M. D. Razario*

Personality of the Headmaster

To justify his place as the inspiring leader and guide, the Headmaster must have a strong personality. R.A. Lamb remarks, "To make the perfect head of the school, there is needed in addition to all these, a quality which is undefinable—and which resides in the personality of the individuality. It is not possible to analyse this quality and more than it is possible by dissecting a man's brain to find wherein resides the soul or the spirit of life. But that it exists is beyond question."

Human Relations of the Head of the School with the Teachers

Milo Stuart has very beautifully illustrated the nature of relations with the staff, "The relation of the principal to his teachers should be the most intimate of any. If a teacher fails, the principal fails; if the teacher succeeds, the principal succeeds. To sum up what the principal's job is, I shall call him a referee—the captain of the ship—the boss of the firm—a juvenile judge before whose tribunal come out not only the culprits but the adults who frequently contribute to the pupil's shortcomings. He is a promoter who must project the future of his institution and convert the public to his plan. He is a social physician to every parent who has a wayward son who needs attention. He is a friend is need to pupils and to all the homes in which misfortune comes. His power, his activities, even the good he does, cannot be measured by a material yardstick."

Principles of Developing Harmonious Staff Relations

1. *Principle of Democratic Administration:* We have already discussed that a Head should follow the principles of democratic administration. According to K.G. Saiyidain, "To my mind a good Headmaster is one who can inspire and enthuse his colleagues without dominating over them like a hard task master."

2. *Principle of Sharing Responsibility:* He should be prepared to share the control and authority with his colleagues. He should not think that he is born to rule and should not desire to be on the top of everything in the school, *i.e.,* the president of games, the chairman of literary societies and the patron of social service and health unions, etc. The different departments should be placed under the charge of the senior members of the staff. Principle of 'Sharing Responsibility' should be the keynote of his policy. Supervision of the examinations, school cleanliness, morning assembly, funds, hostel, scouting, literary and social activities are some of the chief duties which would be delegated by the Headmaster to the other members of the staff. This will develop in them a sense of responsibility for the school.

3. *Principle of Mutual Consultation:* The headmaster should frequently consult his colleagues regarding improvement in school discipline and instruction. Such consultations instil in them the spirit that they belong to

the school and are as responsible to it as the Headmaster is. Staff meetings should be convened from time to time.

4. *Principle of Constructive Criticism:* The criticism offered by the Headmaster should be judicious, fair and constructive rather than destructive. Supervision should be a matter of inspiration to teachers. It should be moderate. Excessive supervision kills all the initiative and drive of teachers. The role of a policeman or a military officer does more harm than good.

5. *Principle of Co-operation:* On the close co-operation of the Headmaster and the staff depends the efficiency of the school and the head of the institution is to a great extent responsible for securing co-operation of teachers. According to Reavis, "No matter what his personal characteristics are, he will not be successful unless he is able to inspire his associates and collaborators with the desire to work co-operatively for the goals for which the school stands. He will be judged by his ability to enlist and to utilise their ability in participating in the solution of school problems and in formulating educational policies that have the common objective of advancing the welfare of the children enrolled in the school. He does not attempt to conceal that he is their leader, but he does not on the other hand remind them what he is."

6. *Principle of Friendly Supervision:* Speaking about administrators of tomorrow D.I. Lal observes, "He gives up the time-old tradition of checking his teachers, frightening his teachers, weakening his teachers and examining them, but manipulates things so as to train his teachers, inspire his teachers and trust them. In this way he will not only create an excellent professional moral among the teaching staff but will also cultivate a vital interest in them for educational philosophy so that they can continually test and re-test their plans and purposes, ideas, ideals, methods and procedures, systems and organisations."

Jacobson observes, "The Principal should not interrupt classes, create disturbances on entering and leaving, or to take the class away from the teacher, unless invited to do so. If the Principal stays to the end of the class period he should observe good manners by expressing in a sentence or two his pleasure in visiting the class but refrain from making condemnatory statements until there is sufficient time to discuss them at length, if indeed he indulges in them at all."

Suggestions for Promoting Staff Harmony

1. Take the first step in being friendly.
2. Be cheerful.
3. Remember and use names.
4. Be easily accessible to the staff.
5. Avoid taking special privileges.
6. Be polite and courteous.

7. Avoid keeping teachers waiting.
8. Ask teachers if they are willing to assume responsibility.
9. Take prompt action on requests.
10. Keep a record of promises and live up to them.
11. Attempt to see actions and decisions from the other persons' point of view.
12. Give credit to the persons responsible when the school receives praise.
13. Let teachers know when their work is good.
14. Be concerned about the way a teacher feels about his job and his out of school life.
15. Be willing to listen to teachers.
16. Avoid any evidence of authority.
17. Ask questions that relieve anxiety about discussing a problem.
18. Give praise for reporting facts accurately.
19. Become fully informed about the social structure of the staff.
20. Refuse to accept the assumption that conflicting groups in staff are unavoidable.
21. Offer services to assist in seeking agreement when disagreements arise in the group.
22. Do not show any undue favour to any member of the staff.
23. Inform new teachers on matters of school regulation.
24. Visit teachers who are ill.
25. Keep in mind while preparing your schedule that other teachers are not put to inconvenience.
26. Show consideration for bashful teachers.
27. Give teachers a chance to tell their side of the story.
28. Do not make personal remarks to shame them.
29. Show consideration for the feeling of other teachers.
30. Do not embarrass a teacher of inferior ability or one who has physical defects.
31. Do not laugh at the actions which seem funny to you.
32. Learn to work, to play, to live successfully with your associates.
33. Learn to like people.
34. Find out how different teachers wished to be treated and treat them accordingly.
35. Be willing to help teachers secure better positions.
36. Make changes slowly, preferably at teachers' suggestions.
37. Seek the help of teachers as co-workers and special advisers.
38. Be sincerely interested in teachers, like them as persons. Lincoln said, "If you would win a man to your cause, first convince him that you are his sincere friend."
39. Give teachers your undivided attention both when listening and when talking to them.

40. Criticise only in private.
41. Smile! As they say in the Navy, "A happy ship is a good ship, so, too, a happy school is a good school"
42. Always ask a teacher's permission to break into a classroom activity.
43. Help teachers in difficulty with pupils, parents or other teachers.
44. Meet staff in informal situations.
45. Use the word 'co-workers' in place of 'subordinates' and treat them as such.
46. Motivate desirable action through commendation.
47. Share knowledge of coming events with colleagues.
48. Give reasons for and interpret instructions and order.
49. Earn respect of colleagues by character and behaviour rather than gain respect through 'position'.
50. Deal appropriately with outside criticism of staff members or the organisation.
51. Encourage suggestions, evaluate them carefully, and accept them on merit.
52. Regard yourself as a member of the group rather than command respect through 'position'.

Staff Meeting

Importance: Efficient running of the school demands that members of the staff should occasionally meet for sharing responsibilities as well as experiences. These meetings should be presided over by the Principal.

These may be convened from time to time.

Briggs found that teachers expected the following things in a staff meeting:

(i) Help in their problems.
(ii) A wider outlook on education.
(iii) Meeting to be happy and wholesome.
(iv) Meeting based on appreciation of effort and accomplishment rather than shortcomings and faults.

Planning of Staff Meetings: The teachers should be informed in advance of the problems to be discussed in the meetings. It is very important for the head to listen to every teacher with attention and care. Minutes of staff meetings should be kept if possible.

A limit must be put to staff meetings and the best appears to be once a month. Of course, there need not be any rigidity in observing this principle. Occasional meetings for some particular purposes may have to be called. Sometimes it may become necessary for the head to convey staff meeting to clarify certain points of written order issued by him. An atmosphere of cheerfulness should prevail in all such meetings.

The head of the institution should take note of the teachers' problems and accordingly give his suggestions for the solution of the problems concerned. His attempt should be to help the teachers as much as possible.

Staff meetings should not be too long. Usually not more than one and a half hours be spent upon these.

Characteristics of Staff Meetings

1. All discussions should be above the personal level.
2. They should be economical in time.
3. Discussion should not go off the track.
4. They should start in time.
5. They should result in concrete suggestions.

Staff Club

The formation of Staff Club will facilitate intimate contacts between the head and the members of the staff and also among the members of the staff themselves. One members of the staff should serve as a secretary who should be elected every year so that most of the members get a chance of leading others.

The functions of the club would be recreational-cum-educational. It may arrange tea during recess for the staff members. Its another function would be to arrange welcome and farewell parties. Its third function will be to arrange excursions and picnics on holidays. Its fourth function will be to arrange discussions on important school problems.

The Head should not look upon this club with suspicion. He should occasionally attend meetings of the club. Through such informal meetings, he will learn more about the members of the staff and this will also help in cementing the bonds of friendship, goodwill and mutual understanding.

The Head's Human Relationships with Students

Often it is seen that the Headmaster makes the error of not coming into direct contact with the pupils. He should not forget that he can directly influence them to a considerable extent and as such he must avail himself of every opportunity of addressing them and attending various functions organised in the school. Regarding his work and relations with the students, we may quote Dr. V.S. Jha: "A good Headmaster or Principal is not merely a scholar, he is a man of sound character, deep sympathy and understanding and considerable tact and experience dealing with pupils. He should be profoundly sensitive to the physical, mental, moral and spiritual needs of the pupils and should know how to minister them."

The headmaster must view the educational programme as a whole and assist students directly in having a balanced experience in terms of individual needs. To accomplish this he should:

— Show by action and in discussion that he places value in educational objectives including but over and beyond academic achievement: positive attitudes, citizenship skills, aesthetic appreciation, individual initiative, cooperative tendencies, etc.

— Give leadership to planning student activities, clubs and projects which will supplement and complement the academic class work.

— Approach individual student's problems from a guidance point of view, and help teachers to recognise individual differences in teaching and in dealing with students' problems.

— Make it a practice to get to know students personally, showing friendship to them and expressing interest in what they are doing.

— Involve students in real responsibility for the operation of significant aspects of the school, through student government, the house system and other techniques.

The great headmasters have always been great friends of their pupils. The headmaster should possess the following skills:

1. Loves them intensely.
2. Shows interest in student activities.
3. Shows due regard to their personality.
4. Shows friendliness towards individual students.
5. Shows a spirit of 'oneness' and 'belongingness' with them.
6. Gives due regard to student opinion.
7. Takes a keen interest in the welfare of the students.
8. Spares time for conferences.
9. Shows a keen interest in solving their problems.
10. Shares responsibility with them.

Head's Human Relations with Parents

Educators and administrators are now fast realising that effective and intimate relations with parents are very necessary for the efficient organisation of school work and activities. The head of an institution must find out ways and means for establishing happy contacts with student's parents and guardians.

His treatment with the parents should be very courteous. As Ryburn puts it, "He should always treat parents with scrupulous courtesy when they come to the school."

Schools serving the public in a democracy should be responsive to the wishes of parents regarding the school programme. Also, the school programme should be related to the community. Towards these ends the headmaster should:

— Arrange a variety of activities and programmes for keeping the public informed about the school programme; new projects, progress in achieving objectives.

— Encourage parents to make constructive suggestions regarding ways of improving the school, providing avenues through which parents' ideas are reported and discussed.

— Assist the school staff in knowing the community and in teaching students different ways through which they can contribute to community development.

— Make the school facilities available for use by appropriate community groups for meetings, recreation and adult education.
— Organise ways in which parents and community groups can help the school, through funds raising for specific activities, making community educational resources more readily available to the school, and assisting teachers and students in studying the community.
— Organise parent-teacher meets from time to time.
— Make the school a centre of community service.

The Head and Development of Human Relations with the Community

1. The head should encourage the parents of the pupils to visit the school frequently.
2. He should see that parents are cordially received when they visit the school.
3. He should regularly inform the parents of the progress of their wards.
4. He should encourage the parents to consult the teachers as well as him on special problems of their wards.
5. He should visit the homes of the pupils in special situations and should suggest to the teachers also to do the same.
6. He should organise parents-study-groups from time to time.
7. He should provide adequate facilities for the organisation and proper functioning of the Parent-Teacher Association in the school.
8. The principal should plan school programme with reference to the needs of the community.
9. He should encourage the use of community resources for vitalizing classroom instruction through excursions, field trips, study of local history, etc.
10. He should encourage and organise and social service programmes to render public services.
11. He should allow the community to use school facilities and services like school-building, library, and dispensary seeing at the same time that the work of the school does not suffer.
12. He should organise social and cultural activities in the school to interpret the school programme to the community.
13. He should actively participate in the social and cultural functions of the community.
14. He should be above politics and religion in organising school programmes.
15. He should not allow the school to become a tool in the hands of any pressure group.

16. He should not allow his political beliefs to influence his administration of school.

(*See also chapter on Parent-Teacher Association*)

Teacher-Pupil Human Relations

Total development of the child as his primary responsibility: In the words of Dr. E.A. Pires, "He (teacher) has to concern himself with the total development of the child and not only with one or two aspects. He must be friend him and help him in his emotional and social development. He must be a philosopher illumining the way of this intellectual and spiritual progress. He must be his guide in his moral and aesthetic advancement. In fact, he must be 'all things' to all his pupils—a physician concerned about their physical health, a mental hygienist leading them carefully to sound mental health, a philosopher guiding them painstakingly in their search for truth, a moralist assisting and encouraging them to acquire goodness, an artist helping them to find beauty. In fact, he must be a minister ministering to their every need. Such a ministry calls for educated service."

Teacher's Roles in the Development of Harmonious and Friendly Relations with the Students

With a view to achieve the goal of total development of the child, it is very essential to create wholesome relations with the students. For this, the teacher should play the following roles.

1. *Confidant:* A teacher is expected to win the confidence of the students so that they express their feelings freely, if need be in private.
2. *Democrat:* He is expected to observe democratic values so as to prepare his students for a democratic way of life.
3. *Detective:* He acts as a detective to find out the shortcomings of the students—committing of offences and law breaking tendencies also.
4. *Ego-supporter:* He is supposed to build up and maintain a healthy strong 'ego' and 'self concept' among students.
5. *Equaliser:* He should treat all students on the basis of equality. He should work for developing an egalitarian outlook in students.
6. *Facilitator of learning:* He works for the promotion of significant learning in his students.
7. *Friend and philosopher:* He must perform the role of a friend and philosopher to his students.
8. *Group leader:* As a leader of the social group in the clan, he must develop a suitable climate and cohesion.
9. *Guidance counsellor and helper:* He provides an academic career and personal guidance to his students.
10. *Initiator:* He is supposed to play the role of an initiator by exploring the new technology to the best advantage of the students and the

progress of education. He should play the role of an innovator of educational ideas, practices and systems.

11. *Role model:* He is envisaged to behave in a manner whereby traits exemplified by him may be emulated by his students.
12. *Judge:* He evaluates the academic and other performance of the students in an impartial manner.
13. *Limiter or reducer of anxiety:* He can help students control their impulses and reduce anxiety about their conduct and performance in different problematic situations.
16. *Rationalist:* He should set an example of a rationalist by basing his actions on reason.
17. *Referee:* He is expected to settle disputes among students in an objective manner.
18. *Reformer:* His entire work consists of bringing about appropriate changes in his students for their full development.
19. *Resource person:* He is expected to serve as a resource person for his students as he possesses knowledge of the subject-matter and skills, better than his pupils.
20. *Secularist:* He should play the role of a secularist by having an open mind on the beliefs of students.
21. *Upholder of the norms and values:* He must present the norms and values of society in a dignified manner.

Suggestive Measures for Developing Ideal Relations with Students

1. Creates an atmosphere of purposeful order, enlists pupil's assistance in orderly, friendly, courteous and co-operative inter-personal relations.
2. Develops a respect for the rights, privileges and opinions of students.
3. Creates group situations which will develop desirable leadership and followership qualities in the pupils.
4. Sets a standard of classroom and school environment behaviour which conforms to socially acceptable behaviour.
5. Directs discussion and develops understanding on moral and other ethical issues in order to develop the understanding of the reasons for ethical standard.
6. Encourages each pupil's thinking and action.
7. Selects materials, teaching aids and methods which will facilitate the learning process and stimulate the desire for further learning.
8. Meets the needs, background and capacities of the children being taught.
9. Teaches by use of a suitable variety of teaching methods like lectures, discussions, demonstrations, visual and oral presentations, recitation, directed group effort, experimentation, special projects

and field trips.

10. Analyses and evaluating the effectiveness of various teaching techniques in order to improve the learning process.
11. Endeavours to obtain and maintain pupil interest and attention so that teaching is done in a receptive environment.
12. Endeavours to assure that material taught is applied in such a manner so as to develop a pattern of understanding for future use in other areas.
13. Encourages and guiding critical thinking by pupils.
14. Develops desirable work and study skills and habits.
15. Enlists pupil participation in the lesson planning process.
16. Attempts to meet individual differences of pupils.

Specific Qualities Needed in Teachers for Developing Proper Human Relations with Pupils

1. *Cooperative attitude:* The success of an institutions depends upon the co-operation among all. A teacher must co-operate with his colleagues, head of the institution, parents and all others engaged in the welfare of children and other tasks.

2. *Democratic attitude:* A teacher cannot afford to be an autocrat. Present day education lays much stress on the inculcation of democratic ideals in the students. A teacher who is to show the way of democracy to the students must develop in himself a democratic attitude. His role is of a friend, philosopher and guide and not of a policeman.

3. *Political neutrality:* The students should not be exploited for political purposes. The programmes of the various political parties must be placed before them in their true perspective.

4. *Religious tolerance:* The minds of the young should not be poisoned though narrow-mindedness and bigotry. The partition of the country has shown what wrong fanaticism can do.

5. *Judicious use of praise and blame:* Praise and blame are the two importance weapons in the armoury of the teacher and these should be used very judiciously. "Praise like gold and diamond owes its value to scarcity," writes Robinson Johnson. A word of praise or commendation will easily enhance the pupil's interest in any course of action. Praise, rightly employed, is forceful incentive at the disposal of the teacher. Rebukes and scolding are to be used very sparingly, otherwise they lose their value.

6. *Character and personality:* The character and personality of the pupils cannot be developed if the teacher who is the model to be followed lacks character and personality. 'Example is better than precept' is an old saying and is absolutely true in the teaching profession. No amount of sermons from the teacher can make much headway. A teacher teaches not only by 'what he says and does' but very largely by 'what he is'. Children are imitative and suggestive by nature. They imitate the dress, voice, habits and

manners of their teachers. The likes and dislikes of the teachers become their likes and desires. Children who are in the plastic period of their life are easily influenced by their teachers. The teachers should teach what they practise. Gandhi strongly denounces those teachers who teach one thing with lips and carry another in their heart. 'Man know thyself' is the advice given by Socrates in Greece and Yajnvalkya in India. The teachers must undergo an inner training. They should try to find out their own shortcomings and try to remove them. Ryburn says, 'Self analysis on the part of a teacher is a necessary equipment'. Montessori stresses that every teacher worth his salt must destroy these sins: pride, anger, sloth, sensuality, gluttony and envy. The teacher should be partly a scientist, partly a doctor and completely religious. He must acquire a moral alertness; mingling of patience, love and humility. He should always be frank, sincere and honest. Prof. Raymount urges that the teacher must avoid everything that is petty and mean. Gandhi observes, "Woe to the teacher who teaches one thing with the lips and carries another in the heart."

7. *Love for children:* It has been said that if a teacher does not actually like boys and girls, he should give up teaching. A good teacher feels that some sort of energy is constantly supplied by the young. "Love the child and the child will love you; hate the child and the child will hate you," is a famous maxim.

8. *Respect for the individuality of each child:* A child should not be treated just like dumb driven cattle. He has his own individuality. He thinks and feels; his sense of respect should not be injured. Emerson has rightly stated, "The secret of education lies in respecting the pupil." A child wants to be heard. His opinion should not be brushed aside merely because he is a child.

9. *Knowledge of child psychology and educational psychology:* Knowledge of psychology goes a long way in providing that basic orientation towards problems of education and child development without which there would be a considerable waste of time, energy and human resources.

10. *Mastery of the subject-matter:* He must be master of his subject. Any weakness on his part will lower his prestige in the eyes of his student. K.G. Saiyidain writes, "You cannot pour out of a vessel except what you have put into it and, if a teacher is poor and shallow from within, if there is no sparking wire in him, he cannot quicken the mind or humanise the emotions of his children."

11. *Grasp over the method:* Two farmers may possess an equal amount of land and an equally great desire of good crops but the one who uses the best methods of farming will, other factors being same, get better results. Similarly, a teacher who adopts proper methods of teaching will show good results and his teaching will be more effective.

12. *Emotional stability:* Various research studies show clearly that the

emotional stability of teachers affect that of pupils. The unhappy, frustrated, dissatisfied teachers cannot help their pupils to become happy, well adjusted young people.

Significance of Each Letter of the Word 'Teacher'

Each letter of the word teacher signifies some traits or values to be possessed by him.

T stands for — Tact. Tolerance. Truth. Training, Technology
E stands for — Efficiency. Enthusiasm. Ethics. Etiquette
A stands for — Adaptability. Affection. Alertness
C stands for — Character. Clarity. Co-operation. Constructiveness. Creativity.
H stands for — Hard work. Humility. Humour. Honesty. Human Relations.
E stands for — Eagerness, Efficiency, Emotional Stability.
R stands for — Rationality. Relationship. Resourcefulness

The teacher should be an integration of all these.

Teacher and Community Relationships

A teacher plays his role in the community in two ways. (a) Inside the school by preparing students for effective citizenship, (b) Outside the school by assuming the role of a social worker and an agent of social change. For playing this twin role, he must develop the art of establishing amicable relations.

Following are some of the measures for winning the willing co-operation of the parents and the community.

1. Participating in parent-teacher and similar activities.
2. Participating in community affairs.
3. Making himself available to parents at scheduled times to discuss pupil progress and behaviour.
4. Evincing a sympathetic, helpful and understanding attitude towards parents and their childrens' schooling problems.
5. Reporting and discussing with parents, pupil progress, problems and needs.
6. Assuring through personal behaviour in the community that the school staff-image in the community is favourable.

(*See also Chapter on Parent-Teacher Association*)

8

Parent-Teacher Associations

Close co-operation between the parent who is the first teacher and the teacher who is the second parent, is the very foundation on which rests the fruitfulness of the training imparted in our institutions.

—*S. Balakrishna Joshi*

Need for Parent-Teacher Cooperation

Both the school and the family have similar objectives i.e. the harmonious development of children. Parents are interested in the welfare of their children. They want their children develop aesthetically, culturally, ethically, mentally, morally, physically, socially, spiritually and vocationally. So is the case with parents. Hence the need for concerned, sincere and united efforts on the part of parents and teachers. Both the groups are the custodians of the progress and welfare of children.

George Tomilnson has stressed the need for cooperation between the home and the school in these words, "Let us fashion our schools with the well-being of children always in mind. In particular, remember that any clash between parents and teachers must be harmful to the child. Harmonious working together can bring us the results we want.

Need for Parent-Teacher Cooperation from the Parents Point of View

(i) They need information regarding the progress' of their children in academic and co-curricular areas.

(ii) They want necessary information well in time regarding expenditure on books etc.

(iii) They need information about problem situations before they become serious.

(iv) They want regular assignment and their careful checking.

(v) They need advice as to how they could supplement the efforts of the school in promoting the progress of their children.

(vi) They are interested to know the new changes to be carried out in curriculum and methods of teaching.

(vii) They need information about school's performance at the public examinations.

(viii) They want to know about the subject combinations available in the school.

(ix) They want to know about the financial position of the school.
(x) They want to know the manner in which they could help the school.

Need for Parent-Teacher Cooperation from the Point of View of Teachers

(i) To seek maximum information from the parents about the child to have fuller understanding of him.
(ii) For getting help from the parents in the regular attendance of the child.
(iii) For getting help in regular supervision of home work of the child.
(iv) For providing the child necessary equipment at proper time.
(v) For getting help in stressing upon the child the necessity of having respect for the school laws.
(vi) For securing necessary financial and other help for the school.
(vii) For understanding the parents of the limitations of the school.
(viii) For expecting the parents to read progress reports of their wards.
(ix) For visiting the school when required to discuss the problems of the child and to take up appropriate follow-up.

Difficulties and Problems in the Way of Parent-Teacher Cooperation

(a) *From the Side of the Parents*
   (i) Indifference of the parents to the school work.
   (ii) Busy life of the parents and the lack of time to contact teachers.
   (iii) Ignorance on the part of the parents as to how they can render any assistance to the child in his work.
   (iv) Their suspicious nature regarding the motives of school authorities.
(b) *From the Side of the Teachers*
   (i) Their unwillingness to face criticism.
   (ii) Their conservative outlook and doubts about the success of this programme.
   (iii) Lack of time to make sincere efforts in this direction.

Methods of Securing Parent-Teacher Cooperation

On account of the mass illiteracy of the parents, the initiative and encouragement must come from the parents. In this regard, S. Balakrishna Joshi's observations deserve careful consideration, "Parental cooperation cannot be had by learned discourses on the subject or periodical pamphlets posted to the parents. It cannot be created overnight. We cannot wake up one fine morning and find the parents pitchforked into cooperation. It is based on a series of silent acts of sincere service to children. It is the natural consummation of devoted deeds of dedication at the shrine of Duty." All possible avenues should be explored to establish contacts with the parents. Following are some of the important methods of securing cooperation of the parents and to make them interested in school work.

1. *Good Treatment:* Proper courtesy should be shown to the parents whenever they visit the school. Patient hearing should be given to their views and complaints. The parents must get the impression that they are wanted in the school.

2. *Personal Contacts:* The parents of those children who do not show good results in monthly tests or terminal examinations, may be requested to visit the school occasionally. Positive suggestions regarding the future progress of the children should be given to them. Frank and free talks would result in active cooperation. Similarly at some other specific situations, the parents should be sent for. Parents of bright and other children may also be requested to visit the school occasionally.

3. *School Reports:* These include:

(a) *Casual letters:* These should be used only when it is not possible to have personal contact with the parents. The parents of those students who reside in the hostel may have to be contacted through letters.

(b) *Progress reports:* These are sent to the parents from time to time. Progress report should be very comprehensive, covering progress in all the different aspects of the life of the child—mental, moral, physical, academic and aesthetic etc.

4. *Participation by the Parents in School Programmes*

(a) Some parents can lend a helping hand in raising funds for the school. Their help should be secured. This will develop in them 'a sense of belongingness' to the school. There are many other ways through which the parents can help the school authorities, *e.g.,* donating or lending books, giving stipends to the poor students, arranging mid-day meals for the poor, etc.

(b) The school authorities should not hesitate to utilise the knowledge, skill and experiences of the parents in supplementing class teaching. A doctor may be requested to give lectures on Hygiene and Physiology. Similarly the services of the parents in other fields may be utilised.

5. *Home Visits by the Teachers:* These should always be friendly. The false notions of prestige should not stand in the way.

6. *Association of the Parents in the Management of the School:* Some representation should be given to the parents on the managing committee. But in some cases this may prove very harmful to the efficient working of the school.

7. *Making the School as a Centre of Community Service:* National, social and cultural functions should be organised in the school.

8. *Community Service:* Labour weeks may be orgnised wherein students render some social service to the community.

9. *Celebration of Parents' Days:* Parents may be invited once or twice a

year to visit the school and see its normal working.

10. *Parent-Teachers Association:* Parent-teacher association has immense potentials in making the school programmes more effective.

The need and importance of parent-teacher may be summed up in the words of Thring: "The ordinary machinery for good school life is a thing of calculation and measurement but all discussion is in vain unless parents are interested."

Parent-Teacher Associations (PTA's)

Meaning of Parent-Teacher Association: PTA is the association of the parents of the students and the teaching staff of a school. Its meetings are expected to be attended by all the parents and the school staff. It works through an executive committee—a representative body of parents.

Significance of PTA: The PTA is the most powerful instrument in the hands of the dynamic, enlightened and progressive head of the school for developing good human relations with the parents and seeking their effective and meaningful cooperation for the all round development of the students.

Objectives of PTA: Important objectives of the PTA are as under:

1. To promote the all round welfare of the students.
2. To bring into closer contact the parents and teachers so that they fully cooperate in the education and training of the child.
3. To appreciate the assets and liabilities of the school and the parents and work within their parameter.
4. To secure for every student the optimum development from the resources of the school and the community/parents.
5. To seek means and way of securing cooperation between the parents and the school.

Main Activities of the PTA

Following are the important activities of the PTA:

1. *Organising parent study groups:* The PTA organises study groups of the parents, the programmes of which are participated by experts also who enlighten the parents of the students on various academic, curricular and vocational pursuits.

2. *Organising parent-teacher conferences:* Parent-teacher conferences are organised from time to time to discuss the progress of the students and to find out ways and means for bringing about improvement.

3. *Organising talks and lectures:* Successful professionals in various fields provide useful information to the parents about various professions and vocations.

4. *Interpreting the needs of the parents:* The PTA interprets the needs of the parents so that the school authorities may take appropriate action.

5. *Interpreting the needs of the school:* The PTA enlightens the parents

as to what is expected of than as to what is expected of than in bettering the material and physical conditions of the school.

6. *Organising prize distribution function of the school:* The PTA renders useful assistance to the school in organizing prize distribution functions. It awards prizes also.

7. *Providing compensatory education:* The PTA organises week boys classes from its own funds.

8. *Providing incentives to talented students:* PTA arranges special stipends and free special coaching from the gifted children of the school.

9. *Conducting adult education programmes:* PTA conducts literacy classes in the school premises. It organises community functions also.

10. *Celebrating Parents' Day*

Importance of Parents' Day

(i) It provides the parents an excellent opportunity to see the actual working of the school.
(ii) It provides them an opportunity to know what their children are doing at school.
(iii) It enables them to discuss certain specific problems of their children with the teachers.

Importance of Parents' Day from Teachers Viewpoint

(i) They get an opportunity to acquaint the parents with the various activities and programmes of the school.
(ii) They get an opportunity to explain to the parents what future plans the school has for the welfare of the students.
(iii) They get an opportunity to request the parents to render assistance to the school.
(iv) They get an opportunity to exchange views on several issues concerning education.

Importance of Parents' Day from Pupils' Point of View

(a) They feel immense joy when they see their parents visiting the school.
(b) They try to put in their best for making the programme a success. Esprit de Corps is developed in them and they feel love for the school.

Programme of a Parents' Day

It should be a full working day. The parents should be taken round the school so that they may see how classes are held and where their children sit. They may get occasions to see the actual teaching done in the school.

Different co-curricular activities such as debates, dramatics, etc., may be organised.

Children's work like calligraphy, models, maps, charts, etc., may be exhibited.

The parents may be taken to special rooms, *e.g.,* Geography, History, Science, Craft etc.

School sports may be organised on this day or it may take the form of prize distribution or School Annual Day.

Adequate preparations should be made so as to give a good show of school activities.

A light refreshment to the parents may be served if the funds allow.

Factors for the Success of PTA

Following suggestions are offered for the successful functioning of the PTA:

1. It is the duty of every class teacher to establish and maintain rapport with the parents of the pupils. This contact helps in making the parents interested in the working of the PTA.
2. Due attention and courtesy should be given to the parents wherever they visit the school.
3. The staff members should not feel that the parents' association will create unnecessary hindrances in their work. They must discard the old-age notion that it is in the nature parents to criticise them.
4. Both the parents and the teachers should appreciate each other's assets and limitations, unreasonable demands on either side will create difficulties and problems.
5. Problems discussed in the PTA meetings should be real ones.
6. The solutions to the problems should flow from the cooperative endeavour of the parents and teachers alike. Discussions should be constructive.
7. The executive committee of the PTA should meet at least six times during the academic session.
8. Elections to the PTA should be held regularly.
9. Proceedings of all meetings should be recorded and follow-up action taken.
10. Politics should not be allowed to influence the functioning of the PTA.

Ways in which Parents can cooperate with the School and also Render Some Assistance

A parent can help the school in the following ways. In fact this help would go a long way in making teaching-learning effective.

(i) He should ensure that the child is regular and punctual in attending school.

(ii) He should recognise that the child's presence at school is more important than to attend marriage parties or other festivities etc.

(iii) He should provide the child with necessary books and equipment.
(iv) He should make sure that the child is regular in home work.
(v) He should see that the child is regular in games.
(vi) He should not insist on sending his child to the school if he is suffering from some contagious disease.
(vii) He should be prompt to take up follow-up work regarding medical inspection.
(viii) He should ensure that the child is adequately fed.
(ix) A check on the company of the child should be kept.
(x) He should see that the home provides a congenial atmosphere to the child.
(xi) By speaking highly of the teachers, he can give immense encouragement to the teachers.
(x) He can render monetary or other help to the school for providing better facilities and enriching cultural life of the school.
(xi) He should visit school from tome to time.
(xii) He should take interest in the functioning of the PTA.

9

School Records

School Office is really the king-pin in the enterprise.

—Dr. Jaswant Singh

Indispensability of School Records

Proper maintenance, accuracy and effective use of records go a long way in the efficient working of any institution or organisation and school is no exception. There is no doubt that the success of a school in each of its elements and its totality depends to a large measure on the scientific and systematic manner in which records are kept.

Purposes of School Records

Records are needed for the following purposes:

1. *Legal Requirements:* School records and reports are used to satisfy the legal requirements of the State Education Department, Examination Board etc.

2. *Relationships with Home and the Community:* School is a social institution answerable to the parents, the managing committee, the department and the public in general and the records kept by the school help to understand the problems and limitations of the school.

3. *Records Essential for the All-Round Growth of the Child:* School is entrusted with the task of the all-round development of the personality of each child and to discharge this function it is absolutely essential to keep a record of his day-to-day growth and development.

4. *Financial Requirements of the School:* The school has to supply a variety of data to justify its financial needs. Financial grants are sanctioned for equipment, library books and furniture etc. by the Education Department, Local Bodies and School Management Committee as the case may be.

5. *Records and Grants-in-Aid:* Sometimes certain conditions are laid down by the department for the payment of grants-in-aid to schools. This requires the supply of certain facts and statistics.

6. *Educational Reform:* Educational reforms can be undertaken only when the school records provide comprehensive data to those who are asked

to shoulder the responsibility of educational reforms.

7. *Assessment of an Institution:* School records are helpful to assess the progress and needs of particular locality.

8. *Cooperation of Parents:* To make the parents interested in school work and in their wards, schools send progress reports from time to time. This helps in establishing closer contacts between the home and the school.

9. *Examination and Evaluation Needs:* Promotions of students are made on their performance which is reflected through the records of tests and examinations.

10. *Guidance and Counselling:* Records of performance of students on psychological tests and measurement prove very helpful in the counselling process.

11. *Future Reference:* It is only through records that the history of the school can be written. Past records may also help in improving the tone of the school and its performance also.

L.M. Camberlain and L.W. Kindred give the following advantages of the school records:

Records Help the School

1. To locate each pupil quickly.
2. To have available the facts significant about each pupil.
3. to explain and remove undesirable conditions.
4. To find if all legal requirements are met.
5. To determine if any administrative or other changes are desirable.
6. To make important investigations and case studies possible.
7. To find if school funds are adequate and wisely expanded.
8. To reduce retardation and failure to a minimum.

Records Help the Classroom Teachers

1. To determine what work a pupil is capable of doing.
2. To provide learning activities suitable to each pupil.
3. To formulate a basis for the intelligent guidance of pupils.
4. To explain the behaviour characteristics or unhappy conditions of any pupil.
5. To make possible the development of unusual capacities or exceptional talents.
6. To identify and make proper provision for the mentally slow children.
7. To make assignments to committee work.
8. To make periodic reports correctly and in time.
9. To be properly informed when conferring with parents and others about a pupil.

Records Help the Pupil

1. To receive fair consideration in his classification.
2. To do his best in making a good record.
3. To make progress in accordance with his ability.
4. To secure development of his natural capabilities.
5. To secure transfer of correct information to other schools when desired.
6. To receive proper adjustment and guidance.

Essential Requisites of School Records

1. *Accuracy:* All information contained in the school records should be accurate, well-organised, pertinent and justified solely on grounds of the contribution it can make either directly or indirectly to the welfare of the students.

2. *Completeness:* Data about a child should be gathered continuously, should be kept up-to-date and include information that reveals his true condition at any given time. In the case of his transfer from one school to another, his records should follow him.

3. *Utility:* Record system should provide for collecting and recording information that is relevant and useful in working with children.

4. *Comprehensiveness:* In view of the emphasis on the harmonious development of the child, different kinds of records will have to be kept. All members of the staff have a responsibility for keeping records peculiar to their field of activity.

5. *Easy Maintenance:* The records and reports should be easily maintained and should require a minimum of time and energy for making entries.

6. *Systematic Maintenance:* School records should be maintenance and located where they will be used to the greatest advantage by staff personnel. Separate files or note-books should be kept for each separate record or report.

7. *Availability:* School records should always be available in the school premises and school not be removed from the school premises for the purpose of scrutiny.

A record system then should be designed carefully, kept efficiently, located strategically and should contain all information that is essential to the achievement of the aim for which it was established.

Mode of Keeping Records

1. Prepare a stock list of registers maintained in the school.
2. Write distinctly the following particulars on the outer cover of each register.
   (a) The name of the school.
   (b) The serial number of the register.
   (c) The name of the register.

(d) The number of volume.
(e) The number of pages of the volume.
(f) The opening and closing dates.

3. Number the pages consecutively either in the red ink or with a number machine when a register is opened.
4. Keep the register tidy. Avoid overwriting.
5. Make all the entries in ink.
6. Get each cutting attested by the Head.
7. Do not open a new volume of a register every year, if the previous volume contains some blank pages.
8. Fill up every column provided in a prescribed register and do not leave any blank space between entries.

School Office: As a general rule every high secondary or senior secondary school must have one separate room for office. The office-in-charge must be a person trained for the type of work to be done in schools. The head must be relieved of the mechanical details of the officer routine if he is to make the best use of his abilities and to discharge his functions of guidance and counselling and supervising. The school office should be spacious and well-ventilated.

Types of School Records : Broad Classification

1	2	3	4	5	6	7
Accounts	Corres-pondence	Educa-tional	Equip-ment	Financial	General	Vocational / Productive Service Matters

1. *Accounts Registers:* (i) Cash Book for daily receipts and expenditure, (ii) General Ledger or Classified Abstract of the monthly totals, (iii) Register of pay bill, (iv) Remittance register.

2. *Correspondence:* (1) 'From' and 'To' Registers, (2) Peon Book, (3) Memo Book, (4) File of Departmental Orders and Circulars, (5) Register of Casual Leave Granted.

3. *Educational:* (1) Pupil's Attendance Register, (2) Teachers' Attendance Register, (3) Time-Tables' Records, (4) Examinations' Results Record, (5) Monthly Progress Register, (6) Private Tuition Register, (7) Public Examination Register, (8) Register of Corporal Punishment, (9) Teacher's Diaries, (10) Cumulative Records, (11) Staff participation in Oriental Courses, (12) Honours Roll.

4. *Equipment:* (1) Stock Book of Furniture and School Appliances, (2) Library Catalogue, (3) Accession Register, (4) Issue Book, (5) Register of Newspapers and Magazines received, (6) Stock and Issue Register of Sports Materials.

5. *Financial:* (1) Contingent Register, (2) Acquittance Roll. (3) Contingent Order Book, (4) Fee Collection Register, (5) Abstract Register

of Fees, (6) Bill Register, (7) Register of Donations, (8) Register of Scholarship, (9) Boys' Fund Registers.

6. *General Records:* (1) School Calender, (2) Log Book, (3) Visitor's Book. (4) Service Registers, (5) Admission and Withdrawal Register, (6) Transfer Certificate Book, (7) General Order Book, (8) Casual Leave Register, (9) Staff Meeting

7. *Service Matters:* (1) Personal Files, (2) Service condition rules etc.

8. *Vocational/Production/Related to Socially Useful Productive Work:* (1) Craft Work, (2) Farm Work, (3) Producer's Register, (4) Art Work Record etc.

The list is no way a comprehensive and complete one. It includes only those registers which are commonly used. Additions will have to be made to suit the needs and requirements of individual schools. A few of the important school records, relating mainly to the educational aspect of school administration are described below:

Description of Some Important School Registers and Records

Educational Records

Admission and Withdrawal Register: This is one of the most important school registers. The head of the institution is personally responsible for its sanctity. According to departmental rules, it is to be kept permanently and therefore it should be specially got bound and arrangements made for its safe custody. Entries should be made as soon as a pupil is admitted or at any rate before the close of the day. Every admission or re-admission made in any part of the year should be entered in it. Successive numbers should be given to the pupils on admission. Each child should retain this number as long as he remains in the school. A new entry should be made if a pupil leaves a school and rejoins it with a leaving certificate issued by another school. This register contains the following information: (a) The number of the child in the register. (b) Date of admission or re-admission, (c) Name of the child in full. (d) The exact date of birth of the child. (e) Name and address of the parent or guardian, (f) The class to which admitted, (g) The date of leaving and the class in which the child was at that time.

Special care is to be taken in recording the date of birth of every child. The entry once made should not be altered unless authorised by competent authority and that too in writing. The entries are to be made both in words as well as in figures. This exact day, month and the year of the birth should be recorded. The entry regarding date of birth is very important as it is also required as evidence in important matters.

Pupils' Attendance Register: Each class has its own register showing the names of the pupils on the rolls of a class during a month. As far as possible only one attendance register should be kept by any one teacher. Attendance should be marked both for the beginning of the school day in the morning and its and towards the evening. Ink or ball pen should be used for marking attendance. No blanks should be left. It is also not a good practice to put dots. The students are to be marked as "leave" or 'sick' only when their leave applications are sanctioned by the competent authority. Holidays should be indicated in red ink. The name of the boy who has been absent without leave for 12 consecutive attendances should be struck off the rolls. Names of girls should be struck off the rolls for absence without leave after ten consecutive days (Departmental rules differ in States). The reason for this action should be given in the remarks column against the name of the boy or girl and the necessary information should be given to the school clerk. The entries thus made should be got signed by the Head simultaneously both in the attendance register and withdrawal register. On the last working day of each month, the summary at the end of each page in the register should be carefully prepared and the register got checked by the teacher deputed for this purpose and then got countersigned by the Head. All amounts received by way of fees and funds must be entered in the register immediately on their receipt.

Truants should be noted particularly and their cases reported to the Head and the parents concerned.

Leave application for long sick periods should be supported by medical certificates.

School Calendar: The school calendar is very conducive to the better and more systematic organisation of school activities. It is drawn up at the beginning of each school session. If possible all schools in the same area should have a uniform school year so that the migrating children are not handicapped and put to troubles. It should contain the following items of information:

(i) All types of holidays.

(ii) Dates for the submission of monthly, quarterly, half-yearly and annual reports and returns.

(iii) Dates of public and school examinations.

(iv) Dates of Meeting of School Committees, Teachers' Associations, Local Excursions; School Tournament, etc.

(v) Schedule of monthly tests.

Teachers' Attendance Register: This register shows the daily attendance of the teachers in a school, their time of arrival and departure, leave taken by them, holidays and their nature. It is generally placed in the Head Office. Every teacher must sign this register every-day when he comes into the school in the morning and leave at the termination of the school day.

The Log Book: In our schools it is devoted to the remarks of the inspecting staff in relation to the school and the members of the school staff.

Progress Report: A Progress Report serves three important purposes as given below:

(a) a Progress Report helps the parents to know about the progress of their children in the curricular as well as co-curricular work and thereby enables them to take necessary steps to improve their children.

(b) It serves as a link between the home and the school which is very important for the progress of the children.

(c) It has a psychological effect on the children who have a natural desire to please their parents. They try to put forth consistent and strenuous efforts to show good results and to secure the appreciation of both the parents as well as the teachers.

Specimen of Simple Progress Report

Name of the School...

Month.......................

Student's Progress Records for the Term

Student's name..Class.....................

Admission No.. Date of birth ....

Father's Name................................. Address of Parent/Guardian..................

Academic

Subject	Max Marks	Marks obtained or Grade	Position	Subject Teacher's Remarks
Regional Language				
Second Language				
English				
Elementary Math				
General Science				
Social Studies				
Art/Domestic Science				
Craft Training				
Work Experience				
Diversified Courses				
1.				
2.				
3.				
Total				

Co-curricular Activities and Citizenship

Practical Activities	Remarks	Practical Activities	Remarks
		Conduct	
Games and Sports		Hand-Writing	
Social Behaviour		Home Work	
Cleanliness		Health	
Attendance		Cultural activities	

Class Teacher's Signature Principal/Headmaster's Signature

Guardian/Parent's Signature

(*Note* : Type of progress report depends on the nature of activities in the school.)

Cumulative Record Card

Meaning of a Cumulative Record: A cumulative record is an account of child's history in the school. It contains the results of different assessments and judgments held from time to time during the course of a stay in a school. Usually it covers four consecutive years. It contains information regarding all aspects of the life of the child—mental, physical, psychological and social. It seeks to give as comprehensive a picture as possible of the personality of the child.

Need and Significance of the Cumulative Record

Writing about cumulative record Jane Warters rightly says, "It aids teachers in the study of the individual by making it possible for them to understand his present through an analysis of his past by furnishing clues regarding the cause of his behaviour difficulties and failures, and by disclosing his strengths and weaknesses."

Contents of the Record Card

1. Personal data
2. Schools attended
3. Family history
4. Physical data
5. Medical report
6. Attendance
7. Psychological report
8. Scholastic report
9. Performance in co-curricular activities
10. Position of responsibility held
11. Vocational information
12. Personality traits.
13. Specific remarks by the Head of the School.

Accounts and Financial Records

Cash Book: It contains a record of all money transactions that are being carried through from day to day in the school. The credit side of the cash book shows all the monies received by the school from different sources, *e.g.,* donations, grants-in-aid, fees, boys' funds etc., and its debit side indicates all the payments made, *e.g.,* salaries paid, deposits made in the post office or bank, contingent expenditure incurred, etc.

Cash Book should be well-bound and the pages should be carefully numbered in print.

Cash Book should be written up daily. The entry relating to each item of receipt and expenditure should be made at the time of transaction.

As far as possible the cash balance should be immediately deposited in the post office or bank. Daily balancing of the cash book avoids chances of errors.

Ledger: It is a necessary complement of the cash book. All entries made in the cash book are carried to the ledger in their respective accounts. It facilitates the preparation of monthly and annual accounts. It is also helpful in controlling future financial commitments.

Contingency Register: Every Head is generally provided with a contingency advance which is spent for day-to-day expenses on petty items such as purchase of office stationary, postage, repairs to building and furniture etc. Details of such expenditure are entered in the contingency register. All entries in this register are supported by proper receipts which are placed in a separate file.

Boys' Fund Register: The head of an institution is the sole incharge of the boys' funds. He is responsible for keeping a regular account of the same and rendering it to the departmental auditors and the inspecting staff.

All income and expenditure pertaining to boys' fund should be entered regularly in the Boys' Fund Register.

It will not be out of place to mention that most of the troubles in our educational institutions owe their origin to the use of these funds. Undue funds charged from the students lead to indiscipline. Wrong use of funds leads them to suspect the integrity of the authorities. Unfortunately the present trend is to use funds for all sundry purposes. A wise head will make a very judicious use of these funds. He will take his students into confidence and spend this funds through their committees working under the guidance of teachers.

Miscellaneous Registers

Property Register: All items of a more or less permanent nature bought and placed in the school are entered in the property register. It contains the name of the article, its price and the ordering authority for its purchase.

The Head should get the stock of equipment checked once a year. Room-wise property list facilitates the work of checking. Proper checking of the equipment has a very good advantage. It helps the Head to know which article of equipment or furniture stands in needs of repairs or is missing.

Nothing should be struck off the register without the permission of the Head who is generally competent to do so.

Service Register: This register contains the record of the official life of every employee working in the institution. On the basis of this record, matters concerning promotions, leave, superannuation, etc., are determined. It is, therefore, very important to make correct and complete entries in it. The entries in the service register should tally with other records. The date and the number of the appointment order should be noted in the case of the first appointment and in the case of transfers. No change in the date of birth is permissible except with the permission of the competent authority. All cases of suspension, or other punishment should be noted along with the reasons and the authority awarding the punishment. All questions relating to previous service should be settled immediately. Service registers should not be handed over to the persons concerned on their transfer from one school to another but should be sent to the officer responsible for the custody of the registers. Every Head should make it a point to ensure that the registers are free from faults of omission and erroneous insertion.

10

Classification of Pupil Adjustment Classes

Meaning of Classification of Pupils

Division of pupils into groups for instructional purposes is called classification. A group comprising a number of students is termed as a class. It is not precisely known when the class system came into vogue but since the inception of the school as a formal active agency of education and a useful means of providing systematic instruction to pupils, some form of grouping the pupils has been used. Even in very ancient times, when the pupils whose member was very small, received their education from one 'guru' or teacher, some form of grouping of pupils did exist. The teacher invariably used some method of separating the more advanced learners from the lesser ones. The learners were admitted by the teacher throughout the year. Thus they differed in attainment in several respects. Nevertheless, some sort of grouping learners was inevitable.

Need for Classification of Pupils: Pupils have marked individual differences in different aspects of their learning capacity and also character and personality traits. The need for classification arises to place students in homogenous groups so that they could derive the optimum benefit.

Thus classification aims at placing each child continuously in an educational setting (group or class) which will give him the best opportunity for all-round growth.

So far no plan of classification has been developed which makes the teaching and learning situation in a classroom a simple matter. The very fact that no individuals are alike challenges the ingenuity even of the most competent teachers and administrators. However, homogeneous a class may be at the commencement of the session, by the end of it there will be marked difference in progress made by different individuals, that is, some may have lagged behind while others may have gone ahead. This necessitates reclassification.

Merits of Classification

Following are the merits of classifying students:

1. Instruction becomes less expensive and economical.
2. Time and energy of the teachers are used to the maximum extent.

3. Motivation is provided to the slow as well as fast learners.
4. Socialisation of students becomes easier.

Class as a System of Organisation and Instruction

Meaning of a Class: Class implies a group of pupils regularly scheduled to meet in an administrative/organisation and instructional unit under the teaching-learning situation of a teacher. The relations of members of the group or the classmates are based upon more or less common aims, attainments, aptitudes and interests. About the chief characteristics of a class, Adams states, "It is indeed one of the best examples of homogeneity. The pupils are approximately of the same age, belong to the same grade of society, have the same traditions, the same religion, the same attitude towards sports and in particular have pretty much the same mental/development so far as the classwork is concerned, for their place in that particular class has been selected for the because of their attainments in the subject being taught." This description hardly fits in the changed circumstances. Now we find students belonging to different religions and strata of society. It is very difficult to define a class in view of the complexity of characteristics.

Bases of Classification

Several practices are in vogue in different countries for classifying pupils. However, following are the important practices in this regard.

1. Grouping by Chronological Age (CA).
2. Grouping by Mental Age (MA).
3. Grouping by Biotypological Age (BA)
4. Grouping by Social Age (SA)
5. Grouping by School Subjects (SS)
6. Grouping by Educational Age (EA)

1. *Grouping by Chronological Age:* This is a very simple and crude form. Due to the introduction of free and compulsory education, children join their school practically at the same age and thus form a class. But age is not a reliable basis of classification. Boys of the same age may not be equally intelligent. A child of six may be more intelligent than a child of 10. It is, therefore, the mental and not the chronological age which should determine the class.

2. *Grouping by Mental Age:* Mental age instead of chronological age is now adopted in several countries as the basis of classification. Intelligence tests are used to find the mental age of the child. These tests are very helpful in the classification of pupils on their admission to a primary school. For grades beyond primary, these tests do not provide a satisfactory basis of classification. In the primary school they are very helpful because the pupils are classified according to their capacity, but in higher grades both capacity and attainment determine the basis of classification, and these mental tests

fails to cope with this necessary condition.

3. *Grouping by Biotypological Examination System:* This examination is used in many schools in France to serve as a basis for classification. Biotypological examination touches the following aspects of the personality of a child:

(a) anthropometric;
(b) sexological;
(c) chemical and urinary;
(d) physiological;
(e) psychological;
(f) general medical; and
(g) psychiatric.

This is a good attempt aiming at the application of the individual, psychological as well as the methods of individual biological sciences in the classification of pupils and other problems of school organisation. But it is very difficult to apply this method in our own country due to non-availability of technical personnel and finances.

4. *Grouping by Social Age:* When one is in a position to behave properly in a social set-up, he is known to have attained social maturity. But there is no reliable method of determining the social maturity of an individual because of the difference in these standards of various societies.

5. *Grouping by Attainment in School Subjects:* Classification of the students may be made on the basis of their attainment in some important subjects. This is done in the Dalton Plan.

6. *Educational Age:* It is the traditional method of reclassification of pupils. Nevertheless it is still prevalent in our country. Since during the year, the attainment of students is different, we generally place those children in one class after a year who fulfil the criterion laid down for promotions. Those students who do not show progress are not sent to the next class.

Factors Leading to the Formation of a Class

1. *Increasing School Going Population:* Since the advent of the democratic ideals, almost all the nations of the world have accepted the principle of universal, free and compulsory primary education and there is bound to be a great rush to the schools. Consequently it necessitates the formation of classes.

2. *Economic Factor:* It is a corollary of the factor stated above. All the persons cannot engage full time tutors for their children. The state has its own financial limitations. It is, therefore, a matter of economic necessity that one teacher should teach many students at a time.

3. *Social Factor:* An individual cannot learn in a vacuum. He is a social being and requires company. He learns through social grouping. Proper company is provided in the form of a class thus enabling an individual to

develop sociability. Individual coaching cannot develop sociability.

4. *Administrative Convenience:* It is not administratively feasible to keep all the students of the school in a group. Hence they are divided into different classes.

5. *Intellectual Attainment:* The standard of intellectual attainment of all the students of a school is not the same. Take for instance two concrete cases at the time of admission—one has just to start his studies and the other has received some education at home. Naturally both of them cannot be put in the same category. Separate classes for such students must be started, otherwise if both the students are placed in the same class, it is quite likely that there may not be harmonious development.

Factors Determining the Size of a Class

(i) *Grade of the Class:* Ordinarily the number of students in the lower classes should be less than the higher classes because at the early stages more individual attention is needed to make the foundation strong.

(ii) *The Subject of Instruction:* Subjects like History, Geography, Economics, Nature Study, Drill and Religion require larger classes for the development of 'sympathy of numbers'. Besides there is less of correction work in these subjects. Languages require smaller classes as there is much of correction work. However, in actual practice, it is very difficult to make such arrangements. To meet with the problem of correction work, the teachers of these subjects are given lesser number of periods.

(iii) *School Building and Equipment:* The number of total classrooms in a school, the teachers' strength and the classroom accommodation are the other determining factors of the size of a class. The personality of the teacher also plays its role. Some teachers are capable of managing and teaching large classes while others are not.

(iv) *Special Purpose for Which Class is Formed:* The number of students in a weak boys' class should be small for these students require more help to grasp things.

Merits of Class System

1. *Less Expensive:* According to Adams the class has solid foundations in economic principles. We cannot afford to do away with it. Individual teaching implies 'Single Teacher' for a 'Single Student' and that is very expensive. No state in the world, however wealthy it may be, can afford to have such a system and our case is all the more a different one. We are finding it very difficult to fulfil our obligations to our Constitution regarding universal, free and compulsory Primary Education even on the basis of 'class teaching' not to talk of individual teaching.

2. *Development of Social Attitudes:* It affords opportunities for the development of social attitudes. Man is a social being. He cannot live in isolation. Participation in group activities leads to the formation of social

habits and the class renders a very useful help.

3. *Inspirational Treatment:* Adams remarks that subjects which demand inspirational treatment require collective teaching. Emotional element is the dominating one in literature, religious knowledge, art appreciation and music appreciation, etc., and can be aroused only in larger classes.

4. *Inculcation of the Spirit of Imitation and Emulation:* Imitation and emulation play a very significant role for the progress of both an individual and the society and 'class reaching' provides scope for healthy competition leading to keener interest among the students for studies.

5. *Development of a Cooperative Spirit:* Class system affords opportunities for the development of a cooperative spirit among the students. Students belonging to different castes, religions, regions, races etc. study in the same class and learn to cross the barriers of caste or creed.

6. *Appropriate Use of Time and Energy:* From the point of view of economy and energy, class system has definite advantages. A large number of students receive instruction from the same teacher. There are many common mistakes made by the students and it will be a sheer wastage of time and energy if a teacher were to explain these mistakes to each student individually.

Limitations of Class System

1. *Disregard for Individual Needs:* Class system fails to take into account the individual needs of the students. It is a well known fact that students make progress according to their own rate and speed. Some move like goods trains while others like Mail or Express trains. But a class system is based on average child which is a statistical myth.

Sultan Mohiyuddin rightly states: "Class teaching is just like pouring water from a bucket into bottles with necks of different sizes, some bottles get more and some less and a great part is spilt."

2. *Limited Public-Teacher Contact:* Without intimate contact between the teachers and the students, education fails to serve its purpose. There is very little scope for the teachers to develop intimate relationships with their wards when the classes are very large.

3. *Scope for Indiscipline:* Overcrowding of classes may lead to indiscipline. A teacher finds it very difficult to devote his full attention to all the students with the result that some students remain neglected and get opportunities to make a noise. Proper supervision becomes very difficult.

Class System cannot be Ended but can be Improved upon

The new system of education aims at individualising instruction. The underlying basis of this system is that children differ in intelligence, temperaments, attitudes, capacity to work etc. No two children are alike. They come from homes having different social and physical environments. Instruction to be effective must take into consideration the individual needs of children. It is said by the enthusiasts of the individual teaching that the knell of class teaching has been rung. But it is wrong to think so. At the most we can say that emphasis on individual teaching has led to a decrease in the size of the class but we find class as a vigorous institution enjoying robust health.

Deficiencies and limitations of class system can be improved upon to a considerable extent by compensatory/remedial educational programmes for the weak students and enrichment programmes for the gifted and talented pupils.

Plans of Classification to mitigate the Limitations of the Class System

(a) Dalton Plan
(b) Triple-Track Plan
(c) Double Promotions
(d) Class as a Unit of Organisation but Not a Unit of Instruction
(e) Compensatory/Remedial Instruction
(f) Enrichment Courses and Programmes for the Gifted and the Talented Pupils

(a) Dalton Plan

Miss Helen Parkhurst of America is the originator of the Dalton Plan. This Plan aims at individualising instruction. The Dalton Plan has been described by Adams "as the dramatic and systematic break away from the class unit teaching." This Plan is also known as the 'Laboratory Plan' because in it the student carries his work independently.

Chief Features of the Dalton Plan

1. Subject rooms take the place of classrooms.
2. Subject teachers or special teachers take the place of class teachers.
3. Each child enters into an agreement or what is known as 'contract' and promises to finish his work within a specified period.
4. No restrictions are imposed on him as to how much time he should spend on different subjects. There is no rigidity in the plan and there in no fixed time-table.
5. The child gets guidance from the teacher accordance to his needs and problems.
6. Graphs are prepared in each subject regarding the progress of a child.
7. On certain occasions, collective instruction is also provided.
8. Class as a unit of instruction disappears but not as a unit of organisation.

The Plan seems to be very useful as regards subjects like History, Geography and Civics but as regards Mathematics and Science, it has many limitations. In India, this Plan has not been tried on account of several limitations.

(b) Triple-Track Plan

This plan has been in operation for many years in several American schools. According to this plan there are three parallel courses of study from class III to class VIII.

(i) *Average Course:* This is meant for average children. They are expected to complete the course in six years.

(ii) *Fast Course:* This course covers the same ground in five years and is meant for industrious and intelligent students.

(iii) *Special Course:* This course provides for the completion of the same work in four years and is meant for very superior students.

The students are transferred from one course to another according to the rate of progress shown by them. This system is very useful in so far as it provides different times to the students of varying capacities. It also introduces elasticity in the classification of the students.

(c) Double Promotions

Double promotions are given to those students who have high achievements in academics. If a child shows an extra-ordinary achievement is one class, he may be given a double promotion. The aim of this promotion is to place the superior student in a setting suiting him most. But at occasions such promotions prove to be very detrimental to the child. The child may not show the same progress in the new setting and this would result in his mental retardation. Age, social maturity and health—all these factors should be given due weighatage.

(d) Class as a Unit of Organisation and not a Unit of Instruction

Class is a unit of organisation but not a unit of instruction. In the Dalton Plan for administrative purposes class remains but for teaching purposes it vanishes. This is known as class a unit of organisation but not a unit of instruction. Instruction is individualised.

System of Annual Promotion

Merits of Annual Promotion

(a) It is easier to administer.

(b) It is economical in cost.

(c) The students spend one year with the teachers. This gives them sufficient time to understand them and work accordingly.

(d) It is an conformity with the plan followed in higher grades of education.

(e) The year is quite a long time and it is easy to organise and divide the subject matter of instruction into units.

Demerits and Limitations of the System of Promotion

(a) The student who fails in one subject has to repeat the whole course for full one year, and this imposes unnecessary burden on him.

(b) The loss of one year means a good deal of loss of money to the parents.

(c) As the time for promotion is the same for all, the progress of the superior students is checked.

(d) Since the progress of the students is judged only by the annual examination, they may not work hard throughout the year. Just near the annual examination they burn the mid-night oil. Habits of constant work are not developed in them.

(e) It leads to cramming and memorising. The students depends upon 'chance element'. They lay emphasis on the subjects and the portions which are useful and important from the examination point of view.

Suggestions for Facilitating Promotion Policy

The reclassification or promotion of pupils during the course of the year has become a formidable problem of school organisation. The traditional basis of promotion is the grading of the child on the basis of the annual examination, *i.e.*, promotion of students after a year.

The following types of promotions may facilitate the problem of promotion if properly planned and executed.

Combined Annual and Terminal Promotion: Under this system the superior students are promoted at the end of the first term and the other students recapitulate what they have read in the first term. The yearly work is divided into different terms, preferably two in a year. The work is planned in such a way that the whole course of the year is covered in the first term and revision work in the second term.

Promotion According to Progress in Subjects: Under this scheme a child may read English or any other subject in which he is weak with the students of the lower class and the other subjects with the students of the higher class. The time-table under the scheme is to be framed in such a way as all the subjects in different classes are taught at the same time so that each student may be in a position to attend the class for which he is fit. This scheme possesses the advantage that a child will not lose one year simply because he does not show the required efficiency in the subject. However, this scheme is fraught with many practical difficulties.

Trial Promotion: Students are promoted to the higher class strictly on the understanding that if they fail to make necessary progress in the upper class during the trial period, they will be sent back to the previous class. Such promotions are made very rarely.

Quarterly Promotion: This kind of promotion is in vogue in many schools in America. Each year is divided into four quarters of ten weeks each. Promotions to the higher class may be given at the end of any quarter to those students who have shown satisfactory progress and the weak students repeat the work of that quarter only.

Can We do Away with Promotion and Non-Promotion?

It is very difficult to give a clear-cut answer to this question. Some educationist seek the solution in better classification practices and better adaptation of the subject matter to the needs of individual pupil. They argue that if the pupil is assisted in making a wise choice of a programme of work and if better methods of instruction are adopted, there is no reason for the failure of the pupil. They put the blame of pupil's failure on the school. This may appear to be theoretically sound. A very pertinent question may be put to such educationists. Is not the success or failure the law of nature? As in actual life success and failure have their own place, so they have in school life. However, our attempt should be to give guidance to the students in such a way that they are successful both in and outside the school life to the maximum extent.

Elasticity in Classification and Promotion

Even assuming that children of the same general intelligence and scholastic attainments are admitted to a particular class, there is bound to be difference in performance as the time passes. Some will make repaid progress and others slow. This is due to different rates of mental development of individual pupils, differences in qualities of character and differences in their physical conditions. A dull child may do a quite satisfactory work while at a more-leisurely rate. Dalton Plan is one of the best plans to overcome this difficulty. But this will be a complete departure from the ordinary system of classification and promotion. A certain degrees of elasticity, in order to meet the needs of pupils of different levels of capacity, may be introduced by following the following methods in our ordinary system of classification.

1. By adopting triple-track plan.
2. By grouping students into different sections, according to their intelligence and scholastic attainments.
3. By introducing half-yearly promotion system or double promotion system.

Principles of Promotion

1. Promotion should be a cooperative process in which the participation of the child should be secured. Definite standards of efficiency should be put before him so that he may able to judge his work daily.
2. The parents of the children should be informed of the progress made by their wards from time to time.
3. The teachers should be able to locate the pupil's difficulty and think

out the remedy.

4. In place of promotion by grade, it should be by subjects.

Ideal Approach

Attempts should be made to offer programmes and courses to the child keeping in view his capacities and abilities. All students should not be measured by the same measuring rod. Helping the student set his goals and then helping him to evaluate his progress towards them is time consuming but it should not be considered an extra or additional task for the teacher. However if a student refuses to make a reasonable effort on an appropriate programme, he should fail.

Means of Reducing Pupil Failure Through Changes in Educational Policy and Administrative Reorganisation

1. Organisation of homogeneous grouping.
2. Differentiation of curriculum and courses of study to fit pupils of different levels of ability.
3. Applying rational promotional policies.
4. Providing special practices.
5. Employing better teachers.
6. Using standardised tests.
7. Adapting the schools to meet individual needs of pupils.
8. Reducing size of classes.
9. Developing a consistent programme of child guidance or counselling.
10. Providing a helping or coaching teacher.
11. Providing an efficient supervisory programme.
12. Securing better motivation through project teaching, enriched materials and pupil activity programme.
13. Carrying out a vigorous health programme.
14. Providing better equipment.
15. Administering a well balanced programme of extra-curricular activities.
16. Organising the schools on supervised study plan.
17. Establishing closer contacts with parents.
18. Introducing new methods of organisation and teaching.
19. Employing visiting teachers.
20. Lengthening the school day or the school year.
21. Admitting pupils to first grade only when they are mature enough to do first grade work.
22. Setting up definite educational aims.
23. Revising marking system.
24. Improving faculty meetings and faculty relationship.
25. Providing compensatory and remedial coaching.

Means by which Teachers may Reduce Pupil Failure

1. Using achievement and diagnostic tests followed up by special help and remedial work—test for deficiencies and diagnose pupil difficulties in each subject.
2. Giving individual attention to pupil needs and interests.
3. Learning about pupil's home conditions and securing cooperation of parents.
4. Diagnosing reading difficulties of individual pupils and giving remedial treatment.
5. Improving teaching methods.
6. Providing thorough, purposeful and motivated drill for accuracy.
7. Teaching pupils how to study and how to organise their work.
8. Improving health of children.
9. Securing better school attendance.
10. Having pupils, keep their individual records of achievement.
11. Taking special care in making lesson assignments clear.
12. Providing a working atmosphere in the classroom—this will include suitable teaching equipment, supplies, and supplementary reading.
13. Dividing large classes into small groups.
14. Developing a child centred activity programme, arranging for greater pupil participation.
15. Ensuring that text books suited to the pupil's interests and vocabulary are provided.
16. Giving immediate attention to low achievers.

11

School Library and Reading Room

In a school that educates pupils for a changing world, the school library should be a live workshop —*S.R. Ranganathan*

Importance of the School Liberty: Library as the Hub and Centre of School Life

The Secondary Education Commission has very beautifully described the significance of the school library. "The library will be the hub and the centre of the intellectual and literary life of the recognised school and play the same part *vis-a-vis* all the other subjects as the laboratory plays for science subjects and the workshop for technical subjects."

In the words of K.G. Saiyidain, "No School or University without a library, adequate for its needs and size should be recognised as a worthy centre of education."

According to Bacon, "Libraries are the shelves where all the relics of saints full of virtue and that without delusion and importance are reposed."

The modern philosophy of education stresses more on the child's learning through experience that on anything else. "Individual work, the pursuit of group projects, many academic hobbies and co-curricular activities postulate the existence of a good, efficiently managed library," wrote the Secondary Education Commission. So library—a good library—is one of the essentials of a school. Oliver Lodge writes, "Part of education should consist in familiarity and practice, with the looking up of details, with the use of books in general, not only of books of reference."

The dynamic role and the educational possibilities of the school library have long been realised in all progressive countries. In countries like the United States and Great Britain, the school libraries are usually well-equipped and are used very profitably in the education of children.

Important Functions of a School Library

Edmonson has described the functions of a school library as, "The modern school library is conceived as a service unit. It supplies materials for developing and expanding interests through the reference tools, indexes, bibliographies and catalogues, the realm of knowledge may be explored. The library cooperates with other agencies of instruction in helping students learn to use books and libraries, to find information, and to study. By its bulletin exhibits, posters and atmosphere, the library teaches informally. By its introduction to books, it suggests the life-time use of reading to further any interest."

A properly organised school library serves the following functions:

1. *Self-Study Opportunities:* It provides opportunities for self-study and self-education. It supplements class work by increasing students' vocabulary. There is no doubt that it is not possible for a single student to afford to purchase all the books that he needs. The school library helps him to read a large number of books.

2. *Broadening of Interest:* It broadens the outlook of the students by placing before them a vast store of useful information that has accumulated through the ages.

3. *Helpful Participation in Co-curricular Programme:* It assists the students to prepare themselves for taking part in the various co-curricular activities like debates, declamation contests and writing for the school magazine for a lot of literature is available.

4. *Source of Inspirational Books:* A good library service helps the students to turn to inspirational books which may enable their lives.

5. *Widening of General Knowledge:* It tends to develop habits of the students to derive pleasure and information from recreational and informative books.

6. *Leisure Time Hobby:* Library reading is a good leisure time hobby and it provides an opportunity for the right use of one's leisure time and thus conserves the time and energy otherwise to be used in card-games, etc.

7. *Training in the Proper Use of Books:* The library imparts training to the student in the proper use of books. The library rules demand that the books should be well-kept and thus the students develop in them the habit of keeping books neat and tidy. H.C. Dent observes, "With a good school library widely used, it is possible to teach children how to use books efficiently—a lesson all of us must learn if we are to get the most out of them. It is a lesson not too easily learnt, and far too rarely taught."

8. *Development of Study Habits:* The library develops the habits of silent reading. Reading, borrowing and returning are the watch-words of a library room.

9. *Constructive Discipline:* It lessens the chance of indiscipline in the school by providing an opportunity to the students to make the best use of leisure time.

10. *Moral Training:* The library imparts training in punctuality by impressing upon the students the necessity of borrowing and returning books in time.

11. *Use of Dynamic and Progressive Methods of Teaching-learning:* A well-developed library is a must for the use of methods like Dalton and the Project.

The functions of the school library may be summed up in the words of the Joint Committee of the School Library Association in Britain, "We seek in the library to make children familiar with the sight and use of a collection of books and to help them to grow to love and care for them, to provide material for child's own recreational reading and explorations, to supply additional reading material illustrating the subjects taught in class, to give opportunities for elementary instruction in the use of books and for carrying out group and individual projects, to give scope for the exercising of simple responsibilities and finally to prepare the way for the use of larger libraries including public library, in adult life."

State of School Libraries in India

The Secondary Education Commission lamented on the sad state of affairs of our school libraries. It observed that our libraries are not worth the name and, therefore, do not inspire students to cultivate the love for knowledge. Our schools do not sum to have been influenced by the new trends in education and especially in the school library organisation.

The Secondary Education Commission listed the main defects of the existing libraries. Though five decades have passed since the observations were made, the conditions, by and large, remain the same. Important defects are as under:

First, the books are usually old, outdated, unsuitable, selected without reference to the students' tastes and interests.

Secondly, there is a lack of suitable books for children.

Thirdly, books are stocked in a few book-shelves.

Fourthly, generally speaking there are no trained librarians in schools and library work is entrusted to teachers who are very busy in their teaching work and show little interest in library work.

Fifthly, school library is generally housed in an inadequate and unattractive room.

Sixthly, the general tendency of the school authorities is not to encourage students to read extra books.

Seventhly, the books are beyond the comprehension of students.

Eighthly, the books do not meet the needs of the students. Teachers generally stuff the library with those books which they need for some examination or some other purpose.

Factors responsible for the poor condition of school libraries: These are:

1. Domination of examinations
2. Defective curriculum.
3. Undue emphasis on prescribed textbooks.
4. Over emphasis on textual knowledge.
5. Very little use of progressive methods.
6. Failure to appreciate the value of school library.

Main Characteristics of a Well Managed School Library

Rabindra Nath Tagore has given a very good description of a good library in these words, "My idea of a small library is one that keeps books on every subject, but only select books, not one of which is there merely as an offering of worship to number, but each one of which stands on its own merit; where the librarian is a true devotee, devoid of ulterior seeking, free from pride in the mere loading of shelves, capable of discriminate rejection. A library, in short, which makes just enough provision that can be placed before its guests for their delectation, with a librarian who has the qualities of a host, not a storekeeper."

Organisation of a Good Library

The organisation of a good library may be discussed under the following heads:

1. The librarian
2. Books
3. Cataloguing
4. Library rules
5. Library room and equipment

I. The Librarian

The Secondary Education Commission observed that if the library is to be the hub of the academic and intellectual life of the school, if it is not only to meet but also to guide the reading interests of the students, if it is to work as a centre of free and supervised study as well as group work on projects undertaken by them—if it is to do all these things, the librarian will surely have to be wide awake and remain active.

Arnold Benett states that if libraries spend less on books and more on educated staff, far better results would be obtained. A librarian should possess the following qualifications:

(i) General educational.
(ii) Professional, *i.e.,* indexing and cataloguing.
(iii) Pedagogical, *i.e.,* adept in child psychology, familiar with the present trends in the educational field, sympathetic nature etc.

A librarian is expected to perform the following functions:

1. Preparing and displaying library rules and regulations.
2. Preparing catalogues.
3. Classifying books
4. Numbering books.
5. Stocking books properly
6. Training students in the art of looking up reference and other material.
7. Instructing students to keep books neat and tidy.
8. Taking annual stock of books.

9. Making plans for the purchase of books of different types.
10. Attaining skills in the use of modern technological aids like computers etc.
11. Making an environment of perfect silence and conducive to self-study.
12. Displaying cuttings and foldings on the new books and journals etc. on the library notice board.

II. Books

According to Secondary Education Commission, the guiding principle in selection should be not the teachers' own idea of what books the students *must* read but their natural and psychological interests. The contents of a library may be classified as:

1. *Books for Younger Children:* Well illustrated and attractive books giving information on fairy tales and fables etc.

2. *Books for Older Children:* (i) Books depicting stories of travels, explorations, adventures, discoveries and inventions.

(ii) Biographies of great men and women.
(iii) Suitable works of fiction, fun and hobbies.
(iv) Parallel text book.
(v) Books on different subjects.

3. *Reference Books*

(a) Source books.
(b) Dictionaries.
(c) Encyclopaedias

4. *Books for Teachers:* A faculty committee including representatives of each department should be appointed with the librarian as the convenor. The committee should determine policies for the development of the library, draw up rules, governing its use and use funds in such a way as each department of the school work is provided for equitably.

5. *Books for Adults:* To serve as a centre of community service, the school library should contain books for adults also.

III. Cataloguing

Views of Tagore are worth noting when he writes, "The usual thing is for a library to say: Here is my catalogue, come and select for yourself. But in the usual catalogue there is no introduction, no invitation, no spirit of welcome. That library alone can be called hospitable, which shows an eagerness to invite readers to the feast at its disposal. It is such hospitality that makes a library big, not its size. That the readers make the library is not the whole truth, the library likewise makes the readers."

IV. Library Rules

Among other rules, the following must be included:

(i) Library periods may be allotted.

(ii) For the changing and distribution of books, a certain time may be fixed.

(iii) Each student may be asked to keep a diary wherein name of the books read with date and comments be entered.

V. Library Room and Equipment

Regarding this, S.R. Ranganathan observes, "It should be equipped with plenty of attractive, well-built, well printed, well illustrated, with comfortable furniture, open shelves, charming pictures, flowers, hangings and bright and cheerful out-look, with a librarian who loves children as well as books."

Reading, lending, borrowing and returning should be the watch words of a library room. Spitting, smoking, noise making, sleeping, and quarrelling should be prohibited.

Encouraging Students to Make the Best Use of School Library

Usually it is observed that the students do not take adequate interest in the use of school library. Only a very negligible number of students make the profitable use of library material. Concerted efforts are needed to develop interest in this regard. Following measures may be adopted towards the end:

1. The library should be made the most attractive place in the school so that it may attract the students in large numbers.
2. The cooperation of the students should be sought in decorating the library in order to give them the feeling that the library belongs to them.
3. The librarian should behave very sympathetically with the students.
4. Books suiting different tastes and interests should be provided in large numbers.
5. The teachers should give occasional talks to pupils on the importance of extra-reading.
6. The librarian should give thorough instructions to the students in not only how to find out books and other material in the library but also how to make the best use of the material which the library contains.
7. Library periods should be provided for each class in the time-table.
8. As far as possible the open shelf system should be introduced so that the students may have free access to books.
9. Students should be asked to maintain a diary in which they should enter date-wise the names of all the books they have read. They may also be asked to write brief quotations or extracts from the books that may appeal to them. They may also write short reviews and appreciation of these books.
10. Marks may be allotted for extra-reading and entered in the monthly progress report.
11. Book competitions should be arranged from time to time and questions on titles, authors and subject-matter may be set.

12. The school library should be kept open during the vacation and long holidays.
13. The beautiful picture-cuttings from newspapers and illustrations from current events and topics should be displayed on the library Bulletin Boards.
14. The furniture should suit the needs of the students.
15. A catalogue of library books should be available in the library for ready reference.
16. Library day may be organised once a year to popularise the school library.

We may sum up the discussion with a quotation from Tagore, "In order to bring a library into the fullest use, it is necessary that its contents should be clearly and specifically brought to notice, otherwise it is difficult for the ordinary man to find his way about them, and the library is left as a city of vast accommodation that lacks sufficient means of communication. Those who frequent libraries on some special quest of their own may manage to make a track for themselves by dint of the urgency of their particular pursuit. But the library itself should recognise its share of responsibility in the matter. Because it has the books, it is incumbent on the library to get them read, for then alone it is justified. It is not enough that it passively permits visitors; its intivation should be active. For, as the Sanskrit proverb tells us *tannashtam yannadiyate*, that which is not given is wasted."

Central or Class Library

Both of these have got a definite place in the school. By classroom library we mean library in the room of each class. It contains well-selected books suited to the needs of the class. Class library is not competitive to central library. It should supplement the work of the central library, "The class library is an important and essential adjunct to the central school library," writes the Secondary Education Commission. It has great educational potentialities.

Classroom library is easier to administer. It does not require an elaborate method of recording.

Its organisation can very easily be entrusted in the hands of the students thus giving them an opportunity to manage their own affairs.

Classroom library affords opportunities to the teachers to see how much reading each pupil is doing and can thus encourage the keen students and stimulate the slowgoers. The teachers can also test whether the pupils are reading carefully and intelligently.

As a class teacher spends much of his time with the students, he is in a better position to suggest suitable books to the students according to their tastes and aptitudes.

Subject Libraries

The Secondary Education Commission recommends that besides the class library in every high school, there should be subject-libraries under the charge of subject teachers. In addition to text books, there should be advanced works, reference books, books on related subjects and allied fields. Such collections will help the teachers in enriching their teaching greatly. The students also will get a wide view of the subject in all its bearings.

Role of the Teachers in Encouraging Students to Use Library

Teachers and librarians must make attempts to break down the old barriers that completely separate library and classroom. They must join together so that students make the optimum use of school library.

The teachers should acquaint themselves with the contents and interesting aspects of books and other reading material within the school library and inform students accordingly.

In the day-to-day classroom teaching, they should make pointed references to important books and other reading materials available in the school library.

They should guide the students as to the type of books they should read.

The teachers may give assignments and project work which the students may complete independently by self-study.

They may maintain records of books read by the students.

They may give extra credit to the students when they read supplementary books.

12

School Health Services

A VEDIC PRAYER

May all humanity be happy
May all be without disease
May all witness auspicious sights
May none have to undergo suffering.

Importance of Health and Health Education

Chariuka, a renowned physician of ancient India observed that health was vital for artistc, ethical, material and spiritual development of man. Health is not only basic to leading a happy life for an individual but is also necessary for all the productive activities of the society. It is widely accepted that

"When health is absent
Wisdom cannot reveal itself
Art cannot manifest
Strength cannot fight,
Wealth becomes useless
And intelligence cannot be applied."

Lord Buddha has said that of all the gains, the gains of health are the highest and the best.

Ben Johnson has observed, "O Health! the blessings of the rich! The riches of the poor! who can buy thee at too dear a rate, since there is no enjoying this world without thee."

Likewise Herbert Spencer has stated, "The preservation of health is a duty and a few seem conscious that there is a thing physical morality."

Locke's famous saying 'a sound mind in a sound body is' a true maxim for all ages.

The Secondary Education Commission has stressed the importance of physical well-being in these words, "The physical welfare of the youth of country should be one of the main concerns of the State, and any departure from the normal standards of physical well-being at this period of life may have serious consequences.

Hall has very emphatically stated, "A ton of knowledge bought at the expense of an ounce of health which is the expense most ancient and precious form of wealth and worth costs more than its value".

Carlyle in this regards points out, "We manufacture devils by the thousands because health is not the object of party politics."

Great Seer Swami Vivekanand stresses the importance of well-built bodies in these words, "What India needs to-day is not the *'Bhagwadgita'* but the foot-ball field."

W.M. Ryburn remarked, "We need in Indian education a general philosophy of physical education—we need a conception of education in which physical education takes it rightful place in which its vital importance is recognised."

In view of importance of health, health education should form an integral part of school education.

Meaning of Health: The dictionary defines health as freedom from disease or pain. The physician views health as a normal functioning of the body organs and systems. The World Health Organisation (WHO) has defined health as "a state of complete physical, mental and social well-being, and not merely the absence of disease or infirmity." Health is also taken as the quality of life which enables the individual to live a happy life.

The First Five Year Plan stated, "Health is a positive state of well-being in which harmonious development of mental and physical capacities of the individuals leads to the enjoyment of a rich and fuller life. It implies adjustment of the individual with his total environment—physical and social."

Health Education and Physical Education: Health education and physical education are complementary forces leading to the total development of the individual, family, community and nation. Health education employs the media of acquisition of knowledge about living healthfully and the immediate participation in health practices. Physical education for these purposes employs the media of exercises, games, sports, dances etc.

Health education represents the sum of all experiences in school and elsewhere that favourably influence habits, attitudes and knowledge related to individual and community health.

Health education is a comprehensive term while physical education carries a limited scope. Physical education can be called one of the aspects of health education. Health education is the whole and physical education a part. J. B. Nash has very appropriately remarked, "Health and recreation are the results while physical education activities are the means."

Physical education is the concern of physical instructors and directors of physical education. On the other hand, health education is the work of teachers of hygiene and physiology, medical officers, physical training instructors, local bodies, municipal councils, panchayats etc.

Interrelationships of Health

S.L. Goel in his book *'Health Care Administration'* has explained various relationships as given in Fig. 12.1.

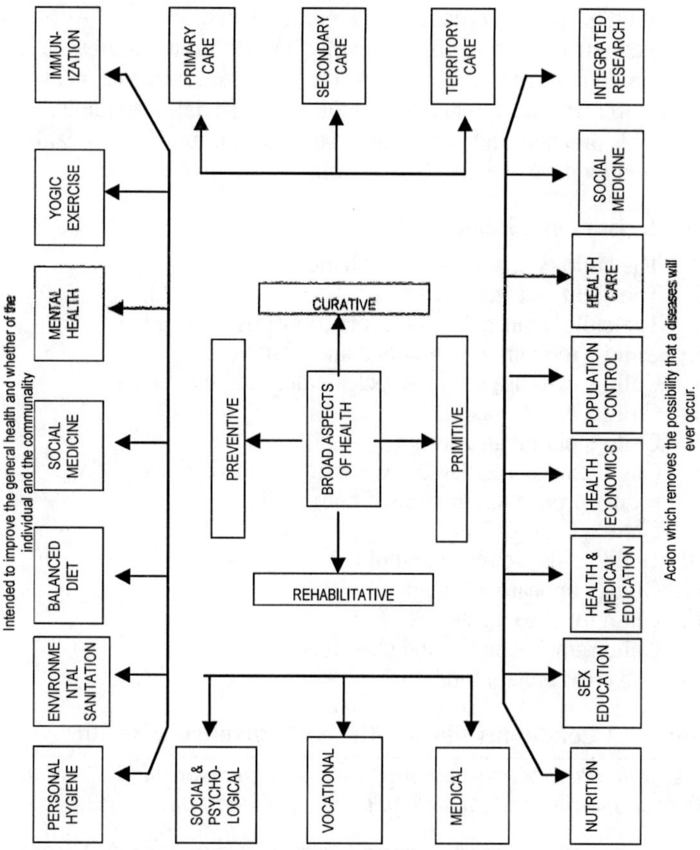

Fig. 12.1 : Health Relationships

The relationship between socio-economic development and progress of health is extremely important. In fact an economy has a health component which has an important bearing on the overall economic development. Health not only affects socio-economic complex but is also affected by it.

Who would deny that a soldier who is not keeping good health cannot be expected to defend the frontiers of his country even if he is provided with the latest sophisticated weapons! Similarly who would deny that an unhealthy farmer with the best possible technological know-how would not succeed in producing the best that can be expected of him! It is equally true in the case of the child.

Poor health results in frustration in life. Likewise emotional disturbance has an adverse impact on the health.

Poor health hinders the development of mental faculties and *vice versa.*

Undoubtedly intellectual efficiency, mental alertness and physical agility, good health and productivity are interrelated.

A disease striken individual can hardly hope to make progress in life.

Factors Influencing Health: A variety of factors influence health. Some of these are: Physical, chemical, biological, social, economic, cultural, educational, prenatal and nutritional. Thus the promotion of health cannot be achieved by measures that derive from any single discipline.

Characteristics of a Healthy Child

1. The child is active and never listless.
2. The child does not tire easily.
3. The child's muscular control is coordinate to age.
4. Child's movements are quick and positive.
5. Child's eyes are bright and clear, alert and interested.
6. Child's hair is glossy.
7. Child's plump and not fat.
8. Child makes regular increases in height and weight which are in proper proportion to age and body build.
9. Child's flesh is firm.
10. Child's lips are moist and pink.
11. Child's appearance is good.
12. Child loves to play.
13. Child remains happy and cheerful.
14. The child enjoys food.

Factors and Conditions which Influence Individual's Health

Favourable Factors and Conditions Influencing an Individual's Health	*Unfavourable Factors and Conditions Influencing an Individual's Health*
1. Good heredity	Poor heredity
2. Healthful and safe living conditions	Pollution and unhygienic conditions
3. Optimal nutrition	Deficient nutrition
4. Adequate exercise	Lack of exercise
5. Play opportunities	Lack of play opportunities
6. Optimism	Pessimism
7. Recreational facilities	Lack of recreational facilities
8. Regulated discipline	Over protective or over strict discipline
9. Desirable health practices	Unhealthy behaviour
10. Emotional maturity	Tension
11. Friendly and cheerful	Choking environment

	environment	
12.	Fun and humour	Boredom
13.	Adequate medical care	Inadequate medical care

General Objectives of Health Education in School

(i) To make the student realise the necessity of having good health.
(ii) To give information regarding health rules.
(iii) To develop health habits among children.
(iv) To develop certain skills concerning health, e.g. training in first aid etc.
(v) To enable students to understand educative value of sanitation, cleanliness and healthful living.
(vi) To develop a will to listen to rules relating to health.
(vii) To develop better human relationship in matters concerning health.
(viii) To acquaint students with the cause and remedies of general diseases.
(ix) To determine the health status of children through health examination and to take up follow-up work.
(x) To take steps to prevent defects or disorders in health aspects.
(xi) To take steps to prevent the occurrence and spread of contagious communicable diseases.
(xii) To provide wholesome school environment.
(xiii) To influence parents and other adults to develop better habits and attitudes through the health programme of school and to make the school an effective agency for the promotion of the social aspects of health education in the family and community as well as the school itself.

Meaning of Social Health Programme: According to a 'Report of the Committee on Terminology in School Health Education in America, the social health programme is defined as "the school procedures that contribute to the maintenance and improvement of the health of pupils and school personnel including health services, healthful living and health education."

Scope of Health Education: It includes all such instruction that enlightens a student about activities and functions contributing to preservation, promotion and restoration of health. By means of a health education programme the spread of disease in the school-going children can be checked. A thorough knowledge of health rules underlines the needs of the study of anatomy and also the symptoms of common diseases of children. Practical knowledge of causes and diagnosis is equally essential. School health education also includes knowledge about the environment, equipment and routine of the school as well.

Components of School Health Programme or Services

Healthful Living	Health Services	Health Instruction
1. This comprises Healthful Physical Environment. 2. Healthful Social Environment 3. Healthful Emotional Environment	1. These include Health or Medical Examination. 2. Follow-up Programme 3. Protective Measures 4. First Aid and Emergency Care 5. Health Examination of School Staff 6. Psychological Services 7. Nutritional Services 8. School Clinic 9. Special classes for exceptional children having physical impair-ments	1. This relates to Formal Health Instruction through talks and other measures regarding the development of health and safety knowledge, altitude and skills. 2. Incidental Instructions 3. Correlated Instruction

Guiding Principles of Health Education Programme and Instruction

Following guiding principles school prove useful in planning and implementing school health education programme.

1. Health education should centre round the health needs and interests of children.
2. The information imparted on health education should be directly related to the level of child's physical, mental and social development.
3. Health education, as far as possible, should be imparted 'by doing'.
4. Problems discussed on health education should be interesting and meaningful.
5. Activities and experiences provided through the health education should be related to home and community needs.

Brief History of School Health Programme

France was the first country to make school authorities look after the health related problems of children. In the year 1833, it introduced the scheme of health programme in schools. Germany follow France in 1896.

School health programme initially includes:

(i) Medical examination of children before entering a school.
(ii) Medical examination of children at least three times during their stay in school.
(iii) Follow-up of the examination by informing parents and referring children to physician.

(iv) Keeping records of health examination of children.

In India, the philosophy of school health programme is still not fully appreciated. Such a programme exists to a considerable extent only in a few public schools. By and large, it is still neglected.

Medical Inspection in Schools

Defects in the Present System of Medical Inspection: Although this system has been in existence for many years, yet it has failed to achieve the desired results. The Secondary Education Commission has observed the following defects in the prevailing system:

(i) It is done in a very superficial manner.
(ii) The remedical measures suggested are often not carried out.
(iii) Follow-up work is practically absent.
(iv) Effective co-operation has not been established between the parents and the school authorities.

Suggestions for Making Medical Inspection Effective

Medical inspection to be effective should be done in the following manner:

1. It should be thorough and comprehensive and should not be treated as a mere routine. It should not merely concern itself with the height, weight and the chest measurements but should also concern itself with ears, teeth, eyes, nose, heart and lungs etc. In fact no part of the body should be left unexamined as far as possible. The first inspection should be at the time of admission of the child in a school. If it is found out that the child is suffering from some chronic disease, he may be refused admission. Child should be examined every year. The last inspection will be just prior to leaving the school which reveals the strength and weakness of the child and helps him to choose some vocation suited to his physical development.

2. Students with serious defects should be examined more frequently.

3. Remedial measures should be taken to remove defects.

4. Three copies of the report should be prepared. One should be sent to the parents, another should be kept by the teacher-in-charge and the third one should be kept by the medical officer.

Follow-up Work: A few words may be said regarding 'follow-up' work. It has been rightly stated that medical inspection is of little or no use unless proper 'follow-up' work is undertaken. In many cases, it does not call for any extra burden. A slight care of the child brings about good results. The parents and the teachers should co-operate. Immediate action should be taken after the medical inspection is over. When the parents are unable to take remedial steps due to poverty, school should take upon itself the responsibility of looking after the health of the child. The State may arrange mobile hospital ambulances for the purpose. "In any case such remedial measures as the school medical officer may suggest should be adopted, and the school authorities should see that they are carried out," thus remarked the Secondary Education Commission.

Apart from medical inspection by the physician, daily inspection of the general cleanliness of the child should be done by the teacher. This costs nothing and can be done in a few minutes.

Personal and Social Aspects of Health Education

Interrelatedness of Personal and Social Aspects of Health Education: There is a very intimate relationship between personal aspects of health education and social aspects of health education. Both are complementary and supplementary. Each influences the other and is influenced in turn. Man is a social being and his individuality has little significance apart from society. Naturally therefore, personal and social aspects of health cannot altogether be separated. Nevertheless for making the subject more vivid, each aspect is dealt with separately to the extent it is possible to do so.

Personal Aspects of Health Education

Personal aspects of health education relate to issues like how to keep oneself in good health by paying attention to the following:

1. Cleanliness of the body, and of each of the organs, viz., eyes, ears, hair, teeth etc.
2. Provision of necessary rest and sleep.
3. Provision of personal comfort through proper clothing, lighting, temperature, ventilation, etc.
4. Maintenance of good postures.
5. Provision of recreation and relaxation through hobbies etc.
6. Toning of various systems of the body—digestive system, nervous system, respiratory system, etc.
7. Provision of nutritious and balanced diet.
8. Provision of exercises.
9. Prevention of diseases in general and infectious diseases in particular.
10. Provision of medical examination.
11. Learning elementary rules of first aid.
12. Inculcation of habits that are beneficial and not hurtful in nature.

Social Aspects of Health Education

Broadly speaking following are the main social aspects of health education:

1. Improving Human Relations in Matters of Health.
2. Developing a Sense of Civic Responsibility.
3. Influencing and Educating Ignorant people.
4. Developing Proper Emotional Environment.
5. Rendering Health Service to the community.

1. *Improving Human Relations in Matter of Health:* In order to become a healthy nation, we must ensure that all the agencies and individuals in the homes schools and the community in matters of health.

2. *Developing a Sense of Civic Responsibility:* An appropriate programme of health education should make people conscious of unhealthy social behaviour like spitting anywhere, urinating anywhere, and every where, coughing and sneezing on other person's face, not isolating oneself when suffering from any infectious disease or throwing rubbish without any consideration for other's health.

3. *Influencing and Educating Ignorant People:* Health education programme of a school should influence the adults of the locality also. The clean, disciplined and healthful way of life imparted to children in the school and followed by them, should be helpful in influencing and educating the ignorant parents and other members of the community.

4. *Developing Proper Emotional Environment:* It should be the endeavour of the school personnel, the parents and the community to provide a suitable emotional environment so that it may have a conducive impact on child's health.

5. *Rendering Health Service to the Community:* Health camps and first aid services can be provided by the school during fairs etc.

PHYSICAL EDUCATION

Meaning of Physical Education

Physical education is an integral part of health education. Following definitions given by experts bring out the meaning of physical education and its important dimensions.

In the words of Jay B. Nash, "Physical education is that field of education which deals with big muscle activities and their related responses."

"Physical education is an integral part of the total education process and has as its aim the development of physically, mentally, emotionally, and socially fit citizens through the medium of physical activities which have been selected with a view to realizing these outcomes."—Charles A. Bucher

"Physical education is the social process of change in the behaviour of the human organism, originating primarily from the stimulus of social big-muscle-play and related activities," —C.C. Cowell.

"Physical education is that phase of education which is concerned, first, with the organisation and leadership of children in big muscle activities, to gain the development and adjustment inherent in the activities according to social standards, and second with the leadership of the activities so that the educational process may go on without growth handicaps."—Clark W. Hetherington.

According to Delbert Obertenffer, "Physical education is the sum of those experiences which come to the individual through movement."

"Physical education is that part of education which proceeds by means of, or predominantly through physical activity, it is not some separate, partially related field."—Edward F. Voltmer, Arthur A. Esslingor.

"Physical education should be defined as that phase of the whole process of education which is concerned with vigorous muscular activities and related responses and with the modifications in the individual resultant from thee responses." —Nixon and Cozens

The *Secondary Education Commission* (1952-53) made it clear "that unless physical education is accepted as an integral part of education, and the educational authorities recognize its need in all schools the youth of the country, which forms its most valuable asset, will never be able to pull their full weight in national welfare".

The old concept of physical education as 'mere drill or a series of regulated exercises' has been rejected. "It includes all forms of physical activities and games which promote the development of the body and mind".

The Education Commission (1964-66) pointed out that the concept of physical education is not merely concerned with physical fitness but also with physical efficiency, mental alertness and the development of qualities like perseverance, team spirit, leadership, obedience to rules moderation in victory and balance in defeat.

Aims of Physical Education

(i) Conservation of health

(ii) Development of well-built bodies

(iii) Development of qualities like courage, endurance and self-control

(iv) Development of social qualities, e.g. followership, obedience, cooperation and leadership.

(v) Development of regular habits of exercise and play

(vi) Development of the whole man as observed by Montaigue, "Physical education neither trains up the soul nor body but the whole man." Froebel aptly stated, "Early education must deal directly with the physical development and influence the spiritual development through the exercise of senses."

Programme of Physical Education

Physical education programme includes the following types of activities:

1. *Developmental Activities:*

(i) Exercise tables, '*dands*', '*baithaks*' and yogic exercises.

(ii) Fundamental movements such as climbing, jumping, running throwing and walking.

(iii) Mimetics and story plays.

(iv) Stunts, pyramids, weight training and conditioning exercises.

2. *Rhythmics:* Rhythm fundamentals, rhythm games, folk dances, social dances, singing games, community singing, Indian rhythmics, *'garha', 'phugdi', 'himma', 'tipri',* etc.

3. *Games, Sports, and Athletics:*

(A) *Games:* (i) Major games, such as *'Kabaddi'*, *'kho-kho'*, volleyball, basketball, hockey, cricket etc.

(ii) Dual games such as tennis, table tennis, badminton, ring-tennis, etc.

(iii) Recreative games, minor games, relays, social games, group games, lead-up games, etc.

(*B*) *Sports:* Cycling, canoeing, shooting, riding, skating etc.

(*C*) *Athletics:* Running, jumping, throwing, walking and relays.

4. *Formal Activities:* Drill and marching, light apparatus, calisthenics, mass P.T. exercises aerobics.

5. *Apparatus:* Parallel bars, vaulting, beam, roman rings, ropes, pommel horse, single bar, 'malkhamb', etc.

6. *Combatives:* Wrestling, boxing, judo, *'lathi'* fight, dagger fight, farigadga, sword fight, simple contests and mass combatives based on 'attack and defence.'

7. *Aquatics:* Swimming, diving and life saving.

8. *Self-Testing Activities:* All types of tests.

9. *Camping and Outdoor Activities:* Hiking, cross country, camping and mountaineering, picnics, excursions etc.

10. *Special Activities:* Demonstrations, ceremonial parades, singing the National Anthem, Flag Salutations, practical projects, citizenship training etc.

11. *Classroom Activities:* Physical education is not merely to be confined to the playground but should pervade the classroom. Physical education in the classroom may take the following forms:

(a) Direct instruction emphasising the necessity of having a good physique.

(b) Suggestions regarding the maintenance of good health.

(c) Emphasis of right postures.

(d) Provision of good seating and lighting arrangements in the classroom, thereby impressing upon them the importance of studying under healthy surroundings.

(e) Providing ample opportunities to the children for physical activity i.e. asking and answering questions, use of audio-visual aids etc.

It should be borne in mind that physical development and mental development are inseparably allied to each other. Classroom should not be devoid of physical activity. Instruction in a play-way manner affords ample opportunities to the students to be physically active and a wise teacher would always bring this spirit of play-way in classroom work. The students should play an active role in the teaching-learning process. They should not remain merely as passive listeners. For pre-primary classes. Kindergarten and Montessori methods afford opportunities for the physical development of the children. Basic system of education is based on the principle of learning by doing. This involves many physical activities. Project Method and the Dalton Plan are the other examples which require many activities on the part of children. Paper cutting and folding may be associated with Elementary Geometry and Arithmetic. Students may learn Nature Study and Geography with the help of clay modelling. A variety of programmes may be introduced in the classroom. Reading, writing, figuring, drawing, etc., should be profitably attempted to provide practical activities. A few minutes drill or music after every lesson of the class may introduce bodily activity among the children. Display of maps and charts etc. bring clarity and vividness in the lesson technology of teaching provides ample opportunities for various kinds of student involvement in the lesson.

Gymnastics and Athletics

Gymnastics and athletics are two important forms of physical education.
The effect of gymnastic exercises is internal and primary. They are based on sound principles. Each exercise has its own value for a specific purpose. Gymnastic exercises are very helpful in teaching correct postures. Gymnastic exercises with apparatus (Bars, Horse, Ladder etc.) are greatly liked by the boys as these involved a great degree of skill and difficulties. Gymnastic exercises like marching, easy exercises in jumping and skipping, aesthetic dancing and folk dancing appeal to the girls.

Athletic activities include running, jumping, disc throwing, hammer throwing and weight throwing, etc.

In carrying out gymnastics, the following points should be taken into consideration:

1. Lessons and exercises should be purposive and not at random.
2. A shirt and shorts are sufficient.
3. The postures should be good.
4. The body should not be held in a straight position for a long time.
5. The gymnastic exercises should be correlated with material and play.
6. All material should be kept in order.

Physical Drill

Physical drill should be organized regularly and properly graded. 'Simple to complex' and 'easy to difficult' should form the basis of physical drill. The duration of the physical drill period should depend on the age and the number of pupils in the group or class. A good system of physical exercises would provide exercise to all parts of the body, *e.g.*, hands, legs, muscles, neck and trunk etc.

Following types of exercises will make the programme effective:

(i) Preparing or warming up exercises, running in a circle, marching etc.

(ii) Corrective exercises

(iii) Recreative exercises
(iv) Psychological exercises

Playground: Games and sports

Playground as the cradle of Democracy: The Battle of Waterloo was won on the play-grounds of Eton

The phrase 'The Battle of Waterloo was won on the playgrounds of Eton' points but that the generals of England who fought the Battle of Waterloo with the foreign enemies had received valuable training in leadership qualities at Eton, which enabled them to win the battle. It may be mentioned that Eton is one of the most prestigious public schools in England. It has produced several eminent personalities of England who have played a leading role in all walks of life and made their mark.

The playground has been rightly called the 'cradle of democracy' as games and sports properly organized and supervised can contribute a lot for the development of ideals and values needed in an enlightened citizen.

Following are the important values of games and sports:

1. *Teach Cooperation:* Team work is the pivot round which the wheel of games revolves. If the members of the team do not work for the team but for their individual distinctions, the team is sure to go to the walls. Games and sports bring home this fact to the students that loyalty and cooperation are the important contributory factors for the honour of the team. They serve to eliminate selfishness and teach the students to subordinate their own interests for the sake of a broader aim of winning the game. This lesson is very important and every citizen is expected to follow it.

2. *Prepare for Life Situations:* The players have to play some times against heavy odds. Courage, patience, steadfastness and perseverance are needed to play well and effectively. The players get accustomed to face very critical situations and this stands in good stead when they enter life. We cannot think of an ideal citizen without possessing these qualities.

3. *Provide Opportunities for Leadershp:* Games and sports provide opportunities for leadership of a very high order. The captain of the team has to put right players at their right places and has to bring about harmony among the different members of the team. Only a man of self-confidence, imagination and enterprise can lead others.

4. *Development of Various Senses:* The games and sports call for a variety of movement—physical and mental. "School games involve a wide range of activity. Most of the senses are called into action. "Comparison and judgment are needed", says William Gowers. The mind has to by kept alert to meet the changing situation of the ball. Body and mind work in harmony.

5. *Physical Development:* Games and sports promote good health, which is perhaps more important than wealth. Good health is also a sign of a good citizen.

6. *Emphasis on Struggle:* They teach the lesson that struggle is more important than success. Baron de Conbertin states, "The important thing in sports is not to win but to take part. The important thing in life is not the triumph but the struggle. The essential thing is not to have conquered but to have fought well. To spread these precepts is to build up a stronger and more scrupulous and more generous humanity."

7. *Satisfaction of Various Urges of Children:* Play is the most important urge of the children. In fact it is a national urge. It is a biological and social necessity for children. Similarly various other urges of children are satisfied.

8. *Development of 'Esprit de Corps':* Tournaments are very helpful in developing 'we feeling' among the students. Team spirit is developed through games and sports.

9. *Profitable Use of Leisure Time:* Games and sports provide recreational avenues.

10. *Character Training:* For promoting qualities of courage, obedience, perseverance, self-control and stead fastness etc., games and sports are very effective.

Concluding Observations

A perusal of the educative value of games and sports leads us to state that playground is an other school.

There is no rose without a thorn. It we do not take precaution to pluck a rose, the thorn is sure to prick us. Likewise it games and sports are not rationally and scientifically organized and supervised, they are likely to do more harm than good.

We may sum up the merits and limitations of games and sports with a quote from Aldous Huxley, "Like every other instrument that man has invented, sports can be used either for good or for evil, purpose. Used well, it can teach endurance and courage, a sense of fair play and a respect for rules, coordinated efforts and the subordination of personal interest to those of the group. Used badly it can encourage personal vanity and group vanity, greedy desire for victory and hatred for rivals, an intolerant *'esprit de corps'* and contempt for people who are beyond arbitrarily selected pole. In either case sports inculcate cooperation."

Tournaments

Merits

Tournaments, understood in the right spirit, are very helpful in developing *'Esprit de Corps'*—sense of corporate life and unity, 'We feeling' comes to the forefront among players and spectators of the respective teams. Love for the institution is clearly manifested in the minds of the students. How thrilling it is to witness the students clapping and encouraging the players. The tournaments also help in raising the standard of sports.

Limitations

However, a few objections are raised to the inter-school tournaments:

1. They benefit only a fair selected players.
2. They are expensive in time and energy.
3. They sometime cause physical injuries to players.
4. They may lead to emotional problems.
5. They tend to faster over specialization.
6. They may encourage unprofessionalism and commercialism.
7. They sometimes lead to serious conflicts and even riots.
8. They create ill-will among institutions.

Right Spirit of Tournaments: It is stated, "To suffer defeat cheerfully and not to burst into rowdyism or even resort to discourtesy, to do one's best against odds and not to lose heart, to be fair to the opponent and to take any mean advantage of him, to play on equal and honourable terms for the sake of play and not try to win by hook and crook; in short to love the game above the prize."

Principles of Organizing Games and Sports

1. A variety of games and sports should be provided to the students to meet their specific needs.
2. Every child should be motivated to take part in one or the other game or sport.
3. Games and sports time-table should be framed and regularly followed.
4. Indian as well as western games and sports should be duly mentioned.
5. The attainments of the students in games and sports should be duly mentioned in important records.
6. Indoor as well as outdoor games should find place in the programme of the school.
7. In case no playgrounds are available to some schools, a cluster of schools may share common playground. A sports complex at suitable place be set up for this purpose.
8. Games and sports should be properly supervised by teachers.
9. Games' fund should be spent for games only.
10. Games' fund should not be utilised on a few selected players.
11. Tournaments should be organized systematically.

Principles and Suggestions for the Promotion of Physical Education

1. The programme of physical education should become an integral part of school education.
2. Physical education should be treated at par with other subjects.
3. Every class/section should be provided with one period daily for physical education in the time-table.

4. Greater facilities should be provided in educational institutions in the form of equipment, playgrounds and funds.
5. Incentives in the form of credit for achievements in sports should be provided.
6. Health, power of endurance, physical well-being of young people should be developed by improvement in nutrition.
7. Planned coaching at all stages in essential. There is a vast talent potential in the country which should be exploited by intensive and planned coaching.
8. Sports and games should be organised in rural areas through Vyayamshalas, Vyayam Mandals, Akharas, etc., and in co-operation with the community.
9. Sports festival should be organised and sports events encouraged on the occasion of fairs. Indigenous sports like *Kabaddi* and indigenous style of wrestling should be encouraged.
10. Where separate playgrounds cannot be made available for each educational institution, a common pool for a group of institutions should be created.
11. Standard equipment should be manufactured in the country so as to be available at cheap rates and facilities for its manufacture should be provided.
12. For the development of sports and games in the country it is essential that umpiring and refereeing should be of a high standard.
13. All teachers below the age of 40 should actively participate in many of the physical activities of students and thus make them a lively part of the school programme.
14. Full records of physical activities of the student must be maintained.
15. The training in physical education should be comprehensive enough to include all aspects of health education.
16. The teachers of physical education should be associated with the teaching of subjects like Physiology and Hygiene and given the same status as other teachers of similar qualifications.
17. The existing facilities for training of teachers of physical education should be expanded by increasing the seats in the existing colleges by opening new colleges where necessary and by reorganising some of the institutions as All India Training Centres to which aid may be given both by the Centre and the States.
18. Leadership in the field of physical education should consist of:
    (a) qualified staff,
    (b) specialist coaches, and
    (c) student leaders
19. In primary schools, classroom teachers should teach physical education. They should be given in-service training in physical education.

20. Periodical refresher courses should be organised for in-service physical education teachers.
21. Special coaching camps should be conducted for school physical education teachers.
22. Playgrounds should be provided by schools as laid down in the National Plan of Physical Education and Recreation. Schools may, however, have playgrounds with the following minimum limits:

Category	*Boys*	*Girls*
(a) High Schools	5 acres	3 acres
(b) Middle Schools	3 acres	2 acres
(c) Primary Schools	1/2 to 1 acre	1/2 to 1 acre

23. Schools having excess open space may be required to permit the use of such open space by the neighbouring schools.
24. Each school should have an indoor gymnasium with the dimensions of 60' × 15'.

Junior Red Cross Society

The Junior Red Cross Society is the School Children's branch of the Red Cross Organisation. The Red Cross Organisation is a world-wide organisation. It is voluntary, non-governmental, non-political, non-sectarian and international in character.

Aims of the Junior Red Cross Society

(a) Promotion of health, personal hygiene, school hygiene and community hygiene.

(b) Service to others especially in relation to health.

(c) Promotion of fellowship among, and friendly helpfulness towards, other young people of all countries.

Activities of a Junior Red Cross Society: For the propagation of health rules, a Junior Red Cross Society takes the aid of posters and charts. Health plays are also staged.

The members of the Junior Red Cross Society can render a very useful assistance to the medical officer at the time of medical inspection of the students. Usually a Junior Red Cross Society runs a small dispensary and a library containing books dealing with health, the rules of health, diseases, their causes and remedies.

The students are encouraged to exchange letters, photos, seeds, plants and handwork with students of other countries in order to promote international friendliness. It also arranges lectures on various diseases and their cures. Its members are expected to set good examples before others by visiting the sick students of the school. The members of a Junior Red Cross Society render first-aid when the students receive minor injuries.

School Dispensary or School Clinic

Large schools should establish a school clinic or dispensary to provide treatment of minor ailments of the students. The school clinic may be put under the charge of a full time/part time doctor/teacher having training in first aid.

First-Aid

Meaning: First-Aid is the immediate and temporary care given to the victim of an accident or sudden illness. Its purpose is to preserve life, assist recovery and prevent aggravation of the condition, until the services of a doctor can be obtained, or during transport to hospital or the casualty's home.

The First-Aider's responsibilities end as soon as medical aid is available; but he should stand by after making his resort to the Doctor in case he can be of further assistance.

First-Aid is definitely limited to the assistance rendered at the time of emergency with such material as may be available. It is not intended that the First-Aider should take the place of the Doctor and it must be clearly understood that the re-dressing of injuries and other such after-treatment are outside the scope of First-Aid.

Origin of the Term: The term 'First-Aid' was adopted officially in England for the first time in 1879 by the St. John Ambulance Association. The expression "First-Aider' was not coined till 1894 and was intended to designate "any person who has received a certificate from an authorised association that he (or she) is qualified to render first hand aid."

The originator of First-Aid was Esmarch (1823-1908). He was born in Schleswing Holstein, became a distinguished surgeon and was appointed Surgeon General in the German Army on the outbreak of the Franco-Prussian War. Later he was appointed Consulting Surgeon to the large military hospital near Berlin and was recognised as one of the greatest authorities on hospital management and military surgery. However, no part of his work was more widely valued than his two manuals, entitled *"First Aid on the Battlefield"* and *"First Aid to the Injured"*. The triangular bandage was invented in 1831 by Dr. Mayor of Lausanne, Switzerland, but was later popularised by Esmarch.

Management of the Case

1. Respond quickly to calls for assistance.
2. Give Artificial Respiration if breathing has stopped—every second counts.
3. Stop any bleeding.
4. Guard against or treat for shock by moving the casualty as little as possible and handling him gently.
5. Do not attempt too much—do the minimum that is essential to save life and prevent the condition from worsening.

6. Reassure the casualty and those around and to help to lessen anxiety.
7. Do not allow people to crowd round as fresh air is essential.
8. Do not remove clothes unnecessarily.
9. Arrange for the removal of the casualty to the care of a Doctor or hospital as soon as possible.

First-Aid Equipment

1. Set of splints with metal connections
2. Splint straps for securing splints in lieu of bandages
3. Triangular bandages
4. 1-inch roller bandages
5. 2-inch roller bandages
6. 1/2 oz. packets of cotton wool
7. 1/2 oz. packets of lint or guaze, plain white.
8. Grey (unbleached) wool (for padding)
9. Adhesive plaster, 2 cm × 4 mts.
10. Scissors
11. Medicine glass, graduated or bakelete measure
12. Safety-pin box
13. 15 cm kidney basin
14. Dressing forceps
15. Note-book and pencil
16. Torch, electric (with spare battery)
17. Smaller size prepared sterile dressings
18. Medium size prepared sterile dressings
19. Large size prepared sterile dressings
20. Glucose sweets or lump sugar
21. Assorted adhesive wound dressings
22. Constrictive bandage (Rubber)
23. Small square of mackintosh or plasting sheeting
24. Smelling salts.

(*Note :* This is a suggestive list and by no means an exhaustive list).

Suggestive School Health Programme by the National School Health Committee

The School Health Committee was appointed by the Government of India in February 1960 under the chairmanship of Shrimati Renuka Ray to assess the present standard of health and nutrition of school children and suggest ways and means of improving them.

Terms of Reference

(a) To examine the present position of school health programme in the country in all its aspects (excluding physical education, games and sports), *e.g.*, prevention of diseases, medical care and follow-up service nutrition, health education, healthy environment, etc., of the students at all stages of education and to suggest: (i) further survey of studies if required; and (ii) how the work of various agencies such as medical, social and welfare association can be co-ordinated to assist in the promotion of health of school children.

(b) To examine studies and surveys so far made to assess the nutritional standard of school children and to indicate: (i) further survey of studies needed in any specific areas; (ii) to give concrete suggestions to institute appropriate measures to improve standards of nutrition among school children recommending *inter alia*, ways and means for financing and organising such a programme.

(c) To examine and recommended the possibility of entrusting Primary Health Centre and other organisations for conducting a comprehensive and realistic school health programme in association with the local education administration. The recommendation should include measures to develop an effective school medical service suitable to the country.

(d) To examine the present facilities available for promoting nutritional standards of pre-school children and to suggest practical measures to improve the present position.

Major Recommendations

1. *School Health Services:*
   (i) All children should be provided with school health services.
   (ii) The functions of the school health services should be the provision of health measures, both preventive and curative. These should include the detection and treatment of defects and the creation and maintenance of a hygienic environment in and around the school.
   (iii) All newly admitted children should have medical examination first and then again after four years, as the limited facilities available at present do not permit medical examination at frequent intervals.
   (iv) Prevention and control of communicable diseases in schools should be the responsibility of public health authorities.
   (v) Emphasis should be laid on compulsory primary and revaccination against smallpox immediately. Immunization against diphtheria, whooping cough and tetanus should be made compulsory in the immediate future.
   (vi) With adequate training in health education and school health services, it should be possible for the teacher to undertake certain functions connected with school health services such as: (a) observation of children with view to spot out any deviations from normal health; (b) recording of height and weight and simple testing of vision and hearing; (c) maintaining of health records of children; and (d) giving first-aid.
2. *School Meal*
   (i) The primary aim of the school meal programme should be to improve health and encourage sound dietary habits among

children.

(ii) The school meal should be based on cheap nutritious and locally available foods. A simple menu may comprise a minimum of cereals and millet—2.5 oz. pulses—1 oz, non-leafy vegetable—1 oz, oil—1/4, and condiments and salt.

(iii) Every school should be provided with protected water supply and facilities for drainage; sanitary environment; facilities for storage; preparation and distribution of food: adequate space for feeding children; and sanitary disposal of garbage.

(iv) It is necessary that the Government should support the school meal programme besides the contribution of the community at the rate of 50 per cent of the total cost

3. *Pre-School Child*

(i) A comprehensive health and welfare service for pre-school children should be introduced.

(ii) Services of 'Balwadis', Mahila Samitis, maternity and child welfare centres, health centres, clinics and nursery schools, the pre-primary schools, pediatric centres of hospitals and social welfare and similar organisations should be utilised for the distribution of milk to pre-school children.

4. *School Health Education*

(i) Health education should be included as a part of general education in the primary, middle and secondary schools.

(ii) The State Administration should take immediate steps to publish text-books on health education and to have health lessons included in other appropriate text-books.

5. *Training, Studies and Research*

(i) In teacher training programmes, heath education and school health should be a required part of training. The teacher should have the knowledge of the growth and development of children, personal health, community health, school health practices and methods of health education.

(ii) For the teachers who are already in service, special short term courses should be organised in the local school organisations with the technical assistance from the health personnel.

(iii) Future school health and school meal policies and programmes should be developed from the results obtained through scientific surveys and studies. Studies and research are quite essential for making school health programme efficient, effective and economical.

6. *School Environment*

(i) School buildings should be simple, safe, attractive and sanitary.

(ii) Every school building in urban areas, where public water supply is available, should have water supply connection and adequate number of taps. In rural areas, an independent water supply system is desirable for each school.

(iii) In urban areas wherever drainage facilities exist, these should be extended to all schools. In rural areas, drains should be constructed for the removal of waste water.

(iv) The sale of food by hawkers in and around the school should be prohibited.

7. *School Health Administration*

(i) At the Centre, there should be National School Health Council. Such a Council will facilitate co-operation and co-ordination of many individuals and groups that are concerned with the health of the children.

(ii) Each State should have a State Council of School Health. The Director of Education and the Director of Health Services should alternatively be Secretary and Joint Secretary of the Council.

(iii) At district level, School Health and School Meal Committees should be set up as sub-committees of the District Development Councils.

(iv) The district health and education organisations should be strengthened appropriately to plan, implement and supervise this additional work.

13

Common Ailments and Physical Defects of Children

Common Cold or Nasal Catarrh

Common cold is a common ailment and when uncared for, it may become very serious. The child suffering from common cold loses health slowly.

This ailment is caused by virus.

Symptoms of Common Cold: There are: (i) Heaviness in the nose, (ii) Sneezing, (iii) Shivering, (iv) Swelling of the nose and eyes.

Treatment: (i) Isolate the child, (ii) Let him take rest, (iii) Give hot tea, (iv) Refer to the doctor.

Precautions: (i) Nasal catarrh is a communicable disease. Hence other students should not come into direct contact with the student who suffers from cold.

(ii) Child should be asked to use a clean handkerchief when coughing or sneezing.

(iii) The clothes such as handkerchief, pillows and bedsheets used by the patient should be disinfected with boiling water.

Sore Throat

Meaning: It is the inflammation of the throat and like common cold it is also a communicable disease and spreads like fire. Some children get sore throat with a slight change in humidity and temperature.

Symptoms: (i) Slight fever, (ii) Headache, (iii) Pain in the body, (iv) Shivering, (v) Pain in swallowing food, (vi) Redness in the throat, (vii) Dried up mucous membrane and discharge, (viii) Change in voice, (ix) Restlessness, (x) Rapid pulse, (xi) Fast breathing.

Treatment: (a) Giving rest to the patient, (b) Letting the patient lie down in warm bed in a ventilated sunlit room, (c) Applying hot dry heat or hot compress from outside, (d) Letting the patient gargle with fresh warm water in which potassium permanganate is mixed, (e) Giving nutrious food.

Constipation

Constipation is related to the digestive system. The symptoms of constipation are: headache, loss of appetite, loss of vitality and vomiting sensation. It is retention of forces, the excretion though the bowel and is usually caused by rotten food, irregular meals, lack of exercise and fresh vegetables in the food.

Constipation, if not checked may result is appendicitis and ulcer.

Constipation can be cured by taking green vegetables, taking a proper amount of water, taking meals at regular hours and doing regular exercises and especially morning walk.

Dyspepsia

Dyspepsia means indigestion. It occurs when the digestive system fails to dissolve solids and make food capable of assimilation by tissues. It implies that either the food has been bolted and has not been converted into sugar in the mouth. In such a situation, additional work has to be done by other organs which increases risk of indigestion. Indigestion also occurs when food is taken in an excess quantity and an undue strain is caused to organs of digestion and excretion.

In the event of indigestion, these steps are recommended: (i) Taking light food, (ii) Administering hot water to produce vomiting, (iii) Administering some purgative to empty the bowels.

Diarrhoea

Diarrhoea is the disorder of the bowels or intestine attended by frequent motions. It is usually caused by a special bacteria which is deposited by flies on food. The bacteria passes into the digestive tract through food, water and various eatables. It is prevented by drinking boiled water, freshly cooked light food, and keeping flies off the food stuff.

This disorder of diarrhoea can be cured by taking proper medicine.

Contagious and Infectious Diseases

Meaning of Contagious and Infectious Diseases: Contagious diseases are those diseases that directly spread from one person to another. Their germs are so strong and so numerous that they are sure to reach from patient to another. On the other hand infectious diseases are those diseases which spread from one person to another, but without the direct knowledge of the patient.

Causes of Infectious Diseases: These are caused by germs which are organisms that are either invisible or visible only under a very powerful microscope. They invade the body and multiply rapidly. The poisons manufactured by the germs circulate in the blood and give rise to the symptoms of particular diseases. Germs are carried from one person to another and the diseases spread. Germs can be carried by flies and other insects, human beings, articles used by the infected persons and public conveyances.

These are caused either through the mouth due to contaminated food or liquid or uncleaned or unwashed hands. These can also take place through the skin where there are wounds or cuts on it.

Spread of infections Diseases: These spread either by direct or indirect contact. In direct contact one touches or is touched by a patient. This includes hand to body and hand to mouth contact, inhaling of the air containing germs of infection, sexual intercourse, kissing, remaining face to face for long, shaking hands and embracing etc. Indirect contact takes place through contaminated food or contaminated materials like beds, books, clothes, doors, utensils, etc.

Diseases According to the Agents that Spread Them

Agent	*Diseases*
1. Air	Chickenpox, Diphtheria, Measles, Mumps, Influenza, Smallpox, Scarlet fever, Whooping cough.
2. Clothing's and Excretions	Ringworm, scabies and other rashes.
3. Insects	Malaria, Plague, Yellow fever etc.
4. Water and Food	Cholera, Dysentery, Diarrhoea, Diphtheria.
5. Wounds and Abrasion	Blood poisoning, Tetanus

Symptoms of Infectious Diseases

1. Unsteady temperature
2. Shivering
3. Pain in some part of the body
4. Appearance of some granules on different parts of the body. There are poisonous in nature.
5. Appearance of raised patches on the forehead below the hair which spread out to other parts of the body. These patches are more or less red in colour.

Prevention of Infectious Diseases

The following steps should be taken to prevent the spread of the disease.

1. *Notification:* The health officer or the municipal committee should be informed at once when a case of infectious disease occurs in the home or in the school.

2. *Isolation:* The student should be separated from healthy individuals.

3. *Quarantine:* Neighbours and relatives of the patient and all those people who have come in contact with the patient should be separated for a specific length of time, equal to the incubation period of the disease.

4. *Vaccination:* Vaccination and inoculation should take place from time to time even without the on set of a disease to keep the student population immune from such diseases.

5. *Chlorinating drinking water:* Drinking water to be supplied to the school should be chrominated properly.

6. *Environmental Sanitation:* Environmental sanitation is an essential preventive measure. School campus, school canteen, classrooms, corridors, toilets, wash-basins, urinals etc. need disinfectants. Disinfectants like carbolic acid, iodine, phenyl and sulphur dioxide are quite effective in destroying germs.

7. *Disinfecting the belongings:* The articles used by the students suffering from infectious diseases need to be thoroughly disinfected.

8. *Testing drinks and food stuffs:* A close check should be exercised over the vendors near the school. The rotten, infected and adulterated articles of food should not be allowed to be sold.

9. *Disposal of garbage, sewage and waste:* Arrangements should be made for the speedy disposal and removal of garbage, sevrage and waste. These dirty materials become breeding places for germs and insects.

10. *Education:* Students and the public need to be properly educated about these diseases—how they are caused, how they are communicated, how they spread, how they are prevented and what steps should be taken to control their spread.

Stages of Diseases

There are three distinct stages in every disease caused by germs: (i) The incubation stage, (ii) The acute stage or that of disease, (iii) Convalescence.

Description of Various Diseases

Disease	*Incubation Period*	*Symptoms*	*Affected Age*	*Precaution to be Taken in the School*
1. Chicken Pox	11 to 19 days	Rashes consisting of red spots, blisters, scabs	All ages	1. Student to be sent home 2. Student not to be allowed to attend school for about three weeks
2. Cholera	A few hours to a few days	Severe pain in the abdomen vomiting, diarrhoea	All ages	Cleanliness of urinals and lavatories
3. Diphtheria	2 to 10 days	White patches on the soft palate, tonsils and throat	Before 2 or 3 years of age	Child should not be allowed to attend the school
4. Influenza	A few hours to a few days	Pain in the head, back, and limbs, shivering, rise in temperature, running of eyes and nose, sneezing and coughing	Children and Adults	1. Students to be advised not to visit crowdy places 2. Use of handkerchief 3. Students to be separated from the school

Disease	*Incubation Period*	*Symptoms*	*Affected Age*	*Precaution to be Taken in the School*
5. Malaria	7 to 21 days	High fever, shivering	All ages	1. Boiled water to be arranged 2. Less eating
6. Measles	One or two weeks	Cold, rise in temperature, reddish rash on the body	Usually before 10 years of age	1. Consultation of the doctor 2. Sending the child home 3. The child to be kept away from school for at least 3 weeks
7. Mumps	14 to 28 days	Swelling from ear to ear, painful eating		Child to be separated from the school for about 20 days
8. Small Pox	10 to 15 days	Severe headache, Backache, high fever	All ages	1. Vaccination 2. Students to be sent home
9. Typhoid	12 to 15 days	Severe headache and vomiting, high temperature	All ages	1. Inoculation, 2. Cleanliness and disinfection
10. Whooping Cough	6 to 18 days	Common cold Running of nose continuous coughing for semitone along with vomiting	Childhood before 5	Child to be kept at home for allowed 2 monthly.

Physical Impairment

Identification

Following are the usually observable impairments:

1. Deformity in fingers, hands, legs, neck and waist.
2. Difficulty in sitting, standing and walking.
3. Difficulty in handling objects, picking up and putting down at appropriate places.
4. Frequent complaints of pains.
5. Difficulty in holding pen to write.
6. Walking with jerks.
7. Involuntary movements of jerks.
8. Ampulated legs.
9. Difficulty in seeing the writing on the blackboard.
10. Difficulty in hearing.

Role of the Teacher

1. Parents should be informed as soon as some defect is noticed.
2. Medical inspection should be arranged whenever any physical

impairment is noticed.

3. Front seats may be provided to students having low vision.
4. Front seats may be given to students with crutches and wheel chairs.
5. Recreational needs of such children should be attended to.
6. Students free from such impairments may be motivated to show due regard to students with impairments.
7. Special attention should be paid to the postures of students.
8. Peers may be encouraged to assist such students.
9. Special cases may be referred to appropriate authorities dealing with impairments, with parents' consent.

Minor Physical Ailments and Defects

There are several minor physical ailments and defects which can be cured at school. Treatment of some common physical ailments and defects is given here.

I. Shock

Signs of Shock

(a) Weakness after fainting especially on standing up
(b) Vomiting feeling
(c) Cold damp skin
(d) Too much sweating even in cold weather
(e) Severe thirst
(f) Restlessness, mental confusion or loss of consciousness
(g) Weak rapid pulse (more than 100 per minute.)

Treatment of Shock

(1). Have the pupil lie down with his feet high than his head. If the shock is due to a head injury do not raise his feet. Make him sit propped up (half sitting position against a pillow.
(2). If the pupil feels cold, cover him with a blanket.
(3). If he is conscious, give him warm water or other lukewarm drinks. If shock is due to injury (accidents, stab wounds) then do not give him anything to drink. He may need surgery. Get medical help fast.
(4). If he is in pain, give him aspirin or another pain medicine.
(5). Keep calm and reassure the person.

II. Loss of Consciousness

Common causes of loss of consciousness are:

(a) A hit on the head (getting knocked out)
(b) Shock
(c) Poisoning
(d) Diabetes
(e) Fainting (from fright, weakness, etc.)

(f) Heat stroke
(g) Stroke
(h) Heart attack
(i) Epilepsy

Treatment: If pupil is unconscious and you do not know why, immediately check each of the following:

1. Is he breathing well? If not, tilt his head way back and pull the jaw and tongue forward. If something is stuck in his throat, pull it out. If he is not breathing, use mouth-to-mouth breathing at once.
2. Is he losing a lot of blood? If so, control the bleeding.
3. Is he is shock (moist, pale skin; weak, rapid pulse)? If so, lay him with his head lower than his feet and loosen his clothing.
4. Could it be heat stroke (no sweat, high fever, hot, red skin)? If so, shade him from the sun, keep his head higher than his feet, and soak him with cold water (ice water of possible).
5. It is best not to move him until he becomes conscious. If you have to move him, do so with great care, because if his neck or back is broken, any change of position may cause greater injury.
6. Look for wounds or broken bones, but move the person as little as possible. Do not bend his back or neck.
7. Never give anything by mouth to a person who is unconscious.

III. When Something Gets Stuck in the Throat

When food or something else sticks in a person's throat and he cannot breathe, quickly do this:

1. Stand behind him and wrap your arms around his waist.
2. Put your first against his belly above the naval and below the ribs.
3. Press into his belly with a sudden strong upward jerk. This forces the air from his lungs and should free his throat. Repeat this several times, if necessary.
4. If the pupil is a bit bigger than you, or is already unconscious, quickly do this:
   (a) Lay him on his back.
   (b) Sit over him like this, with the heel of your lower hand on his belly between his naval and ribs.
   (c) Make a quick, strong upward push. Repeat several times if necessary.
   (d) If he still cannot breathe, try mouth-to-mouth breathing.

IV. Drowning

1. Start mouth-to-mouth breathing at once.
2. If you cannot blow air into his lungs, when you reach the shore, quickly put him with his head lower than his feet and push his belly as described above. Then continue mouth-to-mouth breathing at once.

V. Heat Cramps

In hot weather people who work hard and sweat a lot sometimes get painful cramps in their legs, arms, or stomach. These occur because the body lacks salt.

Treatment. Put a teaspoon of salt in a litre of boiled water and drink it. You can add a little sugar and lime juice to the drink.

VI. Heat Exhaustion

Signs: A person who works and sweats a lot in hot weather may become very pale and weak and perhaps feel faint. The skin is cool and moist. The pulse is rapid and weak. The most striking thing is that on a very hot day the skin is cold and moist.

Treatment: Have the person lie down in a cool place, raise his feet, and rub his legs, Give salt water to drink: 1 teaspoon of salt in a litre of water. (Give nothing by mouth while the person is unconscious.)

VII. Heat Stroke

Heat stroke is not common, but is very dangerous. It occurs especially in older people and alcoholics during hot weather.

Signs: The skin is red, very hot, and dry. Not even the armpits are moist. The person has a very high fever, sometimes more than 42°C. Often he is unconscious.

Treatment: The body temperature must be lowered immediately.

Put the person in the shade.

Take off his clothes and pour cold water over him.

Fan him.

Give ice cold water enema.

Take the temperature every 10 minutes.

When the temperature comes down to 38°C, stop pouring cold water on him.

Seek medical help.

VIII. Cuts, Scraps, and Small Wounds

1. Cleanliness is of first importance in preventing infection and helping wounds to heal.
2. To treat a wound, first, wash your hands very well with soap and water. Then wash the wound well with soap and boiled water.
3. When cleaning the wound, be careful to clean out all the dirt. Lift up and clean under any flaps of skin. You can use a clean tweezers or other instruments to remove bits of dirt, but always boil them first to be sure they are sterile.
4. If a pupil gets a cut, scrape or wound, give him an injection of tetanus toxiod immediately. If he has not been immunized against tetanus, give him one injection each month for the next two months.

IX. Nose-bleeding

1. Patient should sit quietly.
2. Pinch the nose firmly for 10 minutes or until the bleeding has stopped and if this does not control the bleeding, pack the nostril with a wad of cotton, leaving part of it outside the nose. If possible, first wet the cotton with hydrogen peroxide, Vaseline, cardon cactus juice or lidocaine with epinephrine. Then pinch the nose firmly again. Do not leg to for 10 minutes or more.
3. Leave the cotton in a place for a few hours after the bleeding stops; then take it out very carefully.
4. Do not dig into the nose or try to remove clotted blood. Bleeding will start again.
5. If a pupil's nose bleeds often, smear a little Vaseline inside the nostrus twice a day.

X. Burns

(a) Minor Burns that Do not Form Blisters (1st Degree): To help ease the pain and lessen damage caused by a minor burn, put the burned part in cold water at once. No other treatment is needed. Give aspirin for pain.

(b) Burns that Cause Blisters (2nd Degree):

1. Do not break blisters.
2. If the blisters are broken, wash gently with soap and boiled water that has been cooled. Sterilize a little Vaseline by heating it until it boils and spread it on a piece of sterile gauze. Then put the gauze on the burn.
3. If there is no Vaseline, put some gentian violet, leave the burn uncovered.
4. It is very important to keep the burn as clean as possible. Protect it from dirt, dust, and flies.
5. If signs of infection appear—pus, bad smell, fever, or swollen lymph nodes—apply compresses of potassium permanganate solution 3 times a day. If potassium permanganate is not available, you can use warm salt water (1 teaspoon salt to 1 litre water). Boil both the water and cloth before use. With great care, remove the dead skin and flesh. You can spread on a little antibiotic ointment such as neosporin. In severe cases, consider taking an antibiotic such as penicillin or ampicillin by mouth.

(c) Deep Burns (3rd Degree): These destroy the skin and expose raw or charred fresh and are always serious. They cover large areas of the body. Take the pupil to a health centre at once. In the meantime wrap the burned part with a very clean cloth or towel.

If it is not possible to get medical help, treat the burn as described above. If you do not have vaseline, put some gentian violet and leave the burns in the open air, covering it only with a loose cotton cloth or sheet to protect it from dust and flies. Keep the cloth very clean and change it each time it gets dirty with liquid or blood from the burn. Give penicillin.

Never put grease, fat, hides, coffee of feces on burns.

XI. Poisonous Cases

Symptoms are:

1. Eyes become red.
2. The body becomes inactive and unconsciousness develops.
3. Speech sensation is lost.
4. Foam may come out of the mouth.
5. The lips and the tongue get choked and assume scarlet colour.

Common Poisons and their Treatment

1. *Acids (Strong)*
   i) Do not make the patient vomit.
   ii) Give plenty of water to dilute the acid.
   iii) Add if possible, 2 tablets of chalk, milk of magnesia, plaster or white wash to a pint of water.
2. *Lead*
   i) Make the casualty vomit.
   ii) Give a desert spoon of Epson salt in a cup of water.
3. *Mercury*
   Get white of egg in water, followed by milk. Then make the causality vomit.
4. *Opium*
   i) Give a few crystals of permanganate of potash dissolved in a tumbler of water.
   ii) Give hot coffee.
   iii) Make the causality awake.

XII. Snake Bite Treatment

1. If bitten on a limb, arrest the circulation of blood immediately in the arteries and veins by means of a constriction placed round the upper arm, between the wound and the heart but not round the forearm or leg.
2. The constriction may consist of rubber tubing or elastic braces or of non-elastic strips of clothing, e.g., pugree, puttee, a tie or handkerchief, tied loosely round the limb tightened with a stick.
3. Wash the wound with a solution of potassium permanganate in order to remove any venom.
4. Make an incision 3/4 inch deep into the bitten area with a sharp knife or razor blade.
5. Rub crystals of potassium permanganate into the incision as a neutralising agent.
6. Keep the patient warm.

7. Keep the patient at rest.
8. Give hot drinks such as tea, coffee, or milk if the patient is able to swallow.
9. Reassure the patient with encouraging words.
10. Apply artificial respiration if breathing is falling.

XIII. Treatment of Rabies and Dog Bites

1. Immediately send for the doctor.
2. Wash the whole abraded surface with soap and water whether licked, scratched or lacerated.
3. Pain carefully the abraded surfaces if pure carbolic acid is available.
4. Crystals or a saturated solution of permanganate potash may be applied.
5. If the dog is known, insist on the owner to chain it for the doctor's inspection and to prevent any further mischief.

XIV. Headache

It may be on account of poor sleep, too much exertion, fatigue, eye disease, defective vision etc.

1. Rest should be taken and one should lie down on a dark quiet place.
2. Light food should be taken.
3. Asprine tablets may be taken.

XV. Vomiting

It is often due to a problem in the stomach or guts.

Treatment

1. Nothing should be eaten when vomiting is severe.
2. Some tea may be sipped with sugar but without milk. Ginger or lime juice may be added.
3. Frequent sips of cola, tea may be taken.

Bandages

1. Bandages are used to help keep wounds clean. For this reason, bandages or pieces of cloth used to cover wounds must always be clean. Cloth used for bandages should be washed and then dried with an iron or in the sun, in a clean, dust-free place.
2. If possible, cover the wound with a sterile gauze pad before bandaging. These pads are often sold in sealed envelopes in pharmacies. Or prepare your own sterile gauze of cloth. Wrap it in thick paper, seal it with tape, and bake it for 20 minutes in an oven. Putting a pan of water in the oven under the cloth will keep it from charring.
4. If a bandage gets wet or dirt gets under it, take the bandage off, wash the cut again, and put on a clean bandage.
5. Be careful that a bandage that goes around a limb is not so tight it

cuts off the flow of blood.

6. Many small scrapes and cuts do not need bandages. They heal best if washed with soap and water and left open to the air. The most important thing is to keep them clean.

Education of Children with Visual Impairments (Other than Blindness)

Several children do not have sufficient vision. They find it difficult to read the writing on the blackboard clearly. There are partially sighted children also. Some can read only large print. Visual impairment results in several learning problems. Children with visual impairments may have enormous capacity to work. However, this depends upon the nature of the impairment.

Identification of Children with Visual Impairments: It is very necessary to identify each category of children with visual impairments. Medical treatment may become necessary in some cases. Parents also need to be informed.

Children with visual impairment may be identified from the following symptoms:

1. Having watery eyes.
2. Rubbing eyes frequently.
3. Reddening of eyes frequently.
4. Covering one eye and titling the head forward.
5. Holding objects and books close to the eyes.
6. Asking help from others when taking notes from the blackboard.
7. Blinking frequently—squinting eyelids together.
8. Complaining about headache following close eye work.
9. Bumpening into people or objects.
10. Skipping words or lines while reading.
11. Having poor eye-hand coordination.
12. Moving head forward and backward while looking at distant objects.

Role of the School and the Teacher in the Education of Students with Visual Impairment

1. Children with visual impairment may be seated in the front rows so that they can read the writing on the blackboard without any difficulty or pressure.
2. Such children may be given training in listening with comprehension.
3. Books with bold letters may be provided to such children.
4. Radio and T.V. broadcasts may be arranged for to such children.
5. Efforts may be made to procure cassettes in different curricular areas. State Institutes of Education or State Councils of Educational Research and Training or District Institutes of Education and Training or Centres or Institutes of Educational Technology may be approached for this purpose.

6. Blind children need Braille script books.
7. School doctor may be consulted from time to time.
8. Co-operation of the parents be sought in the follow-up work.

Education and Identification of Children with Hearing and Speech Impairment

Listening plays an important role in academic learning. Hearing problems interfere with the achievement of the students. It is, therefore, desirable to identify such children and take steps to meet their educational needs. Such children may be identified as under:

—Some observable deformity of the ear or ears.
—Frequent complaints of pain in ears.
—Frequent scratching of ears.
—Frequent discharge from ears.
—Turning head on one side to hear better.
—Frequent requests to teachers to repeat questions and directions etc.
—Making errors in taking dictation or notes.
—Displaying speech difficulty.

Guidelines for Education of Children with Hearing and Speech Impairment

1. Children with hearing problems may be given front seats.
2. While speaking, the teacher may use a reasonable level of pitch.
3. The teacher should avoid mumbling.
4. The teacher should avoid speaking too fast.
5. Students should be encouraged to speak gradually and steadily.
6. Other students of the class may be asked to give due consideration to such students.
7. A lot of visual aids may be used in the classroom.
8. Some of the hearing problems can be corrected through drill and practice.
9. Medical help may be needed if speech disorder is due to an organic defect in speech mechanism.

Education of Children with Orthopaedic and Locomotor Impairment/Disability

Identification

Such children can be easily identified as their impairment is usually observable.

1. Deformity may be observable in fingers, hands, legs, neck or waist etc.
2. Showing difficulty in sitting, standing and walking.
3. Showing difficulty in picking up and holding objects and putting

them on the ground.

4. Frequently complaining of pains in the joints.
5. Experiencing difficulty in holding the pen to write.
6. Walking with jerks.
7. Experiencing difficulty in the movement of limbs.
8. Amputated limbs.

Education of Children with Orthopaedic and Locomotor Impairment

1. The teacher should accept such children in the meaner he accepts other children.
2. The teacher should avoid sarcasm for the disability of the child.
3. Other children should be advised to appreciate the disability and show due regard to such children. They should be made to understand the disability.
4. Seating arrangement in the class may be adjusted to the specific needs of such students.
5. Reasonable opportunities for participation in recreational activities, sports and games should be provided to these children.
6. Remedial teaching may also be arranged for them.

14

Healthy Physical Life in the School

All Round Attractive, Calm, Captivating, Enchanting, Serence, Spiritual and Vibrant Environment of the School

It is an established fact that school environment has a direct bearing on ethical, mental, physical, social and spiritual development and well-being of students. Next to home, students spend most of their time in school and therefore the school environment and its programme have a great impact on them. Proper conditions for healthy physical life in the school are: proper location and building of the school, sanitation, water supply, recreational programmes, games and sports, emotional set-up and happy group relations, along with effective teaching-learning process.

1. *Physical Environment of the School:* This includes

(i) The site of the school: The school should be located in an attractive, clean, congenial, healthy and pleasant environment. As far as possible, its natural surrounding should have a touch of beauty. The site should be free from dampness, dust, noise, smoke and other unhygienic conditions.

(ii) The school building: The building in its totality—classrooms, laboratory, library and playgrounds etc. should be beautiful, clean, neat and spacious to a reasonable extent. Its maintenance should be properly attended to. There should be suitable arrangement for its annual repairs and white washing.

(iii) Light and air: Adequate arrangements for light and ventilation should exist. There should be no glare from light. During summer there should be no scope for the sunlight to enter the rooms. The purpose should be to have maximum sunlight in winter and minimum in summer. There should be provision for both artificial and natural light and ventilation.

(iv) Furniture: The seats should be comfortable for the students. It should be possible to keep the entire furniture neat and clean. There should be arrangement for its annual repairs and polishing. Blackboard should be of appropriate size and colour and placed in such a location that the students do not have to tax their eyes to see the writings on it.

(v) Canteen: Regular supervision of the school canteen is very important from the print of view of hygiene, cleanliness, and nutrition.

(vi) Drinking water: Suitable provision of clean and fresh water has to be

ensured.

(vii) Toilet: The hygienic environment of the school toilets is an index of the state of its concern for health of the child. Toilet facilities should not only be adequate but also its cleanliness and disinfections should be ensured.

(viii) Dustbins: Dustbins should be provided at suitable spots so that it may be convenient to the students to throw pieces of waste paper, frist skins etc. in them.

(ix) Hygiene and sanitation: There should be no places or spots in the school where water may stagnate and provide a breeding place for mosquitoes and other germs. Disinfectants should be regularly used at all the places where necessary.

(x) Condition of the laboratories, farm and workshops: All these places of work should be kept next and clean. Appropriate safety measures should be adopted.

2. *Instruction and Supervision of Personal Hygiene of the Students:* This includes (i) Cleanliness of body, (ii) Cleanliness of clothes, (iii) Check on unhygienic habits like blowing of noise everywhere, spitting, passing of urine at any place and the like bad habits.

3. *Emotional Environment:* The emotional development of the students is greatly influenced by the emotional balance of the teachers. Sense of humour of the teacher is very helpful in creating and maintaining a healthy classroom environment. He should pay due regard to the personality of the child. He should be fair and just. His own healthy habits generate similar habits among students.

4. *Healthy Postures of the Students:* Suitable postures of reading, writing, sitting, standing, walking, running and lying in the bed should be stressed upon as they form an essential part of any physical and health education programme. A wrong posture is very harmful and it may lead to deformities and stunted growth.

5. *Games, Sports and Exercises:* Physical education including games, sports and exercises go a long way in enabling the students to enjoy reasonable good health.

6. *Mid-day Meals:* Proper arrangement of nutritive mid-day meals should exist in the school. The school should supplement and enrich the lunch packets of the students. A clear and comfortable seating or standing arrangement as the case may be should also be provided for the students to take the lunch.

7. *School Time-Table:* The school programme and time-table should be so organized that it may not cause fatigue to the teachers and students. The school-hour should be adjusted to the age-level of the students and seasonal changes. The entire teaching and non-teaching programme should be made interesting and inspiring.

8. *Medical Inspection:* Medical examination and its follow-up should be

done regularly.

9. *Social Environment:* Good teacher-pupil relationships keep children mentally healthy. Relationships among other groups have also a great bearing on students.

10. *School Health Services:* School health service programme plays a very important role in achieving the aim of promotion of physical, emotional, mental and social health of the students.

Nutrition

Need and Importance of Nutrition: Food acts as the fuel of the body and provides energy. It makes good of the consumed energy, keeps the body temperature in normal state and invigorates the mind and the nervous system. Both the quantity and quality of food are important for the body.

The quantity of food needed daily by a child or adult varies according to the nature of occupation, general health set-up and metabolism.

Balance Diet: The balanced diet is that which fulfills all the nutritive needs of a normal and healthy individual. It should contain all the constituents like proteins, fats, starch, vitamins etc. in needed quantity. The quantity varies in accordance with the requirements of age, sex, body build, nature of occupation and climatic conditions. In general, the diet of a normal and healthy man should consist of the following diet:

Table 14.1 Balanced Diet

	Food Item	*Quantity*	
		Vegetarian Diet gms.	Non-Vegetarian Diet gms.
1.	Milk	200	100
2.	Vegetables (Leafy Green)	125	125
3.	Vegetables (Other)	75	75
4.	Meat and fish	—	30
5.	Eggs	—	30
6.	Cereals	475	475
7.	Sugar and Jaggery	40	40
8.	Fruits	30	30
9.	Roots and Tubers	100	100
10.	Fats and Oils	40	40
11.	Pulses	80	65

Environmental Cleanliness and Preventing Illness

'Prevention is better than cure' is a true saying. There are a large number of environmental factors which influence our health.

However, it costs nothing to take care of the cleanliness of our environment. A few important suggestions are given below to prevent illness by attending to cleanliness.

1. Illness can be prevented by washing hands with soap and water after contact with faeces (solid waste matter passed out of the body) and before handling food

Washing hands with soap and water removes germs from the hands. This helps to stop germs from getting into food or into the mouth. Soap and water should be easily available for all members of the family to wash their hands.

It is especially important to wash hands after defecating, before handling food, and after cleaning the bottom of a baby or child who has just defecated.

Children often put their hands into their mouths. So it is important for the child to wash hands often, especially before giving food.

A child should wash his face at least once every day. This helps to keep flies away from the face and prevent eye infections. Soap is helpful for washing, but not absolutely essential.

2. Illness can be Prevented by Using latrines

The single most important action which families and schools can take to prevent the spread of germs is to dispose of faeces safely. Many illnesses, especially diarrhoea, come from the germs found in human faeces. Pupils can swallow these germs if the germs get into water, into food, into the hands, or into utensils and surfaces used for preparing food.

To prevent this:

(i) Use latrines.

(ii) If it is not possible to use a latrine, adults and children should defecate well away from houses, paths, water supplies, and anywhere that children play. After defecating, the faeces should be buried. Contrary to common belief, the faeces of babies and young children are even more dangerous than those of adults. So even small children should be asked to use the latrine. If children defecate without using a latrine, then their faeces should be cleared up immediately and either put down the latrine or buried.

(iii) Latrines should be cleaned regularly and kept covered.

(iv) Keep the faeces of animals away from homes and water sources.

3. Illness can be Prevented by using Clean Water

Families and schools who have a plentiful supply of safe piped water, and know how to use it, have fewer illnesses.

Schools and families without a safe piped water supply can reduce illness if they protect their water supply from germs by:

(a) Keeping wells covered. Keeping faeces and waste water (especially from latrines) well away from any water used for cooking, drinking, bathing or washing.

(b) Keeping buckets, ropes and jars used to collect and store water as clean as possible (for example, by hanging up buckets rather than putting them on the ground).

(c) Keeping animals away from drinking water.

(d) Families and schools can keep water clean in the home and in the schools by:

(i) Storing drinking water in a clean, covered container.

(ii) Taking water out of the container with a clean cup.

(iii) Not allowing anyone to put hands into the container or to drink directly from it.

(iv) Keeping animals out of the house.

4. Illness can be prevented by boiling drinking water if it is not from a safe piped supply

Even if water is clear, it may not be free from germs. The safest drinking water is from a piped supply. Water from other sources is more likely to contain germs.

Boiled water kills germs. So, if possible, water drawn from sources such as ponds, streams, springs, wells, tanks or public standpipes should be boiled and cooled before drinking. It is especially important to boil and cool the water which is given to babies and young children, because they have less resistance to germs than adults.

If boiling is not possible, store drinking water in a closed or covered container of clean plastic or glass, and leave it standing in sunlight for two days before using it.

5. Illness can be prevented by keeping food clean

Germs on food can enter the body and cause illness. But food can be kept safe by:

(i) Making sure that food is thoroughly cooked, especially meat and poultry.

(ii) Eating food soon after it has been cooked, so that it does not have time to go bad.

(iii) If food has to be kept for more than five hours, it should either be kept heated or kept cooled.

(iv) If already-cooked food is saved, it should be thoroughly reheated before being used again.

(v) Raw meat, especially poultry, usually contains germs. So it should not be allowed to come into contact with cooked meat. Utensils and food-preparing surfaces should be cleaned after preparing raw meats.

(vi) Keeping food-preparing surfaces clean.

(viii) Keeping food clean and covered and away from flies, rats, mice and other animals.

6. Illness can be prevented by burning or burying household refuse

Germs can be spread by flies, which breed in refuse such as food scraps and peelings from fruit and vegetables. Every family should have a special pit where household-refuse is buried or burned every day.

Malnutrition

Meaning of Malnutrition: Malnutrition means insufficient and unwholesome feeding. A large number of people of our country are ill-fed, ill-clothed and ill-housed. They are unable to give proper diet to their children. This degenerates their health and leads to mental retardation also.

Symptoms of Malnutrition: Cases of malnutrition may be detected by both physical and mental conditions.

(a) Physical Conditions

(i) Bad postures.
(ii) Laziness.
(iii) Easily fatigued.
(iv) Susceptibility to diseases.
(v) Pale and charmless face.
(vi) Drowsiness.
(vii) Under-weight.

(b) Mental Conditions

(i) Gloomy nature.
(ii) Un-enthusiasm.
(iii) Forgetful memory.
(iv) Lack of concentration.
(v) Slow comprehension.
(vi) Irritability.

Causes of Malnutrition

1. *Lack of Sufficient and Proper Food:* When a person does not get proper food according to his age and nature of work, his health is adversely affected and malnutrition is caused.
2. *Unsuitable/Environment:* Lack of fresh air, sun light, physical exercise and unhealthy situations of school buildings also lead to malnutrition.
3. *Over Work:* Over work also adversely affects health.
4. *Lack of Sleep:* Lack of sleep also proves harmful for health.
5. *Irregular Meal:* Irregular and untimely eaten meal causes indigestion, dyspepsia and constipation.

Measures for checking Malnutrition: When the parents fail to provide adequate food to the child, the school must step in and provide the required food. Education is not mere teaching. It is definitely something more. An ill-fed child cannot be properly educated. Malnutrition is the main contributory cause of so many ailments of children. Many progressive countries of the world have realised that it is the responsibility of the schools to make up the deficiency and accordingly they provide mid-day meals to poor children. But for Indian schools the task seems to be a formidable one due to lack of funds. However, some of our well established and richly financed schools can help the poor students by providing them mid-day meals. Help of the charitable people and organisation should be sought. The parents should be guided as to what constitutes a good diet. Sometimes due to ignorance, the parents are unable to provide wholesome food to their children. In view of this the function of the school is two-fold:

(a) To enlighten the parents on the constituents of a good diet.

(b) To provide mid-day meals or some kind of other nourishing material to the needy students.

School Meals

Why School Meals: It is now generally recognized that in the wake of under-nutrition and malnutrition of a large number of the Indian children, the school must take up the responsibility to make up this deficiency. This will not only assist in improving the health and physical development of the child but also assist him in making quick and sounder progress in his studies because a child who is better-fed and healthier makes rapid progress. It also provides motivation to parents to send their children to school. It is, therefore, essential that we must develop a programme of school meals as an integral part of its programme of universal, free and compulsory primary education.

Free Milk: With the help of United Nations International Childrens Emergency Fund (UNICEF) which provided milk powder free of charge, milk was distributed to about 7 lakhs of primary school children for several years.

Contents of Mid-day Meals: The School Health Committee (1960) recommended that it should be based on cheap, nutritious and locally available foods. A menu may comprise a minimum of cereals and millets—2.5 oz; pulses—1 oz; non-leafy vegetable—1 oz; Oil—1 oz. and condiments and salt.

Subsidy by the Government: The Committee recommended that the Government should support the school meal programme besides the contribution of the community at the rate of 50 per cent of the total cost.

The Government of India, initiated the scheme 'Nutritional Support to Primary Education' (NSPE), popularly known as the Mid-day Meals Scheme on August 15, 1995 on a nation-wide scale. The programme intends to give a boost to the universalization of primary education by increasing enrolment, retention and attendance and also to improve the nutritional status of students in the primary classes (I. to V).

The Central support under this scheme is:

(i) Provision of foodgrains free of cost.

(ii) Reimbursement of transportation cost to district authorities from moving foodgrains from godowns of Food Corporation of India to schools.

Nearly 7 lakh children are covered every year under the scheme.

Recreation

Meaning of recreation: By recreation we mean a pursuit generally taken up for the sake of pleasure and the joy which it provides. Profit motive is completely absent in such a pursuit. Enjoyability is its chief characteristic. Of course, creativity may also be considered as its other important characteristic.

Value of recreation: For the all round development of the child's personality, the element of recreation is an important one. Among the 7R's i.e. Reading, Writing, Arithmetic (traditional concept of education in terms of 3 R's), Rights, Responsibilities, Relationships and Recreation, the last 'R' of Recreation is also an integral part of complete education. Harmonious development of the student cannot be considered complete without the development of the element of recreation in one's life.

The present machine age has placed enough time at the disposal of man. Every prudent person would like to make the best use of this opportunity. Hobbies provide a good opportunity to make use of leisure time. School time is the best time to train children to develop suitable habits of recreation. For this purpose, a variety of co-curricular activities may be introduced.

There should be enough scope for games and sports which provide a lot of recreation to the students.

Cycling, mountaineering, skating, swimming, etc. are useful recreational pursuits.

Different types of handwork such as paper-mache card board, clay modelling, toy making, flower making etc. provide recreation.

Stamp collecting, coin collecting and photography etc. are also good means of recreation.

Dramatics, folk dance and music are the other means of recreation.

Radio and T.V. programmes are also very useful media of recreation of students and they need to be properly guided and supervised while participating in such programmes in the school. (See Chapter on Co-curricular Activity)

Safety Education

Importance of Safety: Accidents involve persons of all age groups and they may occur at any place in the home, on the road, on the job, in the school or during recreation. However most of the accidents can be prevented. Accidents are a great economic burden on the individual, his family and also on the society. Safety precautions, therefore, should be the part of our daily life, the school is an important place for providing Erasing and instruction in this regard.

Developing positive attitude towards safety and learning to operate new technological devices is sure to go a long way in making our life free from most of the common accidents.

Guidelines for Safety Habits: The following may be considered as acceptable guidelines to make safety a habit:

1. Looking for possible hazards in whatever we may be doing.
2. Taking precautionary measures for making adjustment in our behaviour.
3. Observing proper safety measures needed for a specific situation.

Accidents at Different Age Groups

In general it may be stated that boys are involved in two to three times as many accidents as girls. Every age has its particular hazards. It is important to be acquainted with chief dangers that beset children at each age level and do all in our power to eliminate them.

Under one year: Choking and suffocation are the chief hazards. Falls cause most of the injuries and even account for several deaths.

One to four years: The child is struck in the lane, street or road. Most accidents involve motor vehicles. The menace of fire is the next cause. Drownings in fish ponds or tanks near the home is the third cause. Poisoning is the fourth cause.

Five to nine years: Motor vehicles are responsible for most fatal accidents. Drownings come next. Cuts are the most frequent injuries.

Ten to fourteen: Motor vehicles continue to be the instruments of death. Drownings run second. Fire accidents come third.

Measures for Minimising Accidents

1. Adequate lighting in stairs.
2. Stairways clear of toys, bottles and brooms etc.
3. Handrails on sides.
4. No electrical equipment near bathroom.
5. Disconnected appliances when not in use.
6. Replacing worn out cords.
7. No slippery throw rugs.
8. Liquids spilled on floor wiped up immediately.
9. Highly polished floors to be avoided.
10. Gas burners turned off tightly.
11. Handles of cooking utensils on stove turned inward.
12. Sharp knives, razor blades, scissors and matches out of reach of children.
13. Medicines safely stored.

14. Children not to be allowed to go to the street or road without any escort.

Common Accidents in School

Generally same types of accidents take place in the school as in the home. However in the school there are special situations which need special care. Such special situations in the school are on account of the school workshop, school canteen, chemical laboratory, school gymnasium and play-ground, school transport etc. uncommon to home.

Safety in the Laboratory: All experiments should be performed under the guidance of the teacher. As a matter of fact laboratory should not be opened for use if there is no teacher available. Students should not be allowed to mix up two chemicals when the result of such a combination is not known. Glass should be handled with care so to avoid cuts.

Safety in Workshop: Sufficient space should be provided for movements. Tools should be maintained in proper condition and at their proper places. Students should be given suitable instructions in the use of tools.

Safety at the Playground: School ground should not be slippery. It should be free from thorns and pebbles. All games and sports should be played under the guidance of teachers.

Safety During Recess and at the Close of the School: It is generally observed that when the bell goes on these two occasions, students are so much excited that sometimes there is a 'mini' stampede to rush out of the classes and several students are hurt. Teachers should be very vigilant on such occasions.

Students' Fights: When the discipline in the school is loose, children get several chances to fight among themselves. It is, therefore, very essential that a close watch is kept on the students.

A First-Aid Box must be kept in every institution.

Road Safety

Children should be instructed to obey the traffic rules. Roads should be crossed only on cross walks, intersections, zebra crossings or walk signals. Subways should be used. Passing through the space between parked cars and buses should be avoided. Small children should be instructed in cycle safety measures also. The cycle must have good brakes and bell. During the night there must be proper headlight. Two children should not ride on a cycle as far as possible. Small children should be instructed not to use cycle on the road as far as possible. Cycle racing by children near the congested places is very dangerous.

School Transport Safety

In recent years, especially in cities, quite a large number of students make use of school transport. Trained drivers and cleaners/helpers should be engaged. Speed should also be kept at the prescribed limit. Overloading should not be done. Necessary precautions should be taken at the time of boarding and dropping children at the spots free from heavy traffic.

Safe Drinking Water

Importance: Safe and adequate water supply is very essential for health both of the individual and the community. Drinking unclean water spreads several diseases of the gut and the digestive tract. Drinking unclean water may lead to jaundice. Water intended for human-consumption should be safe and wholesome and it is defined as water that is (a) free from diseases carrying germs; (b) free form harmful chemical substances; (c) pleasant to taste, and (d) usable for domestic purposes.

Sources of Safe Drinking Water: The water for drinking and used in the preparation of eating and drinking products should come from a tested safe source of water and in case of doubt it should be treated by the individual to make it safe before using it. On a large scale water is usually purified and treated in water supply systems under the control of local bodies or any other approved authority. This water is supplied to the households through water taps.

Poisoning: Most of the victims of poison accidents are children between two and five years of age. However, there are some chances in the school also. All the containers of poisonous substances in the laboratory should be kept out the reach of the children. The bottles of medicines and chemicals should be kept very carefully. Children should be instructed not to eat the heads of matches and bright coloured papers because poisonous substances are used to make dyes.

Choking and Suffocation: Sometimes young children swallow small objects like coins. To avoid this, such things should be kept out of reach of the children. Choking and suffocation is also caused by too much of smoke. A kerosene or coal stove to warm the room during winter and especially when doors and windows are closed can be dangerous.

Sex Education

There was a time when strong objections were raised in certain quarters regarding the imparting of sex education at the school stage. But in recent years, there has been a growing demand that sex education, in one or the other form should find place in the overall programme of the school.

Workable outline of sex education as provided, in a publication entitled '*Sex Education. How and Why*' authored by Dr. W. Mathur, is given here with a view to provide guidance to teachers and others to advise adolescent on sex matters.

Programme of Sex Education for Adolescents : 14-18 years Age Group

	Objectives	*Context*	*Approach*
1.	To help adolescents develop into a responsible adult.	Knowledge of the phenomenon of ovulation, foetal development and birth of a baby. Marriage for reproduction, need of assistance at birth.	a) Talks with the aid of audio-visual aids. b) Emphasis on leading highly moral and ethical life in the interest of family happiness and community peace.
2.	To make adolescents understand venereal diseases.	Different venereal diseases. Their mode of infection and their damaging effect on the patients.	Causes of these diseases, their symptoms and the conditions of the patients should be illustrated by means of films, film strips and pictures.
3.	To make adults aware of promiscuity and prostitution.	Danger's of promiscuous sex relations. Its adverse influence on the family life and its being a great social evil. Prostitutes as chief sources of the spread of venereal diseases.	Frank discussion. Students to be told emphatically that all extramarital sex relations must be avoided in the interest of personal health and family happiness.
4.	To make student careful of homosexuality.	Homosexual an unethical and unnatural practice. An offence under law punishable by imprisonment. Can convey venereal diseases	Adolescents must not be permitted to go out with strangers. They should be motivated to utilise their surplus energy and spare time in sports, cultural programmes, community welfare service and nation building activities. Such programmes should be systematically organised.

(*Note: Sex Yoga in chapter 15*)

15

Functions and Responsibilities of Teachers
With Reference to School Health Education

Many-Sided Efforts for the Health and Physical Development of Pupils

In a school, a child comes into contact with his friends, teachers and the other school staff. All these contacts, besides the physical environment of the school have far reaching effects on the emotional, mental, physical, spiritual and social health of a child. As a matter of fact all these facets of the life of the child are very closely interlinked, and are greatly influenced by the teachers. The teachers' their role in the health and physical development of the child is as important as, their role in his academic or intellectual development. It is a wrong notion that the physical education teacher alone is responsible in this regard.

Measures to be adopted by the Teachers for the Promotion of Health and Physical Fitness of Students

The following measures should be adopted by the teachers for the promotion of health and physical fitness of the students.

1. *Personal Cleanliness:* The daily morning inspection of the cleanliness of the students by the teacher is very helpful in enforcing personal cleanliness. A rapid survey of the class should be made. Competition may be introduced among the students. Cleanliness chart may be prepared and marks allotted to them.

2. *Development of Habits Regarding Air:* Stress should be laid on the need of fresh air at all times and especially while sleeping. The students should be asked not to cover their mouth at night. They should be taught to breathe through their noses.

3. *Training in First-Aid Habits:* The students should be instructed to give immediate attention to cuts and bruises.

4. *Vaccination and Inoculation:* At time of epidemics precautionary measures should be suggested to them and they should be vaccinated and inoculated.

5. *Development of Habits of Hygienic Feeding:* The students should be taught to take right type of food in a suitable quantity. They should be warned of the dangers of over-eating. They should be asked not to take sour food. They should be made to understand the importance of drinking plenty

of water.

6. *Selection of Suitable Physical Exercises:* A variety of physical activity programmes should exist in a school so that the students may choose activity of their liking.

7. *Formation of Good Classroom Habits:* A wise teacher would always pay due attention to the postures of the students. The students may be instructed to keep pens and pencils out of the mouth and to use handkerchiefs while coughing. Such other matters should be attended to.

8. *Development of Better Human Relations in Matters Concerning Health:* Every child should be asked to male it a point to do his best for the betterment of the health of his friends, relatives, neighbours and the whole community.

9. *Medical Inspection and Follow-up Work:* Medical examination should be thorough and the follow-up work taken up seriously.

10. *Training in First Aid:* Teachers themselves should get training in first aid, give first aid training to students and render emergency service.

11. *Vaccination and Inoculation:* Teachers should ensure that each child is regularly vaccinated and inoculated through the arrangements made by the school.

12. *Physical Exercises:* Whenever feasible, all teachers should supervise physical education programmes .

13. *Special Methods of Teaching Health:* The teachers should be in the look out of using a variety of methods of teaching health.

14. *School Dispensary:* Teachers, in turn, can look after the school dispensary.

15. *Assistance to Medical Officer or School Doctor:* At the time of medical inspection of students and its follow up, teachers can render very useful help.

Special Methods of Imparting Health Education to Students

Apart from verbal instructions, teachers can impart health and physical education to the students in an interesting manner through the methods suggested below:

(i) *Health Posters:* Posters depicting correct methods of washing of bodies, about various diseases like plague, malaria, etc., and about food, sleep and exercise, etc., can be made and pasted on the school walls. Health authorities may be requested to supply these. The posters should be very simple. Each poster should illustrate one idea only. Striking headings catch our attention. Students may be asked to help in preparing simple charts and posters regarding health.

(ii) *Health Projects and Weeks:* Once a year, a week may be set apart for the purpose of health education. Cleanliness campaigns in the school and locality go a long way in instilling ideas about health. Various committees of the students regarding different aspects of personal cleanliness, *e.g.,* teeth, hair, nails, etc., may be formed. One teacher may serve as an adviser to each committee. The good posture committee should arrange posture competition and the participants should be asked to show proper postures. Prizes may be awarded to the best ones. Similarly exercise competitions may be arranged. Data regarding height, weight, chest measurements etc. may be collected by respective committees. Special lectures on general hygiene may be arranged. The Panchayat, Health Department or the City Health Department, as the case may be, should be requested to help.

(iii) *Health Book:* Each student should be asked to maintain a health book. One important health rule should be pasted on the top of each page. Pictures illustrating certain health rules may be pasted in it. It should also contain his health records.

(iv) *Healthy Environment:* Attempts be made to make classrooms and the school building very attractive and conducive to health. This has a direct bearing on the child. 'As is the environment so is the individual.'

(v) *Film and Film Strips:* Wall-made health films and film strips are valuable in the teaching of health education.

(vi) *Educational Trips:* 'Seeing is believing' is a true saying. Excursions to good dispensaries, water supply centres, etc. may be planned for health educational purposes.

(vii) *Health Clubs:* Like literary clubs, health clubs should be organised in schools. A definite weekly or monthly programme may be chalked out in co-operation with the school Red Cross Society. Debates and declamation contests on health matters may be arranged. Plays depicting health rules be staged.

(viii) *Radio:* Special programmes for children relating to health should be broadcasted.

(ix) *Television:* Television provides a good medium to telecast features on healthful living. The teachers should take interest in such programmes.

Suggestive Activities to be Organised by Teachers Relating to Health and Physical Education

Following types of activities may be undertaken in schools:

1. Art work relating to health and physical education
2. Body (well-built) exhibitions
3. Bulletin board display
4. Case studies
5. Dramatics
6. Demonstration of vaccination (primary and re-vaccination), inoculation, DDT spraying, leprosy treatment
7. Demonstration of exercises
8. Doctor's visit class
9. Exhibitions
10. Essay competitions

11. Field trips
12. Film demonstrations
13. Group discussion
14. Health projects
15. Health squads
16. Health weeks
17. Laboratory methods
18. Lectures
19. Model making
20. School magazine
21. Panel discussion
22. Parent-teacher activities for bringing home and school closer together.
23. Problem solving
24. Health Projects in the village
25. Sanitary and Health Boards in each school
26. Story telling
27. Safety weeks
28. Students health study record
29. Supervised study
30. Surveys
31. Visitation and observation
32. Practical cleanliness and Health work like
    (i) Cleaning teeth
    (ii) Constructing compost pits
    (iii) Disinfecting wells
    (iv) Keeping water safe
    (v) Keeping refuse in basket
    (vi) Regular cleaning of latrines and urinals
    (vii) Sweeping floor
    (viii) Trimming nails
    (ix) Washing hands
33. Charts and diagrams/Visual aids

Postures of the Students: Instruction and Supervision

Importance of Postures: We can hardly ignore the seriousness of poor postures. It adversely affects health, physical efficiency, mental attitude and appearance of an individual. Most of our diseases are the outcome of poor postures. A teacher can do much in the classroom work and physical instruction period to prevent bad postural habits in the students. As a result of poor postures says, Dr. Mosher, "constipation, diarrhoea, flatulence, disturbance of the circulation, nervous irritability and, most marked of all fatigue out of proportion to the effort expended, lessen the efficiency of the individual and often make life a burden."

Major adverse effects of poor postures: Some of the main adverse effects of poor postures are given below:

(i) They interfere in the normal working of respiration, circulation and digestion.
(ii) They badly affect the eye-sight.
(iii) They spoil handwriting because the students will not be able to hold the pen properly.
(iv) They lead to round shoulders and drooping body.
(v) They decease physical efficiency and develop laziness.
(vi) They develop crooked bodies which are not normal in shape, and look very unpleasant.
(vii) They result in undesirable traits, *e.g.* timidness, lack of courage, etc.

Causes of Poor Postures

(a) Weakness of the muscles which may be due to lack of exercise.
(b) Wrong postural habits due to lack of information regarding correct positions.
(c) Defective desks and seats compelling the students to stretch or cramp their bodies.
(d) Wrong writing positions
(e) Wrong reading positions
(f) Defective eye-sight.
(g) Defective hearing.
(h) Illegible writing of the teacher on the black-board
(i) Wrong postures of the teachers leading to depressing effects on the students.
(j) Illness of the students.
(k) Wrong type of dress of the students.

Classification of Postures

(i) Standing postures.
(ii) Sitting postures.
(iii) Writing postures.
(iv) Reading postures.
(v) Walking postures.

Remedial Measures

(i) The students should be asked to take regular exercise to strengthen muscles.
(ii) Suitable furniture should be provided.
(iii) Good posture habits should be developed.
(iv) Stools should be provided for smaller children so that they may learn to sit without reclining against the chair.
(v) Suitable corrective postural exercises should be recommended to

the students.

(vi) Students having defective eye-sight and hearing should be seated on the front benches.

(vii) Rooms should be suitably ventilated and sufficient accommodation should be provided.

(viii) Bold type books should be selected.

(ix) The aid of school medical officer should be sought.

Sitting Postures: In sitting postures, different organs of the body and the body as a whole are balanced; the legs are crossed, the hips are comfortably and properly placed at the seat; the head, the shoulders and hips are in a straight vertical line and the vertebral column is perfectly vertical.

Standing Posture: In correct standing posture, the body weight should equally fall on both the legs, the entire body should be erect and vertical, the heels should rest evenly on the flat floor; the two arms should rest on the thighs in a straight line, the head and the body should not bend forward, the body should not bend on one of its sides and body as a whole should balanced.

Reading Posture: While reading, the book should not be placed very close to the eyes. It should be placed at least 12 inches away. The hand handling the book should form an angle of 45 degrees with the eyes.

Writing Posture: While writing, the position of the desk or table should be quite close to the body and bent in an upright position and not bent over the note-book. The legs should be on the ground. The note-book should be at a distance of 12 inches from the eyes. The paper should be placed parallel to the edge of the desk and the pen should be held in between the thumb and fingers.

Walking Posture: While walking, the body as a whole should be erect and upright. The eyes should look straight at an angle of go degrees. The arms should swing alternately along with steps preferably upto an angle of 90 degrees with the body. The heels should reach the ground first and then the middle portion and the toes. One should take steps of normal dimension.

Role of the Teachers in the Development of Mental Health of the Students

Importance of Mental Health: It is of paramount importance to give due attention to the development of mental health of children. There are mental laws, principles and situations which result in the development of healthy minds of children. Any disregard to these lead to mental disorders and conflict which ultimately bring frustration, misery and unhappiness. Teachers in the school can play a major role in providing such an environment in which children develop healthy mental attitudes.

What Constitutes a Healthy Mind? Following are the characteristics of a healthy mind:

(i) Appetite-normal

(ii) Calmness
(iii) Cheerful outlook
(iv) Good temper
(v) Habits—socially acceptable
(vi) Instincts well regulated
(vii) Philosophy of life—healthy
(viii) Physical vitality—normal
(ix) Receptivity to new ideas
(x) Sex consciousness—normal
(xi) Temper—good
(xii) Will—energetic and strong

Mental Disorders

(a) Undue anxiety
(b) Easily embarrassed in the presence of others
(c) Lack of courage
(d) Undeveloped habits and will
(e) Low intelligence
(f) Irritability
(g) Moodiness
(h) Depressed and pessimistic outlook
(i) Full of prejudice
(j) Abnormal interest in sex
(k) Bad temper

It is a matter of great relief that our educationists have begun to realise the importance of mental health. 'Feeling of insecurity' and the 'feeling of inferiority' are the two great enemies of mental health. A knowledge of mental hygiene helps us to kill these two demons. A psychological approach is needed. Our attempts should be to provide suitable emotional, physical and intellectual environments in which a child may have the 'feeling of security' and the 'feeling of equality'. He should feel that his personality is respected and is given a suitable place.

Measures to Secure Mental Health

1. *Close Pupil-Teacher Contacts:* The teacher should carefully observe the child in and outside the school and should know the child and his home conditions. This will develop the feeling of 'oneness' in the mind of the child who feels that the teacher is interested in his welfare.

2. *Favourable Home and School Environment:* Unfavourable home and school environment leads to mental disorders. Parents should be guided to adopt good methods of upbringing. The child should be free from unsatisfactory relationships and strict discipline. Treatment by the parents should be just and impartial. Too much fondling may also lead to emotional maladjustment. The treatment of the teachers should be just and fair.

3. *Medical Examination:* There should be provision for the medical

examination in schools and remedial measures be adopted to safeguard the health of the child. Defective physique becomes a contributory factor of mental disorders. Cases requiring special treatment should be sent to child guidance clinics.

4. *Intellectual Life of the School:* Sound methods of teaching suited to the individual needs of the child should be adopted. Activity Methods, e.g. Play-way, Project Method, etc., should be encouraged. Audio-visual aids develop interest in the lesson. Special time and attention is to be devoted to weak students.

5. *Provision of Educational and Vocational Guidance Centres:* Schools should start such centres. It is not necessary to appoint full time psychologists in schools. Trained teachers may be asked to undergo short educational and vocational guidance course and the work of guidance be entrusted to them. For specially difficult cases, intelligence, aptitude and personality tests be conducted.

6. *Provision of Co-curricular Activities:* Properly planned activities are very helpful in providing much needed and useful training in civic sense. Sublimation of instincts is also achieved.

7. *Freedom and Self-discipline:* Unnecessary rules and regulations greatly upset the mental equilibrium of the child. A child who breathes in an atmosphere of freedom develops initiative and courage. Severe punishments result in mental retardation. Let us be wise and remember the useful words of Hobbies, "The fool cannot be mended by flogging, and he who flogs is the greatest fool." Hence the right approach would be to give freedom to the child. A.S. Neill says, "We could abolish caning by an act of Parliament, but no act of Parliament can abolish the fear of teacher or a system."

8. *Teacher's Mental Hygiene and His Dynamic Personality:* The teachers should be mentally alert to develop mental alertness in the students. They should be painstaking, sympathetic, appreciative and trusting. They should not have any prejudice which may have an adverse effect on the emotional and intellectual conditions of children. They should have always higher ideals of life before them.

Yoga: Health, Physical, Mental and Spiritual Development of the Students

Meaning of Yoga: According to sage Patanjali, the author of an ancient book *'Yoga Sastra'* (circa Second B.C.), yoga is a method of controlling the tendencies of mind. Some scholars regard yoga as an attempt of uniting oneself with the Supreme Spirit i.e. *'Parmatma'* or God. Yoga is also described as a way of life for the harmonious development of the body, mind and soul. *What Yoga is Not!* Very often, yoga is misunderstood and thought of in term of certain exercises or *'asans* (postures) for training the body. This is a very narrow concept or meaning of Yoga. It is certainly not a physical act or exercise only. It is much more.

Stages or Branches of Yoga

According to sage Patanjali, following are the eight stages of yoga:

1. *'Yama'.* This refers to the moral discipline for the individual and it includes the practice of *'brahamcharya'* (celibacy), non-stealing, non-receiving of gifts and observance of the creed of non-violence.
2. *'Niyama'.* It means self-purification by practising cleanliness, contentment, studying scriptures and surrendering oneself to God.
3. *'Asana'.* This implies practising certain body-postures for acquiring health and developing steadfastness of mind. *'Asanas'* (exercises or postures) have been developed over the centuries and they help in the exercising every muscle, nerve and gland of the body.
4. *'Pranayama'.* It is the practice of controlling breath for strengthening the respiratory system, purifying blood and soothing the mind.
5. *Pratyahara'.* This is an attempt to free the mind from the domination or control of senses.
6. *'Dharana'.* This is concentration on a single object or point.
7. *'Dhyana'.* It refers to the concentration on the all-pervading divinity through practice.
8. *'Samadhi'.* This is the last stage of yoga. In this stage, the yogi merges himself with the Divine Spirit, although he is alert and conscious.

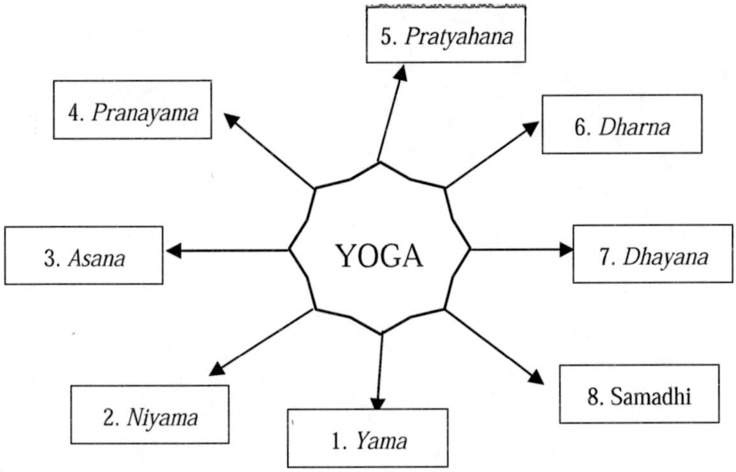

Fig. 15.1: Branches of Yoga

Relevance of Yoga in Modern Times: Yoga is an important contribution of ancient India to the world as a means of not only improving health, curing some maladies, correcting certain postural defects and removing tension but also uniting with the Supreme. It has assumed all the more significance in the modern times when we are confronted with all kinds of fears, stresses, strains, tensions and worries. It is now believed in several quarters of the Western World that yoga can solve man's several problems and bring peace of mind. Rightly followed, it soothens the mind and provides relief from stress which is the main cause of several ailments like high blood pressure, heart problems etc. In view of above, adoption of yoga has become more important in the prevent day society than in the past.

Review Questions and Problems

CHAPTER 1: CONCEPT OF SCHOOL ORGANISATION

1. Explain the meaning of school organisation. State its main objectives and elements.
2. Discuss aims and objectives of modern concept of school organisation as compared with the traditional concept of school organisation.
3. Explain why it is necessary to have an efficient school organisation. State the factors which make school organisation efficient.
4. "Organize the school for the development of the many-sided personality of the child and not to prepare him for the matriculation/secondary or higher secondary examination". Discuss this statement.
5. "The school is to be organized for the children and not the children for the school organisation." Elucidate.
6. "The school is not to be organized merely as a place for study." Explain.
7. In what way does the function of school organisation in the modern times differ from the colonial days? How does this difference influence the modern school organisation?
8. Explain the main features of a well-organized school.
9. "Organisation is like a good servant but a very bad master". Explain this statement and illustrate why it should be kept fluid. State the factors that comprise an efficient school organisation.
10. What is democratic school organisation? Why should we have it? What are its principles? What advantages do we acquire from it?
11. Differentiate between autocratic school organisation and democratic school organisation. Which of the two types would you recommend?
12. Explain the terms school organisation, school management and school administration. Which term would you prefer?

CHAPTER 2 : SCHOOL PLANT AND EQUIPMENT

1. What are the general principles in the planning and designing of school buildings?

2. What considerations should be kept in mind while selecting the site of a school?
3. What are the essential requisites of a good school campus?
4. Prepare a plan for an ideal senior secondary school. What items would you suggest for inclusion besides the main building and why?
5. What do you understand by a school plant? State the essentials of a good school plant. By what considerations would you be guided in the selection of site for a school?
6. "Problem of school buildings is very acute". Explain and state the recommendations made by the Education Commission in solving school building problems. To what extent do you agree with these?
7. How do school building, ground and equipment contribute to the health of the children? Also mention the steps that you will take to introduce aesthetic element in them.

CHAPTER 3 : SCHOOL TIME-TABLE

1. What purposes does a school time serve in the school? State the principles of its construction.
2. Why is it desirable to keep the school time-table fluid? What measures would you adopt regarding this aspect?
3. How can the tyranny of the school time-table be avoided?
4. "Well-arranged time-table is the surest mark of a well-arranged mind!" Explain this statement in the context of framing an ideal time-table of a school.
5. "A good time-table is a good reflection of the smooth work in a school". Explain this statement and indicate the fundamental principles to be kept in mind while planning a balanced time-table.
6. What practical difficulties are faced in planning a balanced time-table for the school? How would solve them?
7. Explain how the element of 'fatigue' can be overcome in planning the school time-table?

CHAPTER 4 : CO-CURRICULAR ACTIVITIES OR EXTRA-CURRICULAR ACTIVITIES

1. "The co-curricular activities are an integral part of school education". Explain.
2. Discuss the value of co-curricular activities in the all round development of the child.
3. What are the limitations in the organisation of co-curricular activities in the school? Give suggestions for their effective organisation.
4. Discuss the role of co-curricular activities in the development of character of the students.
5. Write short notes on the following co-curricular activities with

special reference to their importance and methods of organisation: (i) Morning Assembly, (ii) Labour weak, (iii) Community Service, (iv) School Magazine, (v) Educational Tours, (vi) Literary Activities.

6. Discuss this statement, "It is misnomer to call co-curricular activities as extra-curricular activities. They form a real adjust to curricular work"
7. Explain the relation between discipline and co-curricular activities.
8. "The founder of the Boy-Scouts Movement was a profound psychologist." Illustrate these remarks. State how you would organise a scout troop in your school.

CHAPTER 5 : SELF-GOVERNMENT IN SCHOOLS

1. Explain the meaning of self-government in schools. is it possible to have such a government in school. Give practical sugestions for the introduction of some form of self-government or student participation for developing democrate values in the students.
2. What type of student-self government can be safely introduced in the school? How can it help in the maintenance of discipline in the school?
3. "Students are immature and responsibility of some school affairs cannot be entrusted to them". Explain this statement and state the principles of organizing student councill in a school.
4. Explain the need, activities, principles, limitations and measures for organising student council effectively in the school.
5. Write a brief note on House System in a School.
6. Prepare a list of responsibilities that can be assigned to the students in a school.

CHAPTER 6: REWARDS AND PUNISHMENTS

1. "Spare the rod and spoil the child is an outmoded and discarded notion." Discuss this statement in the light of modern concept of discipline.
2. Examine the place of rewards and punishments in schools.
3. "The object of punishment is training the child and not vengeance." Discuss.
4. State the objectives, types and principles of rewards. What are the objections to them?
5. Indicate the value of punishment as an instrument of learning.
6. State the various types of punishments used in schools. Discuss their merits and limitations.
7. Explain the pros and cons of awarding corporal punishment.
8. What is self-discipline? How can it be achieved?
9. Explain the traditional and modern concept of discipline.

CHAPTER 7 : PRINCIPAL-TEACHER-PUPIL, PARENT RELATIONSHIP IN THE CONTEXT OF ADMINISTRATIVE STYLES OF LEADERSHIP

1. Explain the concept of human-oriented organisation/administration. Suggest measures for developing harmonious relationships.
2. State the meaning and qualities of leadership. Describe styles of administrative leadership. Which of these do you like and why?
3. Explain the various group relations in a school. Elucidate briefly the role of the head of the school in this regard.
4. Discuss the general principles a head should follow in developing harmonious relations in the school. Mention the qualities needed in the head for this purpose.
5. State the importance of staff meetings in the school. What principles should be followed in conducting staff meetings for deriving optimum benefit.
6. "For effective teaching-learning, harmonious relations between the teachers and the students are very essential." Explain this statement and state how such relations can be built by the teachers.
7. State the qualities needed in the teacher for developing balanced relations with the students so that an ideal teaching-learning environment is created.

CHAPTER 8 : PARENT-TEACHER ASSOCIATIONS

1. Explain the need for parent-teacher co-operation. Suggest suitable measures for having maximum co-operation between them.
2. State the meaning of parent-teachers association. What purposes does it serve? Describe its various activities. How can it play an effective role in the education of the child?
3. Why is a parent-teacher association formed? What are the factors for its successful working?
4. State the measures a school should take to win the co-operation of the parents? What are the hurdles in it? How can these hurdles be overcome?
5. State the ways in which parents can help the school.
6. Write a note on 'Parents' Day'.

CHAPTER 9 : SCHOOL RECORDS

1. Explain the importance of school records. What steps should be taken for their efficient maintenance?
2. How does the maintenance of school records help the teachers, students, parents, the department of education and the community?
3. What are the various types of records to be maintained in the school? Mention the academic records. Describe any two academic records.
4. Write notes on the following:

(i) Admission and withdrawal register
(ii) Pupil attendance register
(iii) Cashbook and ledger
(iv) Service book
(v) Cumulative record card

CHAPTER 10 : CLASSIFICATION OF PUPIL ADJUSTMENT CLASSES

1. What do you mean by the term class in a school? What are the factors leading to its formation? How can we determine the true size of the class?
2. Explain the meaning and basis of classification of pupils in a school. Which of the basis would you prefer? Give arguments.
3. Explain the need, advantages and disadvantages of class system. Suggest some alternative to remove the limitations of class system.
4. Explain the plans for the classification of students.
5. State the case for the promotion and non-promotion of students from one class to another. Can we do away with these? State reasons for your answer.
6. Suggest measures for reducing pupil failure through changes in educational policy and administrative reorganisation. Explain the means by which teachers can reduce pupil failure.
7. "Class system can not be ended but can be imposed upon." Discuss this statement and suggest measures for minimising the limitations of class system.

CHAPTER 11 : SCHOOL LIBRARY AND READING ROOM

1. Discuss the importance of a good school library. What are its functions?
2. State the present condition of our school libraries in our country. How can we improve upon the system?
3. You are asked to establish the school library. What considerations would you keep in view in establishing it?
4. Suggest measures for encouraging the students to make full use of school library. State the role of the teachers and the librarian in this regard.

CHAPTER 12 : SCHOOL HEALTH SERVICES

1. State the importance of health education in schools. What are its main objectives?
2. "Health education should form an integral part of school education". Discuss this statement and suggest a suitable programme of school health education.
3. Explain the meaning of school health programme. Describe its components.

4. "School health education revolves around four aspects : (1) Health Instruction, (ii) Healthful living, (iii) Health services, (iv) Health supervision". Discuss this statement.
5. What role a school can play in promoting healthful living among students?
6. Draw up an effective programme of health education in a school.
7. Distinguish between health education and physical education.
8. "Physical education is an integral part of health education." Discuss.
9. What is the importance of medical inspection of school students? How will you make medical inspection and follow up effective?
10. Explain the concept of physical education. What is its importance for the all round development of the child's personality?
11. On what principles would you organise physical education programme in a school?
12. "The playground is the uncovered school." Discuss this statement.
13. "The battle of waterloo was won on the playgrounds of Eton." In this context, explain the importance of games and sports.
14. Write notes on:
    (i) Inter-school tournaments
    (ii) School dispensary
    (iii) Junior Red Cross Society
    (iv) First aid
15. Describe the personal and social aspects of health education. State the role of the teachers and the community in improving these.

CHAPTER 13 : COMMON AILMENTS AND PHYSICAL DEFECTS OF CHILDREN

1. State the role of the teachers in respect of the following:
    (i) Common cold or nasal
    (ii) Sore throat
    (iii) Dyspepsia
2. State the meaning of contagious and infectious diseases. How infectious diseases are spread? What are the agents responsible for the diseases?
3. What are the symptoms of infectious diseases? What preventive precautions should be taken in respect of these diseases?
4. Describe the incubation period, symptoms, affected age and precautions to be taken in respect of the following diseases:
   (i) Measles, (ii) Mumps, (iii) Whooping cough, (iv) Influenza, (v) Malaria, (vi) Cholera
5. State the common physical ailments in students. Explain the role of the teachers in this respect.

CHAPTER 14 : HEALTHY PHYSICAL LIFE IN THE SCHOOL

1. What constitutes healthy physical life in school?
2. What type of physical environment a school should provide for the healthy physical life of the students?
3. Explain the terms nutrition and malnutrition. What is the role of the school in providing nutritious food to the students?
4. Why should the schools provide mid-day meals to students? What should be their contents?
5. State the meaning of posture. Point out some of the defects of incorrect postures of the students. Mention their causes and remedial measures.
6. Write notes on: (i) Safety education in schools, (ii) Sex education in schools

CHAPTER 15 : FUNCTIONS AND RESPONSIBILITIES OF TEACHERS WITH REFERENCE TO SCHOOL HEALTH EDUCATION

1. Explain the role of the teachers in the health education of the students.
2. Suggest measures which the teachers can adopt for the promotion of health and physical fitness of the students.
3. Point out some of the defects of incorrect postures of the students. State their common causes. What roles can the teachers play in the promotion of good postural habits among students?
4. State the meaning of yoga. What is its relevance in present day life? Why should the students be taught yoga?